Internet Telephony

ISBN 0-13-025565-3

Prentice Hall Series In
Advanced Communications Technologies

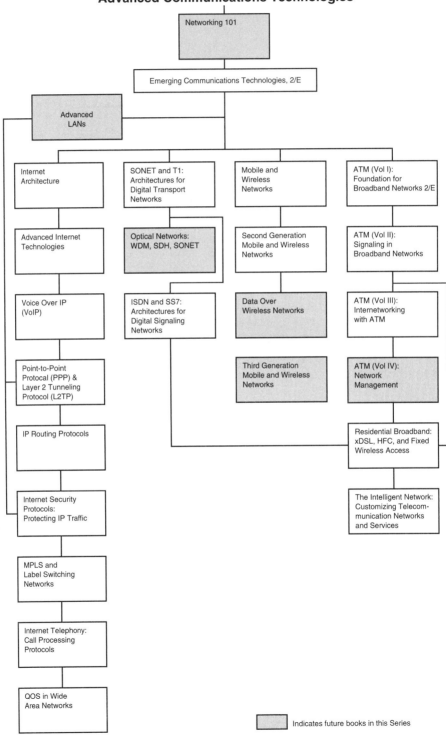

Networking 101

Emerging Communications Technologies, 2/E

Advanced LANs

Internet Architecture

SONET and T1: Architectures for Digital Transport Networks

Mobile and Wireless Networks

ATM (Vol I): Foundation for Broadband Networks 2/E

Advanced Internet Technologies

Optical Networks: WDM, SDH, SONET

Second Generation Mobile and Wireless Networks

ATM (Vol II): Signaling in Broadband Networks

Voice Over IP (VoIP)

ISDN and SS7: Architectures for Digital Signaling Networks

Data Over Wireless Networks

ATM (Vol III): Internetworking with ATM

Point-to-Point Protocal (PPP) & Layer 2 Tunneling Protocol (L2TP)

Third Generation Mobile and Wireless Networks

ATM (Vol IV): Network Management

IP Routing Protocols

Residential Broadband: xDSL, HFC, and Fixed Wireless Access

Internet Security Protocols: Protecting IP Traffic

The Intelligent Network: Customizing Telecommunication Networks and Services

MPLS and Label Switching Networks

Internet Telephony: Call Processing Protocols

QOS in Wide Area Networks

Indicates future books in this Series

Internet Telephony
Call Processing
Protocols

UYLESS BLACK

Prentice Hall PTR
Upper Saddle River, New Jersey 07458
www.phptr.com

Library of Congress Cataloging-in-Publication Data

Black, Uyless D.
    Internet telephony : call processing protocols / Uyless Black.
      p. cm.
    ISBN 0–13–025565–3
    1. Internet telephony I. Title.

TK5105.8865 .B52 2001
621.382′12—dc21   00–047886
                                                       CIP

Acquisitions editor: *Mary Franz*
Editorial assistant: *Noreen Regina*
Cover designer: *Anthony Gemmellaro*
Cover design director: *Jerry Votta*
Buyer: *Maura Zaldivar*
Marketing manager: *Bryan Gambrel*
Project coordinator: *Anne Trowbridge*
Compositor/Production services: *Pine Tree Composition, Inc.*

 © 2001 by Uyless Black
Published by Prentice Hall PTR
Prentice-Hall, Inc.
Upper Saddle River, New Jersey 07458

Prentice Hall books are widely used by corporations and government agencies for training, marketing, and resale.

The publisher offers discounts on this book when ordered in bulk quantities. For more information contact:

        Corporate Sales Department
        Phone: 800–382–3419
        Fax: 201–236–7141
        E-mail: corpsales@prenhall.com

        Or write:

        Prentice Hall PTR
        Corp. Sales Dept.
        One Lake Street
        Upper Saddle River, New Jersey 07458

Printed in the United States of America
10 9 8 7 6 5 4 3 2 1

ISBN: 0-13-025565-3

Prentice-Hall International (UK) Limited, *London*
Prentice-Hall of Australia Pty. Limited, *Sydney*
Prentice-Hall Canada Inc., *Toronto*
Prentice-Hall Hispanoamericana, S.A., *Mexico*
Prentice-Hall of India Private Limited, *New Delhi*
Prentice-Hall of Japan, Inc., *Tokyo*
Pearson Education Asia Pte. Ltd.
Editora Prentice-Hall do Brasil, Ltda., *Rio de Janeiro*

The cover on the forerunner to the book you are reading, *Voice Over IP (VoIP),* shows a parrot in front of a microphone, supposedly chatting on the Internet. As you see, the cover on this book uses the same theme, with the added emphasis on several parrots engaged in a conference call. Multicasting conferencing is a significant part of this book, and several chapters describe the use of the Internet and internets to support voice, video, and data sessions among multiple participants.

In the VoIP book, my assessment of voice calls over the Internet was: "... speech quality on the Internet varies. Sometimes it is acceptable, but some of the time it is not very good, and it is not 'toll' quality." This assessment still holds. The Internet has not yet improved to provide consistent, high-quality audio services.

But this situation has not prevented the growth of voice (and to a lesser extent, video) on the Internet. As examples, a company in Northern Virginia is doing a booming business in building systems that provide telephone calls over the Internet to countries not blessed with a modern telephone plant. I use the Internet about 30 hours a month for conference calls, and to multicast some of my lectures. I am not enamored with the sporadic performance of the Internet to support my voice applications, but it gets the job done, and provides avenues for communicating with my clients and students that are not cost effective in other alternatives.

The cover on this book shows one of the parrots on a screen, implying the birds are participating in a audio/video conference. Certainly, video conferencing is possible on the Internet, but most users do not have sufficient bandwidth to/from the Net to run video applications. However, as high-speed DSL, cable modems, and wireless local loops are deployed on a mass scale, this restriction will change.

In the meantime, the IP Call Processing protocols will find their way into vendor products and the marketplace to support the emerging Internet multimedia services. In the not-too-distant future, audio/video communications will be as common as a call on the telephone network.

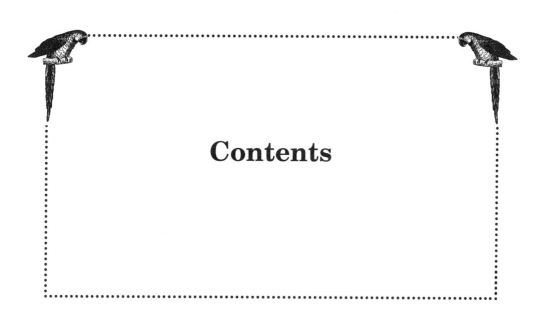

Contents

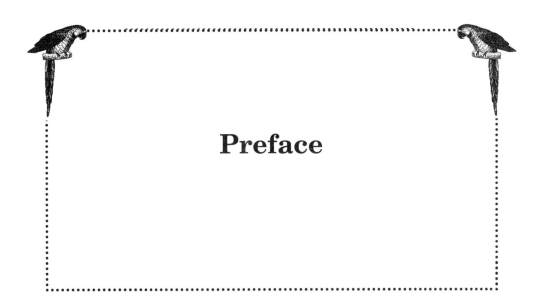

Preface

This book is one in a series of books called, "Advanced Communications Technologies." As the name of the book implies, the focus is on Internet telephony and protocols that support call processing. The book is an expansion of *Advanced Features of the Internet,* also part of this series.

The book has been written as a follow-up to the book in this series titled *Voice Over IP (VOIP).*

While the call processing protocols described in this book are oriented toward telephone calls, they also support calls associated with data and video connections. Examples of their support for all these applications are provided in several chapters.

I hope you find this book a valuable addition to your library.

NOTES TO THE READER

There are four major IP-based Call Processing Protocols being deployed in the industry: H.323, SIP, MGCP, and Megaco. The chapters in this book that deal with other subjects are included because they deal with and support these four protocols.

There are many examples of protocol flows in this book that illustrate how the call processing messages are transported between the call processing nodes. I have prepared some of them, and others are sourced from the Internet RFCs, IETF working papers, and the ISO/ITU-T Recommendations.

These documents use different notations and figures to illustrate the flows. For continuity and to aid your study of these flows, I have modified some of them so that all are similar.

However, in some instances, I left the flows as they are described in the original specification if my potential alteration would have changed the interpretation of the specification in question. For example, some of the authors of the specifications use one "event" to show a message flow though multiple nodes; others describe an event for each instance of the flow at each node. I kept these practices intact; in the event you decide to study the actual specification along with the book, you will find both are consistent.

So, if you do detect some minor differences in my presentations of these important flows, they are there for this reason. Overall, you will find they are quite similar.

ACKNOWLEDGMENTS

In many of my explanations of the Internet call processing operations, I have relied on the Internet Request for Comments (RFCs) and draft standards, published by the Internet Society, and I thank this organization for making the RFCs available to the public. The draft standards are "works in progress," and usually change as they wind their way to an RFC (if indeed they become an RFC). A work in progress cannot be considered final, but many vendors use them in creating products for the marketplace. Notwithstanding, they are subject to change.

For all the Internet standards and draft standards the following applies:

needed for the purpose of developing Internet standards in which case the procedures for copyrights defined in the Internet Standards process must be followed, or as required to translate it into languages other than English.

The limited permissions granted above are perpetual and will not be revoked by the Internet Society or its successors or assigns.

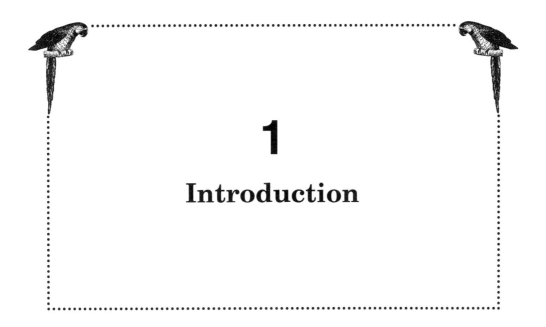

1
Introduction

INTRODUCTION

This chapter explains the motivations behind the interest in Internet telephony and IP Call Processing. It describes the growth of data networks and introduces the concepts of call processing. The chapter concludes with an introduction to the four major IP Call Processing Protocols. This conclusion includes a market survey of the current deployment of VOIP products, as well as current and projected use of the IP Call Processing Protocols.

MOVEMENT TO PACKET-BASED NETWORKS
AND INTERNET ARCHITECTURES

The telecommunications networks in operation today are undergoing dramatic changes. In the next few years, the networks that are based on the conventional voice-based circuit switches (the class 5 switches and class 4 tandem switches [Class4/5 switches]) will migrate to packet-based architectures. Many studies have shown that packet-based networks are considerably less expensive than their circuit-based counter parts. The VOIP book of this series discusses this issue in some detail [BLAC99].[1]

---

[1][BLAC99]. Black, Uyless. *Voice Over IP,* Prentice Hall, 1999. The VOIP book is a prerequisite to the book you are reading.

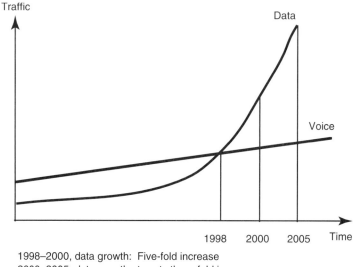

1998–2000, data growth: Five-fold increase
2000–2005, data growth: twenty three-fold increase

Figure 1–1   Comparison of Voice and Data Networks Growth [KNAP00]

Suffice it to say for this book that the "old" telephony-based systems are (a) too expensive, (b) too complex, and (c) not flexible enough. Regarding expense, the newer packet-based systems (using new hardware and software technology) cost as little as 10–20 percent than a class 5 switch [KNAP00].[2] Regarding complexity and inflexibility, the legacy telephone switches are saddled with years of evolutionary add-ons. In addition, they were never designed to support data applications. Furthermore, the telephony-based architectures are just that, telephony-based. They do not interwork easily with the Internet. They are not Web-based and do not use IP addresses.

I may sound dismissive of the PTSN. Quite the contrary. I marvel at its design elegance, and I am aware how effective and robust it is. But automated systems outlive their usefulness. They must adapt, or they will perish. The PTSN is designed for voice traffic, and as explained in the next section, voice traffic is not a high-growth sector of the telecommunications industry.

---

[2][KNAP00]. Knapf, Eric. "Can They Really Rebuild the PTSN?" *Business Communications Review,* May 2000.

THE GROWTH SEGMENT: DATA NETWORKS

A comparison of the growth of data and voice networks is shown in Figure 1–1. The scale for the data is provided at the bottom of the figure, and is quite impressive for the data growth curve. From 1998 to the end of 2000, data network growth is expected to increase five fold. From 2000 to 2005, data growth is expected to increase 23 times. Much of this growth will occur in IP-based data networks, including the public Internet and private internets. Because of the ascendancy of data networks, there is considerable interest to look for ways to place other kinds of traffic (voice and video) onto this technology.

WHY IP CALL PROCESSING?

The VOIP book of this series stated that voice over IP (VOIP) was of keen interest to the communications industry. Several reasons were cited for this interest. These reasons are reviewed here.

- Integration of voice and data networks to support the increased demand for multiservice products that use voice, data, and video traffic.
- Bandwidth consolidation by using one network for all traffic.
- Universal presence of IP (and IP-supporting systems, such as the Web) in most PCs and workstations.
- The shift to data networks and away from expensive, inefficient circuit (telephone-oriented) networks.
- Increasing user demands for more powerful services (such as applications supporting three-dimensional, real-time, voice, full motion video and data displays).
- User demands for the faster provisioning of services, and the ability to negotiate dynamic and tailored services.

Need for IP Call Processing Standards

If Internet-based telephony is to succeed, it follows that there must exist a standard set of IP Call Processing Protocols. In effect, the Internet Engineering Task Forces (IETFs) must assume the role of the old AT&T (Ma Bell). The logic is simple: If Internet telephony is to be an efficient technology, IP Call Processing Protocols common to all vendors and service providers must be in place.

SAVINGS THUS FAR IN INTERNET TELEPHONY?

The previous discussion focused on the advantages of Internet telephony, and the use of IP-based voice systems. However, in some implementations, IP telephony has not yielded significant cost savings, and in some instances, IP telephony in relation to regular telephony, has proven to be more expensive. The reasons for this disparity are the fact that IP telephony is new and the industry is far from settled. Some of the IP telephony products are expensive, and integrating them into an existing telephony infrastructure can be a time-consuming task.

Part of the problem is how IP telephony is implemented. Granted, if an enterprise chooses to acquire IP-based PBXs, and native-mode IP telephones, then the price sticker may not be attractive at this stage in the development of Internet telephony. But I say "may not be," because there are instances where enterprises have indeed saved money, primarily in wide area long distance charges, a subject discussed in more detail later in this book.

Moreover, IP phones have entered the marketplace. PC-based Internet products are becoming common. Many people are now using the Internet to make telephone calls, and the quality is (in my view) suprisingly good.

BEYOND INTERNET TELEPHONY

The focus of this book is on IP Call Processing Protocols. As such, much of the material is oriented toward the protocols that support voice communications. However, voice communications is only part of the picture. Many of the protocols discussed in this book support the processing of calls to support not only voice applications, but data, video, fax, electronic whiteboards, drawing slate images, multi-point conferences, microphone management, and so on. Certainly, the primary interest is on a simple voice conversation, but the intent of these systems is to provide an architecture to support powerful and feature-rich multimedia services.

We are only at the tip of this multimedia iceberg. In the future, we will see Web-based services that parallel the visual and audio images shown in today's movies. It is just a matter of time before our faces are

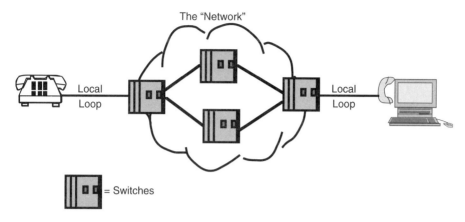

Figure 1–2   Call Processing Operations

morphed though speech phoneme analysis. An original face image will be used to create a truly "talking head."

Call processing in general, and IP Call Processing specifically, will be one of the many tools to support these services. So, let's see what the concept of call processing is all about.

WHAT IS CALL PROCESSING?

Since the publication of the VOIP book, considerable progress has been made in the development of call processing protocols to support VOIP, as well as data and video applications. This part of the chapter introduces the subject of call processing and explains its major attributes. Chapter 2 provides more details about call processing concepts.

The processing of a telephone call entails some very simple as well as complex operations. The goal of course is to connect a calling party to one or more called parties. In some systems, the call processing procedures between the telephone and the telephone provider's facilities (from the customer's local loop to a central office switch, as shown in Figure 1–2) entail the exchange of several different signals, such as the absence or presence of electrical signals on the line, or the sending and receiving of specific signal frequencies, called tones.

In newer systems, these "physical" signals have been replaced by messages or packets,[3] but the messages still do the same thing—set up

---

[3]This book uses the terms message and packet interchangeably.

and tear down calls between the service provider's customers. The basic idea is for the service provider to recognize when a subscriber lifts the telephone from its cradle (going off hook) to make a call, then give this calling subscriber a dial tone to alert the subscriber that a call can be made. The call processing system then accepts the dialed digits, and uses these values to determine the called party's location, all the while monitoring the subscriber's line to detect the subscriber hanging up the telephone (going on hook). To assist in these operations, the "network" must support the call processing operations.

The operations "inside" the network (in Figure 1–2, the operations between switches, and not the subscriber's equipment) to support the relatively simple operations on the local loop are elaborate and complex. First, the call must be set up from the calling to the called party, perhaps through different countries and different service providers. The operations to find the location of the called party, as well as the resources (the available facilities and circuits) to support the end-to-end call is not a trivial process.

Second, the end-to-end connection must be as robust as possible. Inside the network, extensive procedures are in place to provide backup for say a failed switch, or a link between switches. Parts of the telephone network have a fully meshed topology between some of the switches.

Third, the services many of us take for granted, such as call hold, user ID, and call screening must be set up quickly, and in a manner that remains transparent to the customers.

Since the 1970s, almost all the operations inside the network take place through the exchange of call processing messages, and not electrical signals and frequencies. The dominant system for this operation is known an Signaling System Number 7 (SS7), and its call processing protocol, the ISDN User Part (ISUP). The SS7 network is capable of supporting different types of user local loops, such as rotary dialing, touch tone, and ISDN, as well as a wide variety of dialing plans. We will have more to say about SS7 later in this book.

Key Aspects of Modern Call Processing Operations in Data Networks

Since the industry is changing rapidly, and new technologies enter the marketplace frequently, it makes no sense to build a network or user application based on "static technology," such as the legacy telephone network. Some examples support this statement. The progress made in voice codec (coder/decoder) technology in the past few years has resulted in the proliferation of multiple codec standards. The same holds true for the video standards. It is not unusual to find products that support different audio and video specifications, as well as some very good proprietary schemes.

In order for these heterogeneous components to be able to communicate, modern Call Processing Protocols are designed to support (a) the calling and called parties informing each other of their audio and video capabilities, and (b) negotiating the use of a possible subset of these capabilities.

Taking this idea a step further, let's assume a conference needs to use conventional audio and video systems, as well as fax, an interactive whiteboard, plus multiple audio channels for stereo music. IP Call Processing Protocols are designed to support the setting up of the resources to support this type of sophisticated application.

EMERGENCE OF IP-BASED MEDIA GATEWAYS AND GATEWAY CONTROLLERS

While packet telephony and IP call processing is still in its infancy, as it grows, it will require a rethinking of the traditional role of channel banks, PBXs, key systems, data service units (DSUs), and even Centrex. Several Internet task forces are developing standards that provide the interworking of the traditional telephone company (telco) technology with the IP platform, and vendors are already writing the code and building the hardware for these systems. A general view of these systems is provided in Figure 1–3.

The key components to this operation are the Gateway and a node known by four names: (a) Call Agent, (b) Gatekeeper, (c) Media Gateway Controller, or (d) Gateway Controller. Let's use the term Gateway Controller for this discussion.

First, the Gateway is responsible for the connection of the physical links of the various systems. Therefore, telephone network trunks may be terminated with user local loops, and WAN links might be connected with SONET links, and so on.

The Gateway is responsible for any user media stream conversions between the systems. For example, a 64 kbit/s digital voice image stream coming from the telephone network might be translated into a low-bit 8 kbit/s voice image stream for transfer to a personal computer on a LAN, and vice versa.

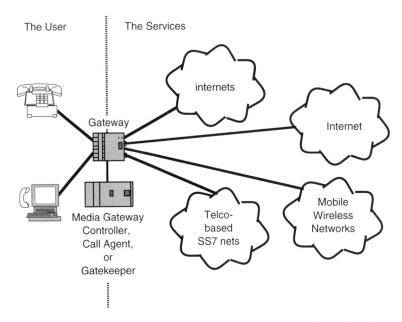

Figure 1-3 Topology for IP-based Multiapplication Networks

The overall controller of the system is the Gateway Controller. Indeed, the Gateway is a slave to the master Gateway Controller, and does not do much until the Gateway Controller gives the orders. For example, the Gateway Controller might direct the Gateway to monitor a particular line for off hook, and then instruct the gateway about how to collect the dialed digits, and how to forward these digits to the Gateway Controller for route determination The Gateway Controller or Gateway may have signaling links to these other networks. These links are not shown in Figure 1-3.

CONCEPT OF A CALLING DOMAIN

Some of the Internet call processing operations use the concept of a calling domain to administer and control the call processing operations. The idea is similar to a telephone network where different service providers (AT&T, Verizon, etc.) are in charge of their respective parts of the overall network. Generally, a Gateway Controller is in charge of a calling domain. This controller is responsible for the overall operations of its calling domain, and all resources (users and Gateways) operate under the directions of the Gateway Controller.

The operations between the calling domains take place as a result of agreements (and resulting configurations) between the administrators of the domains. Afterwards, the call processing messages that flow between the calling domains are (a) the standard call processing messages, and/or (b) a variation of these messages, modified to support the interworking of the different calling domains (for example, between different countries).

THE PRINCIPAL IP CALL PROCESSING PROTOCOLS

As explained in the preface to this book, there are four principal IP-based Call Processing Protocols, all with many supporting systems and protocols. They are:

- H.323
- The Media Gateway Control Protocol (MGCP)
- H.248/Megaco
- The Session Initiation Protocol (SIP)

Our task in this book is to gain an understanding of how these protocols (and their supporting protocols) support call processing. We will also compare them and cite their pros and cons.

Why So Many Protocols?

These protocols have many overlapping functions, and all perform call processing operations. But their many operations vary. For example, the Session Invitation Protocol (SIP) supports features to locate parties in an internet that are to be part of a call. The other protocols do not have this type of service, although H.323 has a similar, but more limited capability.

As another example, H.323, MGCP, SIP, and Megaco all have operations that define how to set up and clear a call across a data network, but their individual rules for this service are different.

These protocols are incompatible and/or have redundant operations. If they are to interwork with each other, there must be some kind of mediation between them, such as protocol converters (another "gateway"). Moreover, some functions that exist in one protocol do not map to another protocol. So, there are situations where one standard does not define a particular operation, but another does. This situation provides an opportunity for a vendor to use more than one of these standards to build a product.

As of this writing, there is no recognized standards body that is providing guidance on how the interworking of the standards will occur (such as a specific profile for a product). It is likely a product that integrates multiple protocols will not be compatible with a product from another vendor.

One can certainly wonder why multiple protocols are published that have so much redundancy. The answer is that some of these procedures are developed by the ITU-T, and others by the Internet task forces, two different standards bodies with their own views of how to go about developing standards. Another answer is that there are often honest differences of opinion about how to design a protocol to meet a stated set of objectives, and these differences may lead to multiple efforts.

In addition, vendors' views come into play, and the standards bodies are influenced greatly by the vendors. Indeed, vendors' employees sit on the standards committees and working groups.

Considerable coordination has occurred between some of these working groups and task forces. This situation sometimes results in the dove-tailing of one standard into another. For example, Megaco is published as part of the ITU-T H Series (H.248).

THE MIER SURVEY

The proliferation of multiple, competing protocols that have overlapping operations are very confusing to an outsider, but one hopes this "competitive" approach will lead to better specifications. However, for the near future, it is going to be a puzzling environment in the IP Call Processing world.

To show why, Mier Communications Inc. conducted a survey of 150 vendors of VOIP hardware and software products [MIER00].[4] About 45% responded with sufficiently complete information to be considered a valid response. This part of the chapter provides a summary of Mier's findings.

Products Offered

Table 1–1 reflects the products offered by the respondents in the survey. As expected, the majority of products are for Gateways, Gate-

---

[4][MIER00]. Mier, Edwin E. and Yocom, Betsy. "Too Many VOIP Standards," *Business Communications Review,* June, 2000. Authors can be reached at *ed@mier.com* and *byocom@mier.com* respectively.

Table 1–1   Products Offered [MIER00]

Product	Percent
Gateways	59%
Software for system integrators	46%
Gatekeepers, Call Agents, Media Gateway Controllers	43%
End-node (IP phones)	34%
Software for end users	33%
Other*	33%
Components	31%
PBXs	30%
Central office switches	15%

*Includes SS7, test equipment, and other components

keepers, and Call Agents. The commitment to PBXs and central office VOIP switches comes from a much smaller vendor population because of the capital and technical expertise needed to build these products.

Standards Supported

Figure 1–4 shows the results of the survey pertaining to the vendors' current support of the standards [Figure 1–4(a)], and their plan to use the standards in new products [Figure 1–4(b)]. H.323 comes in three versions (and soon, a fourth). SIP is published as RFC 3543, and Internet working papers have been added, to yield SIP+. MGCP is published as RFC 2705, and also by the International Software Consortium (ISC).

H.323 has the lead for implementation in current products by a wide margin. The reason H.323 has this lead is that it has been around longer than the others, and the same holds true for the standard in second place, MGCP. SIP and Megaco are relative newcomers to the IP Call Processing arena.

The survey results for the support for these standards in new products [Figure 1–4(b)] shows a marked increase in H.248/Megaco, SIP and MGCP gaining in use, and a decline in the use of all versions of H.323. We will explore the reasons for this "future" trend in later chapters. But a few thoughts are in order here. First, H.323 is a complex set of procedures, and it uses non-Web syntax for its messages [Abstract Syntax Notation.One (ASN.1) and the Basic Encoding Rules (BER)]. In contrast, Megaco, MGCP, and SIP all use the underlying technologies that

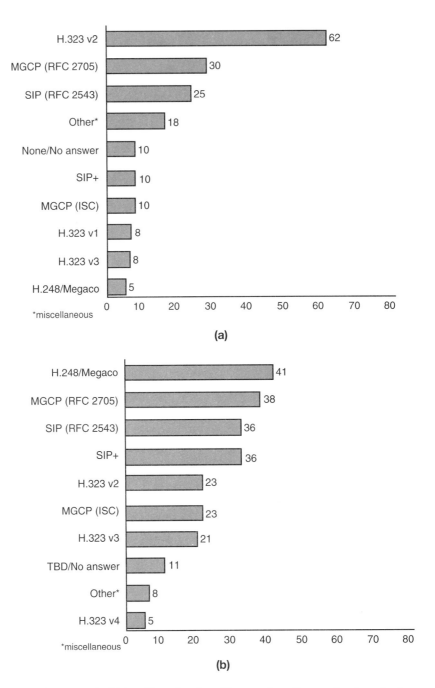

Figure 1–4(a) Standards Support: Current Products [MIER00]; (b) Standard Support: New Products [MIER00]

support the Web: (a) the Domain Name System (DNS), (b) the Universal Resource Locator (URL), and (c) text-based syntax used by the Hypertext Transfer Protocol (HTTP), based on the well-known and widely used RFC 822.

Not everyone is enamored by text-based syntax; some prefer the ASN.1/BER approach. Nonetheless, H.323's versions that are now implemented do not integrate easily into the Web architecture. However, H.323 (in the writer's opinion) will continue as a major presence in the industry.

A LOOK AT THE INTERNET TELEPHONY INDUSTRY

Voice over the public Internet and private internets is now starting to make an impact in the industry. Several companies have deployed their products in the Internet, or have built their own private networks for telephony traffic.

The prices vary among these service providers, as do the services. Some offer PC-to-PC calls; others offer PC-to-telephone calls; some offer national calls; some offer international calls. Other services are online fax services, e-mail, and voice messaging. Table 1–2 lists these services, as well as some of the more prominent service providers. The Web pages for these providers is also listed.

Table 1–2   Voice Over Data Service Providers

- A wide variety of services are now available
- Services and prices vary, with these offerings:
  PC-to-PC calls

  PC-to-telephone calls

  Telephone-to-telephone calls

  Fax service

  E-mail

  Voice messaging
- Examples of Service Providers:
  (a) Deltathree (www.deltathree.com)

  (b) PhoneFree (www.phonefree.com)

  (c) MediaRing (www.mediaring.com)

  (d) Net2Phone (www.Net2Phone.com)

  (e) Dialpad (www.dialpad.com)

SUMMARY

There is little question that the next few years will see a shift to IP-based Call Processing Protocols, and the legacy Central Office switch will undergo an metamorphosis to support telephony networks that are packet-based, instead of circuit-based.

The question is how the diverse IP Call Processing Protocols will be integrated into the vendors' products and the service provider's networks. A great deal remains to be done before we will realize a full-featured network that integrates the IP Call Processing Protocols. But it will happen; it is only a matter of time.

2

The Telephone Network

INTRODUCTION

This chapter provides an introduction to the telephone network, known in telephony circles, as "The Network." Some people use the term network to describe the Internet, and often shorten the term to "The Net."

We begin with a discussion of the outside telephone plant, the link between our telephones and computers to the telephone system. Next the "inside" of the telephone network is explained, with a discussion of switching offices and trunks. The remainder (and the bulk) of the chapter describes the basic signaling (call processing) procedures employed in making a telephone call.

GOALS OF A TELEPHONE SYSTEM

In building the telephone system, the telephone companies established three goals. First, there had to be sufficient direct current flow to operate the customer's station sets. It was decided that all power requirements would be the responsibility of the service provider, and not the

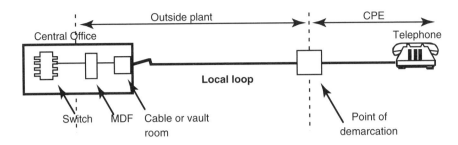

Figure 2–1   The Telephone Plant

customer—a decision that millions of customers take for granted, but provides an very valuable service.[1]

The second goal was to support dc/low-frequency call process signaling (dialing, ringing) and to keep the signaling simple at the customer's terminal.

The third goal was to limit signal loss to acceptable levels such that the voice conversation between the customers would appear as "natural" as possible.

THE TELEPHONE PLANT

Figure 2–1 shows the basic telephone company (telco) set up with a customer's telephone. The line connecting the customer premises equipment (CPE) to the telephone central office (CO) consists of two wires and is called the local loop. The connecting point between the CPE and CO is called the point of demarcation and is usually found in a box (the protection block or station block) on the outside of a house. The outside plant facilities include the wires and supporting hardware to the CO.

At the CO, the lines enter through a cable room (aerial lines) or a cable vault (buried lines). The lines are then spliced to tip cables and di-

---

[1]A native mode IP telephony network (that is, eliminating the telco local loop) will not provide electrical power unless special arrangements are made between a service provider and the customer. And they would have to be very special. One can envision the ISP building a plant to the subscriber that provides UPS!

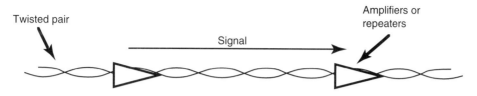

Figure 2–2   Twisted Pair Cable

rected to the main distribution frame (MDF); each wire is attached to a connector at the MDF.[2] From the MDF, the wires are directed to other equipment such as a switch.

THE MEDIA TO THE CUSTOMER

The telephone plant uses copper wires for the sending of the voice traffic between the subscriber and the central office. Call processing signals are also sent on these wires. The systems use wire pairs. The twisting of each pair (in a multipair cable) is staggered, as shown in Figure 2–2. Radiated energy from the current flowing in one wire of the pair is largely canceled by the radiated energy of the current flowing back in the return wire of the same pair. This approach greatly reduces the effect of crosstalk (interference on the pair). Moreover, each pair in the cable is less acceptable to external noise; the pair cancels out much of the noise because noise is coupled almost equally in each wire of the pair.

These characteristics describe a balanced line. Both wires carry current; the current in one wire is 180° out-of-phase with the current in the other wire. Both wires are above ground potential. In contrast, an unbalanced line carries the current on one wire and the other wire is at ground potential.

The two wires on the twisted pair are referred to as tip and ring. As Figure 2–3 shows, the terms originated during the days of the manual telephone switchboards when the conventional telephone plug was used to make the connections through the switchboard. A third wire (if present) is sometimes called a sleeve, once again after the switchboard plug. In a 4-wire system the four leads are called T, R, T1, and R1.

---

[2]Even though the MDF is at the CO, it is usually considered part of the outside plant and CO performance is usually measured between the MDFs.

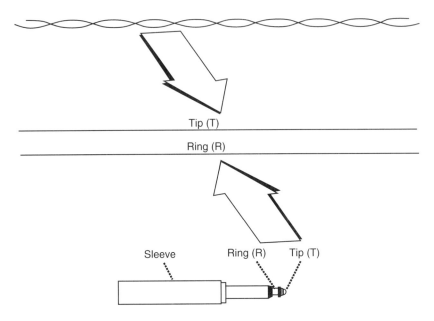

Figure 2–3   Tip and Ring

A MORE DETAILED LOOK AT THE OUTSIDE PLANT

Figure 2–4 depicts several aspects of the local (subscriber) loop. As shown in Figure 2–4(a), the system consists of feeder plant, distribution plant, and the feeder-distribution interface (FDI). The feeder plant consists of the large number of physical wires and signal repeaters. Usually, they are located based on geographical constraints and the customer locations. They often run parallel to roads and highways. The distribution plant consists of a smaller number of cables and connects to the customer's network interface (NI), which is usually located in a "box" attached to the customer's building. The serving area interface (interface plant) is the term used to describe the manual cross-connections between the feeder and distribution plants. This interface is designed to allow any feeder unit to be connected to any distribution pair.

The subscriber loop consists of sections of copper pairs (usually about 500 feet long). The sections are joined together with electrical joints, called splices, at the telephone poles for aerial cables and at a manhole for underground cables. The cable pairs are bundled together in a cable binder group.

Figure 2–4(b) shows the serving area boundary in more detail. This term describes the geographical division of the outside plant into discrete

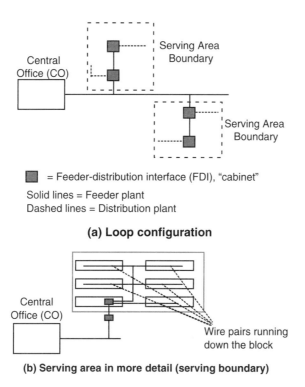

Solid lines = Feeder plant
Dashed lines = Distribution plant

(a) Loop configuration

(b) Serving area in more detail (serving boundary)

Figure 2–4   The Outside Plant

parts. All wires in a serving area are connected to a single serving area interface to the feeder plant, which simplifies ongoing maintenance and record keeping.

Connecting the Business or Residence

As shown in Figure 2–5, the feeder cables provide the links from the central office to the local subscriber area, and then the distribution cables carry on from there to the customer sites (a residence or business). Since the subscriber loop system is usually installed before all the customers are connected, there will be unused distribution cables. The common practice is to connect a twisted pair from a feeder cable to more than one distribution cable, and these unused distribution cables are called bridged taps. These bridged taps must be set up within the loop plant rules to minimize adverse effects on the system, such as signal loss, radiation, and spectrum distortions.

The connection points in the distribution cables are in pedestals for underground cables, and terminals for aerial cables. The connection into the

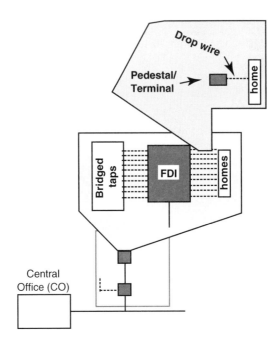

Where:
   FDI   Feeder distribution interface

Figure 2–5   Connecting to the Customer

customer site is called the drop wire. It is short, and can (potentially) pick up other frequency radiations. It might also radiate signals to other devices.

OFFICES AND TRUNKS

Figure 2–6 depicts several lines and types of equipment and types of "offices" found in the public network. Most of the terms in this figure are self-explanatory, but it should prove useful to amplify some of them:

- Trunk: A communication channel between two switching systems.
- Tandem office: A broad category of office that represents systems that connect trunks to trunks. Local tandem offices connect trunks within a metropolitan area. Toll offices connect trunks in the toll part of the network. With some exceptions, the end customer is not connected to a tandem.
- Toll connecting trunk: A trunk between an end office (local office) and a toll office.

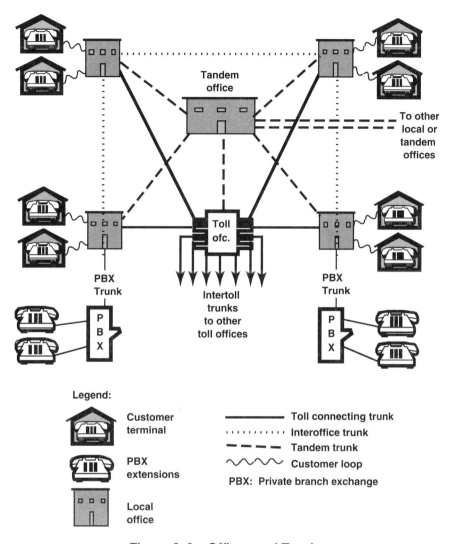

Figure 2–6   Offices and Trunks

THE TELEPHONE DIALING PLAN

The current dialing plan in North America is a seven-digit address to identify each network station (telephone). The address takes the form:

$$NXX\text{-}XXXX$$

where N can be any digit 2 through 9 and X can be 0 through 9. The arbitrarily assigned NXX portion of the address identifies the customer location where the station is homed. It cannot be the same as the NXX digits assigned to the same switch for public network use. The XXXX digits are the numbers of the individual station at the customer location.

This address is preceded with a three-digit area code, and for dialing since the 1984 divestiture, the full dialing address is:

10XXX (to be expanded to 101XXXX) carrier access code

where XXX identifies the specific carrier. The dialing sequence is 10XXX + (0/1) + 7/10 digits (D), where X can be any digit from 0 to 9. The 7/10 digits dialed must conform to the North American Numbering Plan (NANP).

In the local exchange carrier (LEC) network, the complete convention for "Dial 0" services is as follows:

- Intra-exchange: 0   or   0 + /10D
- Interexchange (inside
  world zone 1):   10 xxx +0 +7/10D   or   0 + 7/10D*
- Outside world zone 1: 10 xxx + 01 + CC + NN   or   01 + CC + NN*
- No call address   10 xxx + 0   or   00*

where CC = country code and NN = network number; * represents presubscribed numbers.

BASICS OF TELEPHONY CALL PROCESSING

This part of the chapter provides an introduction to the basics of telephony call processing. To begin this analysis, a few definitions are needed.

Access line signaling defines the operations to connect the customer to the switching system. The signaling can take place across a two-wire or four-wire interface, and signaling is transmitted in various modes, depending on the specific implementation by the network provider. Regardless of the mode of operation, these classes of signals are used during access line operations. These terms and definitions are derived from various Bellcore/ANSI manuals and vendor specifications.

- *Supervisory:* These signals are used to initiate or terminate connections. From the sending customer, the initiator requests a service. From the standpoint of the receiver, they represent the initiation of a connection.

- *Address:* These signals provide information to the network about the destination user. In so many words, they are the called party (and maybe the calling party) numbers.
- *Alerting:* These signals are provided by the network to the receiving customer that an incoming call is taking place, or to alert that some need is being signaled (flashing, recall, etc.).
- *Call progress:* These signals inform the user about the progress or lack-of-progress of a call that has been initiated by this user.
- *Control:* These signals are used for functions that usually remain transparent to the end customer. They are usually associated with network connections to the point-of-termination (POT) or the demarcation point. One example of a control signal is the requirement for party identification.
- *Test signals:* These signals are used for a wide array of circuit validation and quality checks.

Supervisory Signals

The supervisory signals convey the following service conditions.

- *Idle circuit:* Indicated by the combination of an on-hook signal and the absence of any connection in the switching system between loops.
- *Seizure (request for service):* Indicated by an off-hook signal and the absence of any connection to another loop or trunk.
- *Disconnect:* Indicated by an on-hook signal in the presence of a connection to a trunk or another loop.
- *Wink start:* Indicated by an off-hook signal from the called end after a connect signal is sent from the calling end. The signal duration is about 320± ms.
- *Delay start:* Indicated by an off-hook signal sent to the originating end after the terminating end has received a connect signal. It is maintained until the terminating end is ready to receive digits. The signal duration is typically 256± ms.
- *Immediate start:* Refers to outpulsing where the originating end outpulses 120 ms after having sent the connect signal.
- *Answer signal:* Indicated by a sustained off-hook signal toward the originating end.

- *Start dialing:* Indicated by an off-hook signal sent by the terminating end to indicate it can now receive digits. This signal is also called start pulsing. The originating end must delay 70 ms after receiving the start dialing before it can outpulse.

- *Stop/go:* Indicated by an off-hook signal sent by the terminating end within the interdigit interval to halt the outpulsing of digits. The go signal is an on-hook sent by the terminating end, with a duration of about 330 ms.

Off-hook and On-hook

To keep matters simple, the telephone system was designed to perform many of its signaling operations by on-hook and off-hook operations. The on-hook operation means the telephone is not being used, a term derived in the old days when the telephone handset was placed on a hook (later a cradle) when it was not being used. The off-hook is just the opposite; the handset is being used—it is lifted from the telephone.

Name	Type	Direction Originating Terminating	Meaning
Connect	Off-hook	———————→	Request service and hold connection
Disconnect	On-hook	———————→	Release connection
Answer	Off-hook	———————→	Terminating end has answered
Hangup	On-hook	←———————	Message complete
Delay start	Off-hook	←———————	Terminating end not ready for digits
Wink start	Off-hook	←———————	Terminating end ready to receive digits
Start dialing	On-hook	←———————	Terminating end ready for digits
Stop	Off-hook	←———————	Terminating end not ready for further digits
Go	On-hook	←———————	Terminating end ready for further digits
Idle trunk	On-hook	←———————→	
Busy trunk	Off-hook	←———————→	

Figure 2–7   On-hook and Off-hook Operations

The off-hook and on-hook operations change the electrical state of the line between the terminal and the CO (or PBX). The signals shown in Figure 2–7 are on-hook or off-hook signals of various durations to convey different meanings, as summarized in the far right-hand column of the figure.

EXAMPLE OF A CALL

Figure 2–8 builds on the information just explained and shows the typical operations involved in setting up a call. The operations are self-explanatory, based on the previous information provided in this book.

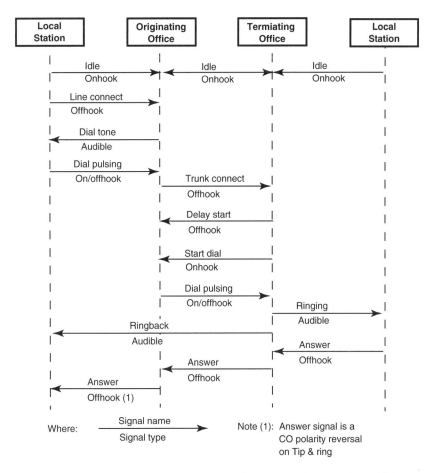

Figure 2–8   Using On-hook and Off-hook End-to-End (Off-hook and On-hook Signals Within Network Are Rare Today)

One point should be made regarding the signaling between the originating office (CO) and the terminating office (CO). The example shows conventional on-hook and off-hook signaling, which has been the method used in the past. Newer systems replace this type of signaling with message-based operations. The same type of information is carried between the offices, but it is conveyed in a signaling protocol, that contains digital codes (fields) in the message. This "new" type of signaling is an example of Signaling System Number 7 (SS7), introduced later in this chapter, and explained in more detail in Appendix B.

MULTIFREQUENCY (MF) SIGNALS

To this point in the discussion, we have discussed several types of signals and tests that are used in telephony systems. Most of these signals are represented with the off-hook/on-hook operations or the measurement of a voltage level on the circuit.

In addition to these simple arrangements, analog telephone systems use multifrequency (MF) pulsing. This type of signaling consists of com-

Table 2–1   Multifrequency (MF) Codes

Frequencies (in Hz)	Digit and Control
700 + 900	1
700 + 1100	2
700 + 1300	4
700 + 1500	7
700 + 1700	
900 + 1100	3
900 + 1300	5
900 + 1500	8
900 + 1700	
1100 + 1300	6
1100 + 1500	9
1100 + 1700	Key pulse (KPP)
1300 + 1500	0
1300 + 1700	
1500 + 1700	Start (ST)

binations of frequencies to send other kinds of information over trunks. The combinations of two frequencies represents a signal and as depicted in Table 2–1, each combination represents a digit. These signals fall within the speech bandwidth, so they can be sent over regular voice channels. MF pulses are used to transfer information to the control equipment that sets up the connections through the switches.

MF pulsing is also used to send information on the call in a BOC Centralized Automatic Message Accounting-Automatic Number Identification (CAMA-ANI) procedure. The calling number is transmitted from the originating end office to the CAMA office after the sending of the called number. For equal access arrangements to an IC, the calling number is sent first, followed by the called number.

A key pulse (KP) signal is a multifrequency tone of 1100 + 1700 Hz ranging form 90 to 120 ms. Its function is to indicate the beginning (the start) of pulsing, that is the dialed number follows the KP signal. The start (ST) signal does not mean the start of the signal. It indicates the end of the pulsing: that is, the end of the dialed telephone number. From the perspective of the telephone exchange, it represents the beginning of the processing of the signal.

DTMF SIGNALING

For customer stations, the signaling arrangement is used called dual-tone multifrequency (DTMF) signaling. DTMF is provided for the push buttons on the telephone set. This form of signaling provides 16 distinct signals, and each signal uses two frequencies selected from two sets of four groups. Table 2–2 shows the arrangement for the DTMF pairs.

Table 2–2 Dual-tone Multifrequency (DTMF) Pairs

| | | High Group (Hz) | | | |
		1209	1336	1477	1633
Low Group (Hz)	697	1	2	3	A
	770	4	5	6	B
	852	7	8	9	C
	941	*	0	#	D

OTHER TONES AND EVENTS ON THE SUBSCRIBER LINE

In addition to the off-hook/on-hook signals, the tones to represent dialed digits, and some additional events, the ITU-T (Recommendation E.182) defines other tones and events that can appear on a subscriber line. The tones explained below are tones that may be heard by the calling party [SCHU99].[3]

- Busy tone: The called line is busy.
- Call waiting tone: Indicates another party wishes to communicate with the subscriber.
- Caller waiting tone: Indicates the called terminal is busy, but has call waiting available.
- Calling card service tone: Used for calling card operations.
- Comfort tone: Indicates the call is being processed. May be used in situations where there is a long delay in dialing the callee, such as an international call.
- Congestion tone: The telco facilities are busy.
- CPE alerting signal (CAS): Used to alert a device of an arriving in-band frequency shift key (FSK) data transmission.
- Dial tone: This tone is placed on the line after the calling party goes off-hook. It indicates the telephone exchange is ready to receive address information (dialed digits).
- Hold tone: Indicates the caller has been placed on hold.
- Intrusion tone: Indicates call is being monitored by an operator.
- Negative indication tone: A supplementary service could not be activated.
- Off-hook warning tone: Indicates a phone as been left off-hook for an extended time.
- PABX internal dial tone: Indicates that a PABX is ready to receive address information.
- Pay tone: Indicates the payphone user is to deposit additional coins to continue the service.
- Positive indication tone: A supplementary service has been activated.

[3][SCHU99]. Schulzrinne, Henning and Petrack, Scott. "RTP Payload DTMF Digits, Telephony Tones, and Telephony Signals." Ietf-avt-tones-o1.ps, August, 1999.

- Record tone: Indicates the caller is connected to an automatic answering device, and is being requested to start speaking.
- Ringing tone: Indicates that a called has been placed to the callee, and a ringing signal has been transmitted to this party.
- Second dial tone: The telco network has accepted the address information but is requesting additional information.
- Special dial tone: Serves the same function as a dial tone, except it indicates the caller's line has a special condition associated with it, such as an indication that voice mail is available.
- Special information tone: The callee cannot be reached, but not because of the callee being busy, nor because of network congestion. Used on automatic equipment.
- Special ringing tone: A special service is active at the called number, such as call forwarding or call wailing.
- Warning tone: Indicates the call is being recorded.

EXAMPLES OF CALL PROCESSING OPERATIONS

Signaling systems must support (interwork with) the older analog signaling systems because analog is still the pervasive technology used in the local loop. The next part of this chapter shows two common operations.

These examples are not all-inclusive, but they represent common implementations. For the reader who needs information on each service option offered by the U.S. BOCs, I refer you to Bellcore Document SR-TSV-002275, Issue 2, April 1994.

Feature Group B (FGB)

The BOCs classify several of their access arrangements with the title "Feature Group." The example in Figure 2–9 is feature group B, which specifies an access agreement between an LEC end office (EO) and an interexchange carrier (IC). With this arrangement, the calls to the IC must use the initial address of: (I) + 950 + WXXX Where: W = 0/1.

Figure 2–9 is largely self-descriptive, but some rules for the signaling sequences shown in the figure should be helpful. For calls from EOs or an access tandem: (a) the carrier returns a wink signal with 4 seconds of trunk seizure, and (b) the carrier returns an off-hook signal within 5 seconds of completion of the address outpulsing. For calls from a carrier to an EO or access tandem: (a) the end office or access tandem returns

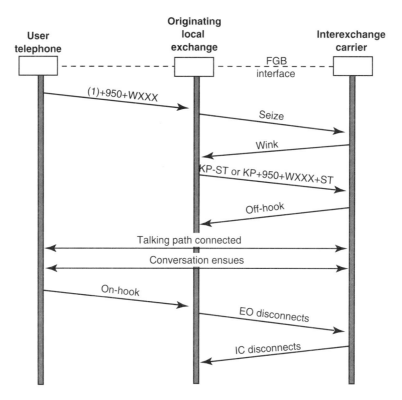

Figure 2–9   Example of Trunk-side Access Arrangement

the wink start signal within 8 seconds of trunk seizure; (b) the carrier starts outpulsing the address with 3.5 seconds of the wink; and (c) the carrier completes sending the address sequence within 20 seconds.

Operator Service Signaling (OSS)

OSS signaling is similar to one of the feature groups, but it has some characteristics that may be more familiar to the reader. Figure 2–10 shows these operations, with six events.

In event 1, the customer dials 10XXX + (1) + 7 or 10, or 10XXX + 0 + 7 or 10. Upon receiving these signals, the EO (event 2) seizes an outgoing trunk. In event 3, the OS facility responds with a wink. Upon receiving the wink signal the EO outpulses in event 4 the called number after a delay of 40 to 200 ms. The outpulsing is KP + 7/10 digits + ST (STP, ST2P, ST3P), or KP + STP(ST3P). In event 5, the OS facility will go off-hook (any time after the start of the ST pulse). Off-hook indicates its ability to receive ANI.

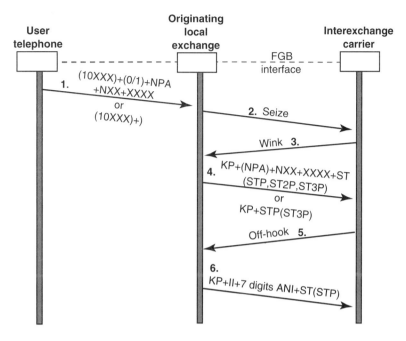

Figure 2–10   Operator Service Signaling (OSS)

In event 6, the EO sends the ANI (after a delay of 40–200 ms). The signals are KP + 02 + ST (STP).

ISDN

In the 1960s and 1970s, as digital technology began to find its way into the telephone providers' networks, and as the costs of digital technology declined, the telephone industry began to look for ways to move this technology into the local loop. The telephone service providers' view was that the superior characteristics of digital technology (over analog) would make it attractive to the customer.

Additionally, the use of analog signaling over the local loop was quite limited with regard to data rates (in bit/s). In fact, when ISDN was first introduced in 1984, the V.22 bis modem was just introduced, operating at 2400 bit/s. So, a 64 kbit/s rate sounded very attractive to the data user.

There was also the recognition that the T1 technology was proving to be effective within the telephone carriers' backbone network—so why not use some version of T1 at the local loop? This "version" is ISDN.

IP Call Processing Protocols must be able to interwork with ISDN, and these interworking examples are shown later in this book. If you are not familiar with ISDN, take a look at Appendix B.

SS7

SS7 is the prevalent signaling system for telephone networks for setting up and clearing calls and furnishing services such as 800 operations. It is designed also to operate with the ISDN technology.

Common channel signaling (CCS) systems were designed in the 1950s and 1960s for analog networks and later adapted for digital telephone switches. In 1976, AT&T implemented the Common Channel Interoffice Signaling (CCIS) into its toll network. This system is referred to as CCS6 and was based on the CCITT Signaling System No. 6 Recommendation.

SS6 and CCS6 were slow and designed to work on low-bit rate channels. Moreover, these architectures were not layered which made changing the code a complex and expensive task. And they were designed for analog networks, which was not the "technology of the future."

Consequently, the CCITT (now the ITU-T) began work in the mid-1970s on a new generation signaling system. These efforts resulted in the publication of SS7 in 1980 with extensive improvements published in 1984 and again in 1988. Today, SS7 and variations are implemented throughout the world. Indeed, SS7 has found its way into other communications architectures such as personal communications services (PCS) and global systems for mobile communications (GSM).

Later chapters offer several examples of how IP Call Processing protocols and Gateways interact with SS7 networks. If you are not familiar with SS7, Appendix B has a short tutorial on the subject.

SUMMARY

The telephone network provides a wide variety of call processing signals and operations which deal with: supervision, addressing, alerting, call progress, and testing. In order to interface with the telephone network and/or a user legacy telephone, the IP Call Processing Protocols must understand the telephony call processing operations.

3

The Internet

INTRODUCTION

This chapter is an introduction to the Internet's architecture and its layered protocol suites. The material is written for the person who is new to TCP/IP and Internet protocols, and it contains information used in subsequent chapters. The advanced reader can skip this chapter and go on to Chapter 4. But keep in mind that this tutorial also explains the subject in relation to IP Call Processing.

THE PROTOCOL SUITE

Figure 3–1 depicts an architectural model of TCP/IP and several of the major related protocols. The notations "L_1, L_2" and so forth refer to the layers of the model.

The choices in the stacking of the layers of this model vary, depending on the needs of network users and the decisions made by network designers. IP is the key protocol at the network layer. Several other protocols are used in conjunction with IP that serve as route discovery and address mapping protocols. The protocols that rest over TCP (and UDP) are examples of the application layer protocols. The lower two layers represent the data link and physical layers and are implemented with a wide choice of standards and protocols.

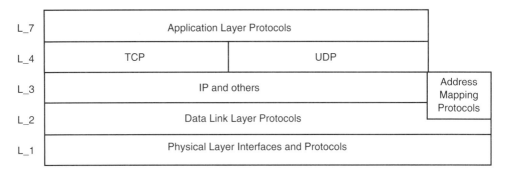

Figure 3–1   The TCP/IP Internet (Model)

The Physical Layer

The lowest layer in the Internet model is called the physical layer, although the Internet standards do not dictate the interfaces and protocols that reside in this layer. The functions within the layer are identical to the OSI Model and are responsible for activating, maintaining, and deactivating a physical circuit between machines. This layer defines the type of physical signals (electrical, optical, etc.), as well as the type of media (wires, coaxial cable, satellite, etc.).

There are many standards published for the physical layer; for example EIA-232-E, V.34, V.35, and V.90 are physical layer protocols. The TCP/IP suite is also implemented widely on local area networks (LANs), usually above the IEEE 802 or ISO 8802 standards.

The Data Link Layer

The data link layer (layer 2 or L_2) is responsible for transferring data across one communications link. It delimits the flow of bits from the physical layer. It also provides for the identity of the bits. It usually ensures that the data arrives safely at the receiving node. It often provides for flow control to ensure that the node does not become overburdened with too much data at any one time. One of its most important functions is to provide for the detection of transmission errors and provide mechanisms to recover from lost, duplicated, or erroneous data.

Common examples of data link control (DLC) protocols are the High Level Data Link Control (HDLC), published by the ISO; Synchronous Data Link Control (SDLC), used by IBM; and the Point-to-Point Protocol (PPP).

The Network Layer

The Internet Protocol (IP) is a simple internetworking protocol operating at the network layer (layer 3, or L_3). It forwards traffic between networks. IP is a connectionless service. It permits the exchange of traffic between two host computers without any prior call setup. It is possible that data could be lost between the two end user's stations. For example, the IP gateway enforces a maximum queue length size, and if this queue length is violated, the buffers will overflow. In this situation, the additional datagrams are discarded in the network.[1]

IP has no error-reporting or error-correcting mechanisms. It relies on a module called the Internet Control Message Protocol (ICMP) to (a) report errors in the processing of a datagram, and (b) provide for some administrative and status messages.

ICMP will notify the host if a destination is unreachable. ICMP is also responsible for managing or creating a time-exceeded message in the event that the lifetime of the datagram expires. ICMP also performs certain editing functions to determine if the IP header is in error or otherwise unintelligible.

IP is not a route discovery protocol, but a forwarding protocol. It makes use of the routing tables that are filled in by gateway protocols; one of which (OSPF) operates directly with the IP header (that is, it does not run on TCP or UDP). The purpose of these protocols is to "find" a good route for the traffic to traverse through an internet. The vast majority of gateway protocols route traffic based on the idea that it makes the best sense to transmit the datagram through the fewest number of networks and gateways (hops). The newer protocols use other criteria such as finding the route with the best throughput or the shortest delay. These newer gateway protocols use adaptive and dynamic methods to update the routing tables to reflect traffic and link conditions.

Layer 2 and Layer 3 Address Resolution Operations

The IP stack provides a protocol for resolving addresses, shown in Figure 3–1 as "Address Mapping Protocols." The Address Resolution Protocol (ARP) is used to take care of the translation of IP addresses to physical addresses and hide these physical addresses from the upper layers.

---

[1]The term *datagram* was the term used in the earlier Internet specifications to describe an IP data unit. Today, the term *packet* is also used.

Generally, ARP works with mapping tables (referred to as the ARP cache). The table provides the mapping between an IP address and a physical address. In a LAN (like Ethernet or an IEEE 802 network), ARP takes an IP address and searches for a corresponding physical address in a mapping table. If it finds the address, it returns the physical address back to the requester, such as a server on a LAN. However, if the needed address is not found in the ARP cache, the ARP module sends a broadcast onto the network.

Another protocol, called Proxy ARP, allows an organization to use only one IP address (network portion of address) for multiple networks. In essence, Proxy ARP maps a single IP network address into multiple physical addresses.

The ARP protocol is a useful technique for determining physical addresses from network addresses. However, some workstations do not know their own IP address. For example, diskless workstations do not have any IP address knowledge when they are booted to a system. The diskless workstations know only their hardware address. The Reverse Address Resolution Protocol (RARP) works in a manner similar to ARP except, as the name suggests, it works in reverse order: it provides an IP address when given a MAC address. RARP is often used on LANs for booting the machines to the network.

The Transport Layer

The Transmission Control Protocol (TCP) resides in the transport layer (layer 4 or L_4) of the Internet Model. It is situated above IP and below the upper layers. It is designed to reside in the host computer or in a machine that is tasked with end-to-end integrity of the transfer of user data.

The tasks of reliability, flow control, sequencing, opens, and closes are given to TCP. TCP and IP are tied together so closely that they are used in the same context "TCP/IP."

The User Datagram Protocol (UDP) is sometimes used in place of TCP in situations where the full services of TCP are not needed. For example the Trivial File Transfer Protocol (TFTP), and the Remote Procedure Call (RPC) use UDP, as do voice and video applications.

UDP serves as a simple application interface to the IP. Since it has no reliability, flow control, nor error-recovery measures, it serves principally as a multiplexer/demultiplexer for the receiving and sending of IP traffic.

The Application Layer

The Internet application layer (layer 7 or L_7) protocols serve as a direct service provider to user applications and workstations. Operations, such as electronic mail, file transfer, name servers, and terminal services are provided in this layer.

Some of the more widely used application layer services include:

- TELNET: For terminal services
- Trivial File Transfer Protocol (TFTP): For simple file transfer services
- File Transfer Protocol (FTP): For more elaborate file transfer services
- Simple Mail Transfer Protocol (SMTP): For message transfer services (electronic mail)
- Domain Name System (DNS): For name server operations
- Hypertext Transfer Protocol (HTTP): For Web message transfers
- Simple Network Management Protocol (SNMP): For network management operations
- Several multimedia protocols: MGCP, Megaco, H.225, H.245, and SIP.

NAMES AND ADDRESSES

A newcomer to data networks is often perplexed when the subject of naming and addressing arises. Addresses in data networks are similar to postal addresses and telephone numbering schemes. Indeed, many of the networks that exist today have derived some of their addressing structures from the concepts of the telephone numbering plan.

It should prove useful to clarify the meaning of names, addresses, and routes. A *name* is an identification of an entity (independent of its physical location), such as a person, an applications program, or even a computer. An *address* is also an identification but it reveals additional information about the entity, principally information about its physical or logical placement in a network. A *route* is information on how to relay traffic to a physical location (address).

A network usually provides a service which allows a network user to furnish the network with a name of something (another user, an application, etc.) that is to receive traffic. A network *name server* then uses this name to determine the address of the receiving entity. This address is then used by a routing protocol to determine the physical route to the receiver.

With this approach, a network user does not become involved and is not aware of physical addresses and the physical location of other users and network resources. This practice allows the network administrator to relocate and reconfigure network resources without affecting end users. Likewise, users can move to other physical locations but their names remain the same. The network changes its naming/routing tables to reflect the relocation.

Physical Addresses

Communications between users through a data network requires several forms of addressing. Typically, two addresses are required: (a) a physical address, also called a data link address, and (b) a network address. Other identifiers are needed for unambiguous end-to-end communications between two users, such as upper-layer names and/or port addresses.

Each device (such as a computer or workstation) on a communications link or network is identified with a physical address. This address is also called the hardware address. Many manufacturers place the physical address on a logic board within the device or in an interface unit connected directly to the device. Two physical addresses are employed in a communications dialogue, one address identifies the sender (source) and the other address identifies the receiver (destination). The length of the physical address varies, and most implementations use two 48-bit addresses.

The address detection operation on a LAN is illustrated in Figure 3–2. Device A transmits a frame onto the channel. It is received by all other stations attached to the channel, namely stations B, C, and D. We assume that the destination physical address contains the value C. Consequently, stations B and D ignore the frame. Station C accepts it, performs several tasks associated with the physical layer, strips away the physical layer headers and trailers, and passes the remainder of the packet to the next upper layer.

The MAC Address.   The IEEE assigns LAN addresses. Previously this work was performed by the Xerox Corporation by administering what were known as block identifiers (Block IDs) for Ethernet addresses. The Xerox Ethernet Administration Office assigned these values, which

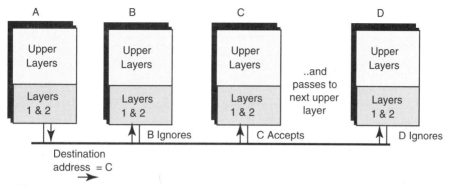

Notes:
    For LANs, address is called a MAC address
    For non-LAN links, address is called a link address, or
    some variation of an "HDLC" address

Where:
    HDLC   High level data link control
    MAC   Media access control

Figure 3–2   Physical Address Detection

were 3 octets (24 bits) in length. The organization that received this address was free to use the remaining 24 bits of the Ethernet address in any way it chose.

Because of the progress made in the IEEE 802 project, it was decided that the IEEE would assume the task of assigning these universal identifiers for all LANs, not just CSMA/CD types of networks. However, the IEEE continues to honor the assignments made by the Ethernet administration office although it now calls the block ID an *organization unique identifier (OUI)*.

The format for the OUI is shown in Figure 3–3. The least significant bit of the address space corresponds to the individual/group (I/G) address bit. The I/G address bit, if set to a zero, means that the address field identifies an individual address. If the value is set to a one, the address field identifies a group address which is used to identify more than one station connected to the LAN. If the entire OUI is set to all ones, it signifies a broadcast address which identifies all stations on the network.

The second bit of the address space is the local or universal bit (U/L). When this bit is set to a zero, it has universal assignment significance—for example, from the IEEE. If it is set to a one it is an address that is locally assigned. Bit position number two must always be set to a zero if it is administered by the IEEE.

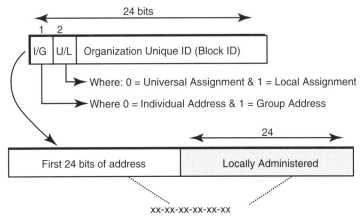

Figure 3–3   Universal Addresses and IDs: The MAC Address

The OUI is extended to include a 48 bit universal LAN address (which is designated as the *media access control [MAC]* address). The 24 bits of the address space is the same as the OUI assigned by the IEEE. The one exception is that the I/G bit may be set to a one or a zero to identify group or individual addresses. The second part of the address space consisting of the remaining 24 bits is locally administered and can be set to any values an organization chooses.

IP Call Processing and MAC Addresses.   The IP Call Processing Protocols do not concern themselves with MAC addresses. If any addressees are used, they are network addresses, such as IP addresses. For native-mode telephony devices, they of course use telephone numbers for their addresses. The resolution of a voice packet to a specific end-point on LAN is not the concern of IP Call Processing; it is handled by the address resolution operations, explained earlier in this chapter.

The Network Address: The IP Address

A network address (or network layer address) identifies a network, or networks. Part of the network address may also designate a computer, a terminal, or anything that a private network administrator wishes to identify within a network (or attached to a network), although the Internet standards place very strict rules on what an IP address identifies.

A network address is a "higher level" address than the physical address. The components in an internet that deal with network addresses need not be concerned with physical addresses until the data has arrived at the network link to which the physical device is attached.

This important concept is illustrated in Figure 3–4. Assume that a user (host computer) in Los Angeles transmits packets to a packet network for relaying to a workstation on a LAN in London. The network in London has a network address of XYZ (this address scheme is explained shortly).

The packets are passed through the packet network (using the network's internal routing mechanisms) to the packet switch in New York. The packet switch in New York routes the packet to the gateway located in London. This gateway examines the destination network address in the packet and determines that the packet is to be routed to network XYZ. It then transmits the packet onto the appropriate communications channel (link) to the node on the LAN that is responsible for communicating with the London gateway.

Notice that this operation did not use any physical addresses in these routing operations. The packet switches and gateway were only concerned with the destination network address of XYZ.

The reader might question how the London LAN is able to pass the packet to the correct device (host). As we learned earlier, a physical address is needed to prevent every packet from being processed by the upper-layer network layer protocols residing in every host attached to the network. Therefore, the answer is that the target network (or gate-

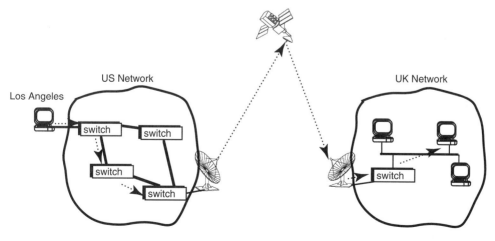

Figure 3–4 Network Layer Addressing

way) must be able to translate a higher layer network destination address to a lower layer physical destination address.

In Figure 3–5, a node on the LAN is a server that is tasked with address resolution. Let us assume that the destination address contains a network address, such as 128.1 *and* a host address, say 3.2. Therefore, the two addresses could be joined (concatenated) to create a full internet network address, which would appear as 128.1.3.2 in the destination address field of the IP datagram.

Once the LAN node receives the datagram from the gateway, it must examine the host address, and either (a) perform a look-up into a table that contains the local physical address and its associated network address, or (b) query the station for its physical address. Then, it encapsulates the user data into the LAN frame, places the appropriate LAN physical layer address in the destination address of the frame, and transmits the frame onto the LAN channel. All devices on the network examine the physical address. If this address matches the device's address, the PDU is passed to the next upper layer; otherwise, it is ignored.

In this manner the two addresses can be associated with each other.

The IP Address.   TCP/IP networks use a 32-bit network layer 3 address to identify a host computer and the network to which the host is attached. The structure of the IP address is depicted in Figure 3–6. Its format is:

IP address = network address + host address

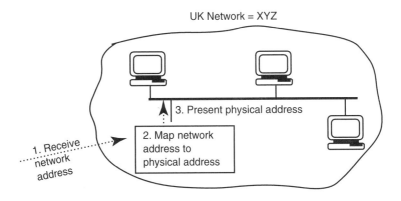

Figure 3–5   Mapping Network Addresses to Physical Addresses

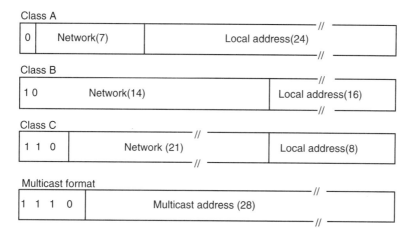

Figure 3–6   Internet Protocol (IP) Address Formats

The IP address identifies a host's connection to its network, that is, a point of attachment. Consequently, if a host machine is moved to another network, its address must be changed. This aspect of the IP address has major implications for mobile systems, discussed in Chapter 11.

In the past, IP addresses have been classified by their formats:[2] class A, class B, class C, or class D formats. As illustrated in Figure 3–6, the first bits of the address specify the format of the remainder of the address field in relation to the network and host subfields. The host address is also called the local address (also called the REST field).

The *class A* addresses provide for networks that have a large number of hosts. The host ID field is 24 bits. Therefore, 2^{24} hosts can be identified. Seven bits are devoted to the network ID, which supports an identification scheme for as many as 127 networks (bit values of 1 to 127).

Class B addresses are used for networks of intermediate size. Fourteen bits are assigned for the network ID, and 16 bits are assigned for the host ID. *Class C* networks contain fewer than 256 hosts (2^8). Twenty-one bits are assigned to the network ID. Finally, *class D* addresses are reserved for multicasting, which is a form of broadcasting but within a limited area.

---

[2]I say "in the past," but this system still prevails. Yet, it is being replaced by a concept called classless addresses, a topic explained in Chapter 7.

IP Call Processing and IP Addresses.   The IP Call Processing Protocols must be able to process IP addresses. Even though they are not tasked with the actual forwarding of the IP datagrams (in which the Call Processing message resides), in many instances they rely on IP addresses for the identification of their sessions (connections) between the calling and called parties.

A BRIEF LOOK AT IP

I mentioned earlier that it is not the intent of this book to describe in detail the current Internet Protocols. So, a productive approach to a general analysis of IP is to examine the fields in the IP datagram (PDU) depicted in Figure 3–7.

The *version* field identifies the version of IP in use. Most protocols contain this field because some network nodes may not have the latest release available of the protocol. The current version of IP is 4, or IPv4.

The *header length* field contains 4 bits which are set to a value to indicate the length of the datagram header. The length is measured in 32-bit words. Typically, a header without QOS options contains 20 octets. Therefore, the value in the length field is usually 5.

The *total length* field specifies the total length of the IP datagram. It is measured in octets and includes the length of the header and the data. IP subtracts the header length field from the total length field to compute the size of the data field. The maximum possible length of a data-

0	1-2	3	4	5-6	7	8	9-14	15	16	17-22	23	24	25-30	31
Version		H-Length		Type of Service (TOS)					Total Length					
Identifier								Flags		Fragment Offset				
Time to Live				Protocol				Header Checksum						
Source Address (32)														
Destination Address (32)														
Options and Padding (Variable)														
Data (Variable)														

Where:
  H-Length   Header Length

Figure 3–7   The IP Datagram

gram is 65,535 octets (2^{16}). Gateways that service IP datagrams are required to accept any datagram that supports the maximum size of a PDU of the attached networks. Additionally, all gateways must accommodate datagrams of 576 octets in total length.

Each 32-bit value is transmitted in this order: (a) bits 0–7, (b) bits 8–15, (c) bits 16–23, and (d) bits 24–31. This is known as big endian byte ordering.

Type of Service (TOS)

The *type of service (TOS)* field can be used to identify several QOS functions provided for an Internet application. Transit delay, throughput, precedence, and reliability can be requested with this field. Therefore, this field can be used as a means for prioritizing traffic in a multiservice internet.

The *TOS field* is not used in some vendors' implementations of IP. Nonetheless, it will be used increasingly in the future as the internet capabilities are increased. For example, it is used in the Open Shortest Path First (OSPF) protocol. Consequently, a user should examine this field for future work and ascertain a vendor's use or intended support of this field.

Fragmentation Fields

The IP protocol uses three fields in the header to control datagram fragmentation and reassembly. These fields are the *identifier, flags,* and *fragmentation offset.* The identifier field is used to uniquely identify all fragments from an original datagram. It is used with the source address at the receiving host to identify the fragment. The flags field contains bits to determine if the datagram may be fragmented, and if fragmented, one of the bits can be set to determine if this fragment is the last fragment of the datagram. The fragmentation offset field contains a value which specifies the relative position of the fragment to the original datagram. The value is initialized as 0 and is subsequently set to the proper number if/when an IP node fragments the data. The value is measured in units of eight octets.

Time-to-live (TTL) Field

The *time-to-live (TTL)* field is used to measure the time a datagram has been in the internet. Each gateway in the internet is required to check this field and discard the datagram if the TTL value equals 0. An IP node is also required to decrement this field in each datagram it processes. In actual implementations, the TTL field is a number of hops value. Therefore, when a datagram proceeds through a gateway (hop), the value in the field is decremented by a value of one. Some implementations of IP use a time-counter in this field and decrement the value in one-second decrements.

The time-to-live (TTL) field is used not only to prevent endless loops, it can also be used by the host to limit the lifetime that datagrams have in an internet. Be aware that if a host is acting as a "route-through" node, it must treat the TTL field by the router rules. The reader should check with the vendor to determine when a host throws away a datagram based on the TTL value.

Ideally, the TTL value could be configured and its value assigned based on observing an internet's performance. Additionally, network management information protocols such as those residing in SNMP might wish to set the TTL value for diagnostic purposes. Finally, if your vendor uses a fixed value that cannot be reconfigured, make certain that it is fixed initially to allow for your internet's growth.

Protocol Field

The *protocol* field is used to identify the next protocol that is to receive the datagram at the final host destination. It is similar to the Ethertype field found in the Ethernet frame, but identifies the payload in the data field of the IP datagram. The Internet standards groups have established a numbering system to identify the most widely used protocols that "reside" in the IP datagram data field. This field is also called the protocol ID (PID).

Header Checksum

The *header checksum* is used to detect an error that may have occurred in the header. Checks are not performed on the user data stream. Some critics of IP have stated that the provision for error detection in the user data should allow the receiving gateway to at least notify the sending host that problems have occurred. (This service is indeed provided by a companion standard to IP [the ICMP].) Whatever one's view on the issue, the current approach keeps the checksum algorithm in IP quite simple. It does not have to operate on many octets, but it does require that a higher level protocol at the receiving host must perform some type of error check on the user data if it cares about its integrity.

Address Fields

IP carries two addresses in the datagram. These are labeled *source* and *destination addresses* and remain the same value throughout the life of the datagram. These fields contain the Internet addresses, described earlier in this chapter.

Options Field

The *options* field is used to identify several additional services.[3] The options field is not used in every datagram. The majority of implementations use this field for network management and diagnostics. Many implementations do not even use this field.

IP provides two options in routing the datagram to the final destination. The first, called *loose source routing,* gives the IP nodes the option of using intermediate hops to reach the addresses obtained in the source list as long as the datagram traverses the nodes listed. Conversely, *strict source routing* requires that the datagram travel only through the networks whose addresses are indicated in the source list. If the strict source route cannot be followed, the originating host IP is notified with an error message. Both loose and strict routing require that the route recording feature be implemented.

A BRIEF LOOK AT TCP AND UDP

The Transmission Control Protocol (TCP) and the User Datagram Protocol (UDP) operate at layer 4 of the Internet protocol stack. TCP is a connection-oriented protocol and is responsible for the reliable transfer of user traffic between two hosts. Consequently, it uses sequence numbers and acknowledgments to make certain all traffic is delivered safely to the destination endpoint.

UDP is a connectionless protocol and does not provide sequencing or acknowledgments. It is used in place of TCP in situations where the full services of TCP are not needed. For example, telephony traffic, the Trivial File Transfer Protocol (TFTP), and the Remote Procedure Call (RPC) use UDP. Since it has no reliability, flow control, nor error-recovery measures, UDP serves principally as a multiplexer/demultiplexer for the receiving and sending of traffic into and out of an application.

---

[3]The option field has fallen into disuse by routers, because of the processing overhead required to support the features it identifies.

The Internet Port

A TCP or UDP user in a host machine is identified by a *port* identifier. The port number is concatenated with the IP internet address to form a *socket*. This address must be unique throughout the internet and a pair of sockets uniquely identifies each endpoint connection. In some of the IP Call Processing literature, the IP address and a port number are called a transport address. Here are two examples of the use of these values:

Sending socket = Source IP address + source port number
Receiving socket = Destination IP address + destination port number

Although the mapping of ports to higher layer processes can be handled as an internal matter in a host, the Internet publishes numbers for frequently used higher level processes. For many of the IP Call Processing operations, the port numbers are set up between a called and calling party during the call processing handshake.

The Segment

The packets exchanged between two TCP modules are called segments. Figure 3–8 illustrates the format for the segment.

The first two fields of the segment are identified as *source port* and *destination port*. These 16-bit fields are used to identify the upper-layer application programs that are using the TCP connection.

The next field is labeled *sequence number*. This field contains the sequence number of the first octet in the user data field. Its value specifies

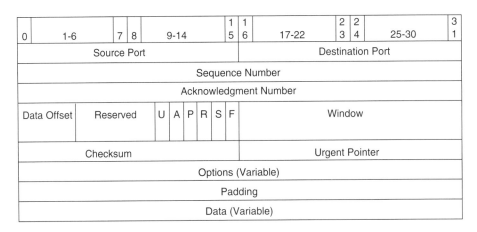

Figure 3–8   The TCP Segment (PDU)

the position of the transmitting module's byte stream. Within the segment, it specifies the first user data octet in the segment.

The sequence number is also used during a connection management operation. If a connection request segment is used between two TCP entities, the sequence number specifies the *initial send sequence (ISS)* number that is to be used for the subsequent numbering of the user data.

The *acknowledgment number* is set to a value which acknowledges data previously received. The value in this field contains the value of the sequence number of the next expected octet from the transmitter. Since this number is set to the next expected octet, it provides an inclusive acknowledgment capability, in that it acknowledges all octets up to and including this number, minus 1.

The *data offset* field specifies the number of 32-bit aligned words that comprise the TCP header. This field is used to determine where the data field begins.

As the reader might expect, the *reserved* field is reserved. It consists of 6 bits which must be set to zero. These bits are reserved for future use.

The next six fields are called flags. They are labeled as control bits by TCP and they are used to specify certain services and operations which are to be used during the session. Some of the bits determine how to interpret other fields in the header. The six bits are used to convey the following information:

- *URG (U):* This flag signifies if the urgent pointer field is significant.
- *ACK (A):* This flag signifies if the acknowledgment field is significant.
- *PSH (P):* This flag signifies that the module is to exercise the push function. Some systems do not support the push function, but rely on TCP to "push" the traffic efficiently.
- *RST (R):* This flag indicates that the connection is to be reset.
- *SYN (S):* This flag is used to indicate that the sequence numbers are to be synchronized; it is used with the connection-establishment segments as a flag to indicate handshaking operations are to take place.
- *FIN (F):* This flag indicates that the sender has no more data to send and is comparable to the end-of-transmission (EOT) signal in other protocols.

The next field is labeled *window*. This value is set to a value indicating how many octets the receiver is willing to accept. The value is established based on the value in the acknowledgment field (acknowledgment number). The window is established by adding the value in the window field to the value of the acknowledgment number field.

The purpose of the checksum calculation is to determine if the segment has arrived error-free from the transmitter.

The next field in the segment is labeled the *urgent pointer*. This field is only used if the URG flag is set. The purpose of the urgent pointer is to signify the data octet in which urgent data follows. Urgent data is also called *out-of-band* data. TCP does not dictate what happens for urgent data. It is implementation specific. It only signifies where the urgent data is located. It is an offset from the sequence number and points to the octet following the urgent data.

The *options* field was conceived to provide for future enhancements to TCP. It is constructed in a manner similar to that of IP datagrams option field, in that each option specification consists of a single byte containing an option number, a field containing the length of the option, and last the option values themselves.

Presently the option field is limited in its use, but options are available dealing with size of the TCP data field, window size, a time-stamp for an echo, and some others under consideration. For more information, see RFC 1323.

Finally, the *padding* field is used to insure that the TCP header is filled to an even multiple of 32 bits. After that, as the figure illustrates, user *data* follows.

The options field in the TCP header can contain a number of options, and the original specification included only the maximum segment size (MSS) option. This option is almost universal, and is found in practically all TCP SYN segments. The MSS value permits the two TCP entities to inform each other about the size of their traffic units, and to reserve buffer of their reception. The other options are relatively new, and their implementation will depend upon the TCP product. For more information, see RFCs 793 and 1323.

THE DOMAIN NAME SYSTEM (DNS)

This section examines the Domain Name System (DNS) specification. DNS is the Internet standard that defines the Internet name server operations. One of its principal jobs is to map (or correlate) a "user-friendly" e-mail name to a routeable address.

This type of service is quite helpful to a user, because the user is not tasked with remembering an abstract address of a person (or application) with whom the user wishes to communicate. Rather, the sending user need only know a "easy-to-remember" text-oriented value (a name) of the recipient. This name is keyed-in during a session, relayed to a name server, which looks-up an associated address.

Figure 3–9 shows the approach used with DNS. In event 1, a person enters a domain name for Uyless Black: ublack@infoinst.com. The name server software in the host forms a query to a local name server (event 2). In effect, this query asks the name server to look-up the name in the DNS database and find an associated address. In event 3, the name server responds with a reply which associates *ublack@infoinst.com* to address 38.146.104.234.

In event 4, this address is placed into the destination IP address field of the IP datagram and in event 5, it is sent to a local router. The router receives the datagram (event 6), and finds a match in its routing table with the identification address in the datagram (event 7), which reveals the node to receive the datagram, as well as the outgoing physical port (interface) through which the datagram is transported to the next node (event 8).

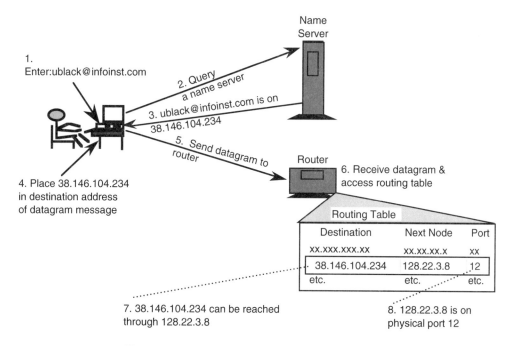

Figure 3–9   Operations with Name Servers

THE DNS ROOT SERVERS

The DNS in the Internet is organized around root servers.[4] The Root Nameserver System is comprised of three major components, the DNS protocol itself, the *root zone file,* and the *root name servers.* This section describes these components in some detail.

The root of the Internet namespace consists of a single file, the root zone file, which describes the delegations of the top level domains and the associated records necessitated by the DNS protocol to implement those delegations. Currently, this file is maintained by Network Solutions Incorporated (NSI) of Herndon, Virginia, and is made available to the 12 secondary servers from the primary a.root-server.net. Change control of this file is held by the IANA. Typically modifications of the name servers for top level domains are made approximately once or twice a week.

The root zone file is made available to the root name servers either in-band via the DNS protocol itself (through zone transfers as described in RFC 1034) or out-of-band via the FTP protocol (as described in RFC 952). Given the relatively small size of the root zone, most updates of the root zone file are propagated via zone transfers.

The root zone file itself is composed of 7-bit ASCII characters and contains an SOA (start of zone authority) record, NS (name server) records for each of the top level domain zone delegations, and associated glue records. As a (human) administrative convenience, the SOA serial number is often represented as a date indicating the last modification to the zone file, typically of the form YYYYMMDDXX where YYYY is the year, MM is the month (1–12), DD is the day (1–31), and XX is a sequence number indicating the number of updates within a day.

The root name servers are the machines that provide access to the root zone file for proper DNS protocol operation. Due to protocol limitations, the number of these machines is currently limited to 13, although efforts are underway to remove this limitation. A conscious effort has been made to diversify the administration of these 13 machines in several areas.

DNS Support of IP Call Processing Operations

The DNS information is organized into specific records in the data bases at the DNS servers. Each record is called a Resource Record (RR),

---

[4]The information from this section is sourced from the Internet Software Consortium (http://www.isc.org/). Their paper was focused on the potential Y2K problem, and I have not included this part of the paper in my summary. I thank the Internet Software Consortium for this information. As you can see from Table 3–1, they run DNS site F.

Table 3–1   Current DNS Root Servers

A	Network Solutions, Inc.	Herndon, VA USA	http://www.netsol.com
B	Information Sciences Institute, USC	Marina Del Rey, CA USA	http://www.isi.edu
C	PSINet	Herndon, VA USA	http://www.psi.net
D	University of Maryland	College Park, MD USA	http://www.umd.edu
E	NASA	Mountain View, CA USA	http://www.nasa.gov
F	Internet Software Consortium	Palo Alto, CA USA	http://www.isc.org
G	Defense Information Systems Agency	Vienna, VA USA	http://www.nic.mil
H	Army Research Laboratory	Aberdeen, MD USA	http://www.arl.mil
I	NORDUNet	Stockholm Sweden	http://www.nordu.net
J	To Be Determined	Herndon, VA USA	
K	RIPE-NCC	London UK	http://www.ripe.net
L	To Be Determined	Marina Del Rey, CA USA	
M	WIDE	Tokyo Japan	http://wide.ad.jp

and it is identified by the type of record, called the RR type. The most common RR is the address record (the A RR). Its entry contains the domain name (such as infoinst.com) and an associated IP address (such as 172.16.14.88).

In a typical name-to-address look up, the exact address of a server is entered into a query or a broadcast is sent out onto a subnet. To provide for more flexibility to this arrangement, RFC 2052 defines a new RR, designated as the SRV RR. It allows the use of multiple servers for a single DSN domain. With this approach, a DNS client can ask for a specific service from a specific domain, yet get back the names of more than one server that can provide the service.

The Uniform Resource Identifier (URI)

One of the attractive features of many of the IP Call Processing protocols is the use of conventional Internet naming and addressing methods. They use the Uniform Resource Identifier (URI) to identify the participants in the session.[5] In addition, since URIs are based on the Do-

---

[5]Tim Berners-Lee, the man behind the invention of the Web, devised the URI, and considers it, in his words, "the most fundamental innovation of the Web." Later, the IETF renamed the URI the URL (L, for Locator). Berners-Lee still prefers the term URI. The IETF considers a URI as a URL. Most people use the two terms synonymously.

main Name System (DNS), and DNS is used to correlate DNS names to IP addresses, these Call Processing protocols take advantage of the ongoing Internet naming and addressing architecture.

RFC 2396 provides guidance on the use of URIs [BERN98].[6] For the reader working with URIs, RFC is a very valuable resource. It also revises and replaces the generic URI definitions in RFC 1738 and RFC 1808.

HTTP, HTML

The HTTP protocol (Hypertext Transfer Protocol) is a request/response protocol, and is descried in RFC 2608. A client sends a request to the server in the form of a request method, URI, and protocol version, followed by a MIME-like message containing request modifiers, client information, and possible body content over a connection with a server. The server responds with a status line, including the message's protocol version and a success or error code, followed by a MIME-like message containing server information, entity metainformation, and possible entity-body content. HTTP uses the augmented Bakus Naur Form (BNR) convention for describing the structure and contents of the messages. Many examples of augmented BNR are provided in this book.

The Hypertex Markup Language (HTML) is used to define the structure of data. HTML is not a conventional programming language, such as C. Rather it is defines the format of a Web document and supports hypertext links to be embedded in the document.

SUMMARY

The Internet protocols explained in this chapter form the bedrock of the Internet. The IP Call Processing Protocols use all these protocols to support their operations. However, with few exceptions, the Call Processing Protocols are unaware of most of these bedrock operations. The notable exceptions are the use of IP addresses and port numbers. Indeed, in most instances, Internet call processing operations are tasked with keeping track of all the media streams flowing among the users. These streams are identified partially with port numbers.

---

[6][BERN98] Berners-Lee, Tim, et al. Uniform Resource Identifiers (URI): Generic Syntax, RFC 2386, August, 1998.

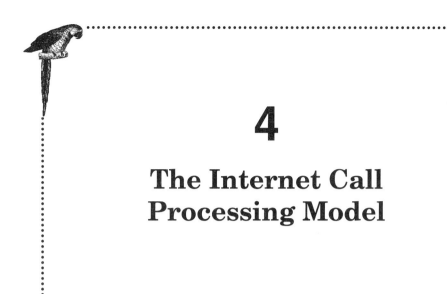

4

The Internet Call Processing Model

INTRODUCTION

This chapter introduces the Internet Call Processing Model. In the first part of the chapter, the key components of the model are explained, such as Gateways, and Gateway Controllers. Several alternatives exist for the implementation of this model, and they are described.

In the second part of the chapter, the Call Processing Model is described in the context of the Internet-layered protocol suite. During this discussion, the principal IP Call Processing Protocols (and key supporting protocols) are introduced.

THE GATEWAY/GATEKEEPER/MEDIA GATEWAY CONTROLLER MODEL

Earlier chapters explained that several terms are used to describe the placement of Internet call processing functions in the physical nodes. This aspect of packet telephony can be confusing because the various specifications use different terms to describe the same or similar functions. For example, H.323 uses the term Gatekeeper to describe a similar entity residing in MGCP as a Call Agent, and in Megaco as a Media Gateway Controller.

To help clarify these terms and concepts, [VAND98][1] has published a model of the Media Gateway Controller and the Media Gateway, which also includes the Gatekeeper, the H.323 terminal, and the Signaling Gateway. This model is shown in Figure 4–1. The model is not yet finished, and some of the references (A, B, C, etc.) have not been fully defined.

In this model, the Gateway is actually made up of the Media Gateway Controller (MGC), the Media Gateway (MG), and the Signaling Gateway (SG). The overall Gateway (made up of these components) is the entity in the network that interfaces an IP-based network and the telephony network. It must provide two-way, real-time communications interfaces between the IP-based network and the telephony network. The three components that make up the Gateway are described next. The nodes labeled "Gatekeeper" and "Backend" are also explained.

Media Gateway

The *Media Gateway* provides the mapping and translation functions between the IP/telephony networks. For example, it might translate G.711 64 kbit/s speech into G.723.1 6.3 kbit/s speech or vice versa. These operations are referred to as stream conditioning and may also include echo cancellation, if necessary. For traffic emanating from the IP network, the packet media termination is performed since packets do not operate on the telephony side. Therefore, these packets must be mapped into telephony bearer channels (a DS0, or a ISDN B channel, as examples). The opposite operations occur when traffic emanates from the telephony network.

The Media Gateway may also be responsible for support services such as playing announcements, and tone generation as necessary. It keeps track of traffic and has statistics available on network usage. The responsibilities may be off-loaded to the Backend, shown in Figure 4–1.

Signaling Gateway

The *Signaling Gateway* is responsible for the signaling operations of the system. It provides the interworking of say, H.323 and SS7 ISUP signaling operations. For example, it might translate an H.323 SETUP mes-

---

[1][VAND98] Vandenameele, Jozef. Requirements for the Reference Point ('N') between Media Gateway Controller and Media Gateway. Draft-vandenameele-tiphon-archgway-decomp-00.txt, November 1988.

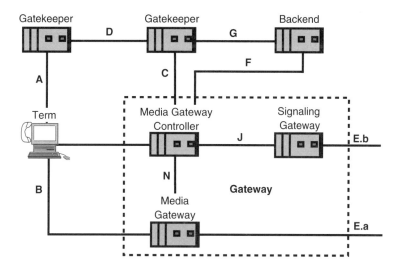

Figure 4-1 The VoIP Gateway/Gatekeeper Reference Model [VAND98]

sage coming from an H.323 Gatekeeper into an SS7 ISUP Initial Address Message (IAM) that is to go to a telephony exchange. It may translate the analog telephone signaling tones to binary numbers for transport over a data network in a packet, and translate the binary representations back to the telephone signaling tones at the receiving end.

Synchronizing Signals. The mapping of the analog tones into binary equivalents is an easy and straightforward task. A more difficult job for the signaling gateway is the ability to accept varying signal streams from the telephone. For example, some people press a button on the telephone pad for a long time, and wait some time before pressing another. At the other extreme, a dialed-digit stream entered automatically from a personal computer dials all the digits in a couple of seconds or so. The signaling gateway must not only be able to accept these signaling variations, but represent them correctly in a data message, for proper translation at the other end of the line. This correct representation is important for purposes of synchronization with telephone systems' equipment and software.

Media Gateway Controller

The *Media Gateway Controller* is the overall controller of the system. That is, it controls the Media Gateway and the Signaling Gateway. It must interwork with the H.232 Gatekeeper, so it is able to process

H.225 and H.245 messages (explained later in this book). It is also responsible for authentication and network security. It monitors the resources of the overall system, and maintains control of all connections.

Other Components

The *Gatekeeper* (an H.323 term) is also a controller and has some of the same responsibilities as the Media Gateway Controller. Its job is to control the H.323 activities on the IP-based network.

The *Backend* may be used by the Gateways and Gatekeepers to provide support functions such as billing, database management, routing and address resolution.

The reference interfaces labeled E are: (a) E.a is the interface for telephony user links (lines and trunks), (b) E.b is the interface for the SS7 signaling links. The J and N reference interfaces are where Megaco and MGCP operate. The H.323 control protocol operates over reference interfaces D, A, G, and C.

A UNIFIED VIEW

The intent of the Internet call processing gateway model is for it to act as an internal service in a distributed system that to the outside of this system, appears as a single "Gateway," as depicted in Figure 4–2.

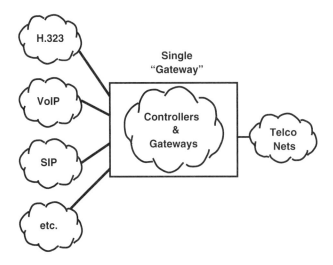

Figure 4–2   Unified View of the Internet Telephony Gateways

The system contains Controllers and Gateways. The system interfaces on one side with a telephony system and on the other with an H.323 conformant system, a SIP system, a basic Internet telephony device, and other systems and protocols.

Therefore, the Internet Gateway model must be "conversant" in the ISDN User Part (ISUP) and other telephony protocols on one side and packet telephony protocols, such as H.323 protocols on the other side.

THE SIGNALING GATEWAY IN MORE DETAIL

As we have learned, the signaling gateway is concerned with interfacing with the user's telephone's control operations. This interface entails accepting the telephone's signals, such as its dialed digits, its off hook indicator, etc., and converting those signals into binary bits (placed in packets), a concept shown in Figure 4–3. This information is then treated as data by the gateway, and are encapsulated into the IP datagram for forwarding, say to a router.

The binary representation of the telephone signals can take one or two forms: (a) assigning a reserved name for each tone (for example, a name for the digit 5), or (b) describing the acoustical property of the signal (for example, 770/1336 DTMF Hz for digit 5). Whatever the option, these binary representations must be converted back to native tones at the called telephone.

The IP datagram has the appearance of any other piece of traffic sent through the Internet. Its distinguishing feature is that it has different performance requirements (in contrast to data), a subject explained in Appendix A.

The "voice packets" are sent through the Internet using the same operations as those for "data packets." At the receiving end, the process is reversed. The IP payload of binary images of telephone events and signals must be translated back into native telephony signals. For example, let us assume that the payload is indeed the dialed number of the called party. The gateway for the called party must be able to analyze the number and place a ringing signal on the correct gateway interface to the called party.

This configuration may not work if these signals must be transported through the telephone network (telco, for telephone company), as shown in Figure 4–4. The circuit-switched telephone network operates on DS1-based signals. The Gateway on the user "line" side converts the DTMF signals to DS1 bits in the DS1 frame for operations on the telco

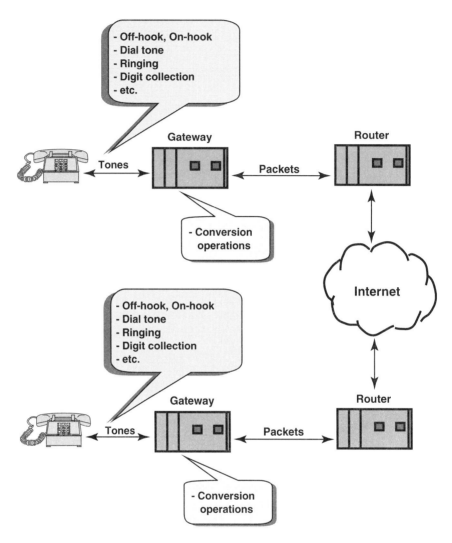

Figure 4–3   Signaling Gateway: Mapping Tones and Packets

signaling network. If the Gateway is interfacing with the circuit switch, as shown in this example, it must be able to accept the conventional signals from the calling party, such as off-hook, a dialed digit, etc., and convert them into the conventional form that is acceptable to the telco signaling network; that is, the telephone trunk signals. For example, the gateway might be required to map the calling party's off-hook signal into a DS1 frame (in the bit robbing bits).

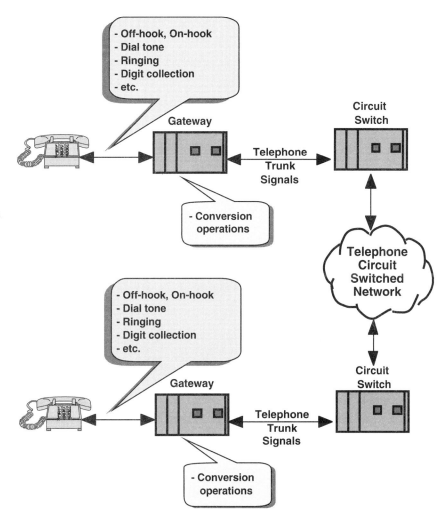

Figure 4–4   An Inefficient Implementation

You may be asking, "What is the point of the configuration in Figure 4–4?" All that has been done is to superimpose a "Gateway" into the operation, and this "Gateway" is already a part of the telco architecture. It is called a circuit switch, and it provides the mapping operations between the local loop and the network trunks.

The point is well-made, and this configuration makes little sense. But consider the configuration in Figure 4–5. Here, we have an IP telephony terminal, in that it is sending and receiving packets (not tones) to and from the gateway. At the other end of the connection, there is a native-mode telephone, operating with conventional analog frequency tones.

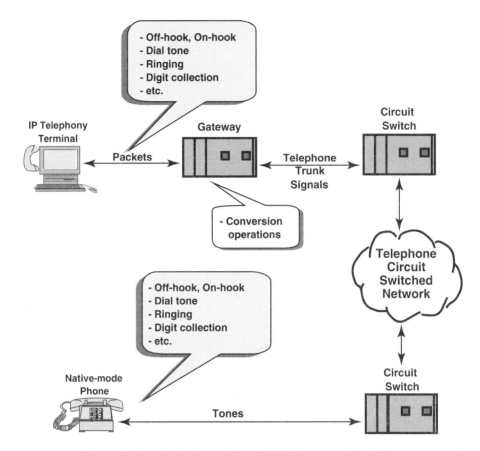

Figure 4–5   Packets on One End, Tones on the Other

The use of the gateway now makes sense. It acts as an interworking unit between the "packet terminal" and the circuit switch. In addition, the gateway must convert the IP-based telephony message (coded in Web-based syntax) to the conventional telco format (for example, the SS7 message syntax [the telephone trunk signals]) for processing through the telco network.

Another extension to these configurations yields some significant advantages to a user, shown in Figure 4–6. Notations have been added representing the several important parts of the modern Internet: (a) the Domain Name System (DNS), and (b) the Web (with its URL, HTML, and HTTP conventions). In addition, the user terminals are now native-mode IP telephony instruments, and the gateway functions have been integrated into the router. This model is the ultimate goal of Internet telephony and call processing, and its advantages were described in Chapter 1.

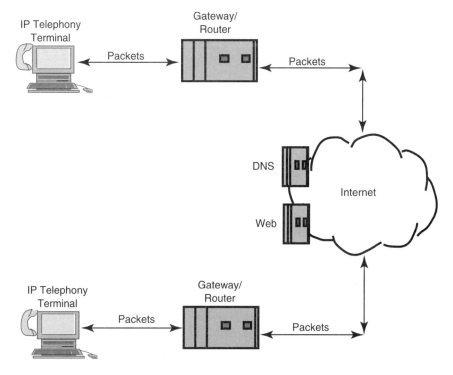

Figure 4–6   The All-Packet System

The configuration in Figure 4–6 may be one to which the world evolves. But for now, it is missing a very important piece of the IP multimedia puzzle: the telco's vast repository of information dealing with 800 numbers, 888 numbers, 911 numbers, credit data, and scores of service features (IN/AIN capabilities, for example).

It is folly to assume one can abandon these sources of information, and develop redundant (and competing) services. Therefore, another gateway is needed, the so-called IP/SS7 gateway, shown in Figure 4–7. This gateway provides the interface into the many service features of the telephone system, including call directories, 800, 900, 888, 911 services, as well as the Advanced Intelligent Network (AIN)/Intelligent Network (IN) databases and software.

One last depiction of the Model shows the legacy telephone services and network being replaced with DNS/Web-based operations. In Figure 4–8, the "Telco cloud" is absorbed into the Internet architecture. This may seem far-fetched. After all, the replacements and transitions would be immense.

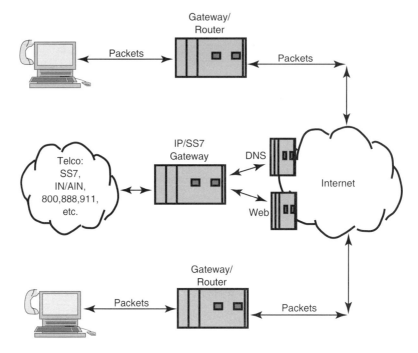

Figure 4–7   Interfacing with the Telco's Service Features

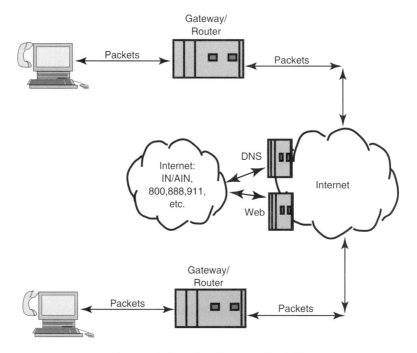

Figure 4–8   The Future Model?

If this "absorption" occurs, it will be on an evolutionary basis. Certainly, we will see extensive Web-based call features in the near future. And as the roles of the traditional telephone service providers meld with those of the Internet service providers, it is likely that we will witness an integration of the public telephone networks with the public Internet.

THE INTERNET LAYERED MODEL AND THE INTERNET CALL PROCESSING MODEL

The Internet Call Processing Model can be viewed another way, that of a layered architecture in relation to the Internet Layered Model. The idea is shown in Figure 4–9. These protocol stacks or planes are shown:

- *Call Processing Protocols:* These protocols form the basis for most of the call processing for voice or video services, and they are the primary subjects of this book.
- *User Protocols:* These protocols form the basis for the user applications and of course the user voice, video and data traffic. Examples are file transfers, e-mail, telephone calls, teleconferences, Web surfing, etc.
- *Support Protocols:* These protocols support the Call Processing Protocols. They do not control a call per se, but assist the Call Processing Protocols.

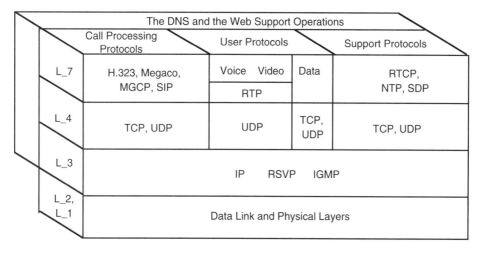

Figure 4–9   The Call Processing Layered Model

- *The DNS and the Web Plane:* These services are positioned as a second plane in the Model to connote the fact that they are supportive of all the other protocols; indeed, they are vital. This second plane reaches down to layers 7, 4, and 3 to support most of the protocols and services shown in the figure.
- *Layers 1 and 2:* These layers remain transparent to the Call Processing operations. Other books in this series describe these layers.

Overview of the Protocols and Planes in the Call Processing Model

As a prelude to the subsequent chapters in this book, this section provides an introduction to the protocols and planes shown in Figure 4–9. We start at the lower layers and work our way up to layer 7.

- *IP:* The Internet Protocol (IP) is essentially a forwarding protocol. It carries a source IP address and a destination IP address in the IP header. The destination IP address is examined at each router and is used to access a routing table, which is then used to forward the IP datagram to the next node. One of the IP address formats is used for multicasting. Thus, IP is an important component in the Internet's multicasting operations.
- *RSVP:* As its name implies, the resource reservation protocol (RSVP) is used to reserve resources for a session in an Internet. RSVP is intended to provide guaranteed performance by reserving the necessary resources at each machine that participates in supporting the flow of traffic (such as a video or audio conference).
- *IGMP:* The Internet Group Management Protocol (IGMP) is designed to support multicasting operations. It allows a user machine (a host) to join a multicast group. After which, the host receives any multicasting traffic sent within this group.
- *TCP:* The Transmission Control Protocol (TCP) operates at layer 4 of the layered model. TCP is responsible for the reliable transfer of user traffic between two computers. Consequently, it uses sequence numbers and acknowledgments to make certain all traffic is delivered safely to the destination endpoint. If something goes wrong, and the traffic does not arrive at the receiver correctly, TCP has the means to resend the traffic. For internet telephony, TCP is not used for voice traffic. Due to its operating characteris-

tics, it introduces too much overhead and delay. It is used extensively for the support of the transmissions of call processing messages, such as a connect request message.

- *UDP:* The user datagram protocol (UDP) has long been a mainstay in an internet. It is a very important tool for multiservice operations, such as telephony and video, because it is used to manage the Internet ports, over which several of the multiservice applications operate. These Internet ports are used to identify each layer 7 application; that is to say, the application that runs on top of UDP. UDP is used in place of TCP for real-time traffic (again, such as voice and video), because it does not have the overhead and delay of TCP's flow control and retransmission operations.

- *H.323:* H.323 is a Call Processing Protocol, with a variety of features, such as multipoint operations, as well as registration and admission procedures into a conference or a single call. It also provides an operation for bandwidth management on the network facilities in which it is in charge.

- *Megaco:* Megaco is a Call Processing Protocol, also with a variety of features, some similar to H.323. Its operations are Web-based in that it uses Web syntax for its messages. Megaco is part of the H.xxx specifications, and acts as a companion to H.323. It is published as H.248.

- *MGCP:* MGCP is yet another Call Processing Protocol, and is quite similar to Megaco. It was developed prior to Megaco. Many of Megaco's features are based on MGCP.

- *SIP:* The Session Initiation Protocol (SIP) is also a Call Processing Protocol. It, too, has similarities to H.323, Megaco, and MGCP. But it also has unique characteristics, such as a heavy reliance on the Domain Name System (DNS), Universal Resource Locators (URLs). Part of its service is to keep track of clients and servers that are part of a "Calling Domain," a concept explained in Chapter 1. Its operations are also Web-based.

- *RTP:* The Real Time Protocol (RTP) is designed for the support of real-time traffic, that is traffic that needs to be sent and received in a very short time period. RTP is also an encapsulation protocol in that the real time traffic runs in the data field of the RTP packet, and the RTP header contains information about the type of traffic that RTP is transporting. (While RTP can perform this function, not all multiservice applications will use RTP. Each IP telephony or video commercial product should be evaluated to determine the exact "protocol mix" in the offering). RTP also has a time-stamp field in its header. It can be used to synchronize the traffic play-out to the receiving application.

- *RTCP:* After a reservation has been established through the use of RSVP (or some other means), the traffic is then sent between machines with RTP. Next, the Real Time Control Protocol (RTCP) may come into the picture by providing the procedure for the parties to keep each other informed about (a) the quality of services they think they are providing (if they are service providers), and/or (b) the quality of services they are receiving (if they are service clients). In concept, a server can adjust its quality of service operations depending on the feedback it receives from its clients. However, the manner in which these adjustments are made is not defined by RTCP.

- *NTP:* The network time protocol (NTP) is used for time-stamping operations. Clocking information for a network is provided through the primary time server designated as a root. The time server obtains its clocking information from master sources. In the United States, this is usually one of four sources: (a) Fort Collins, Colorado: Station WWV operated by the National Institute of Standards and Technology (NIST) using high frequency (HF) frequencies. (b) Kauai, Hawaii: Station WWVH operated by NIST, also operating with HF frequencies. (c) Boulder, Colorado: Station WWVB operating with low frequency transmissions. (d) Geosynchronous Orbiting Environmental Satellite (GOES): Operated by NIST in the UHF range. These "master clocking sources" are used to derive accurate clocks by the primary time server. Other countries may have their own clocks that are used to provide clocking over large areas. Most of these clocks provide very accurate clocking synchronization on the order of less than 1 millisecond. Local clocks are even more accurate.

- *SDP:* The Session Description Protocol (SDP) is designed to convey session information to recipients, as well as media information that pertain to the session. SDP is purely a format for session description—it does not incorporate a transport protocol, and is intended to use different transport protocols as appropriate.

- *Voice traffic:* Figure 4–9 shows the protocol placement of voice in the Call Model. Actually, it can run directly over IP, or over the User Datagram Protocol (UDP) then IP, or over RTP. While products vary in the placement of voice in the Call Model, the running of voice over RTP is preferred, and this statement will be explained in considerable detail later.

Why Multiple Call Processing Protocols?

Four different Call Processing Protocols are shown in the Model: (a) H.323, (b) Megaco, (c) MGCP, and (d) SIP. As we learned, there is considerable overlap in their operations, yet they each have unique attributes. The reasons multiple Call Processing Protocols exist are explained in the following sections.

Different Design Philosophies in the Standards Committees. The people who participate in the task forces and working groups that publish the Call Processing Protocol specifications have different views of how the protocol should operate. These differing views can result in multiple task forces being formed, resulting in the publication of multiple call processing specifications.

Different Standards Groups. As a general statement, the ITU-T, the ISO, the IEEE, the IETF, and others have a very elaborate structure for the creation and publication of "their" standards. In some situations, it is important to these organizations to be the authoritative body for a standard. After all, they are organizations, and organizations must have a reason to exist.

But it is not just a matter of protecting "turf" for turf's sake. Like the designers on the committees, these organizations have philosophical views on how a communications infrastructure should evolve, and call processing is a small part of the total system. For example, historically, the ITU-T has been circuit switch-oriented, and the IETF has been packet-switch-oriented. The ITU-T has preferred to endorse ASN.1 for defining message syntax, while the IETF has preferred text-based message syntax, and so on.

Vendor Preferences. Vendors play a big role in the development of the call processing standards. It is often to the advantage of a vendor to get its views inculcated into a specification. Thus, the task forces and working groups often play the key role in resolving (as best as possible) the different views of the vendors, many of whom sit as members of the task forces and working groups.

SUMMARY

The Internet Call Processing Model is described with two methods. The first method describes the functions and interface relationships of Gateway Controllers, Media Gateways, and Signaling Gateways. The second method describes the functions of the protocols and their relationships in regards to the Internet Layered Protocol Model. Both methods have been described in this chapter.

5
Session Description Protocol (SDP)

INTRODUCTION

This chapter explains the Session Description Protocol (SDP), one of the most important supporting protocols to IP Call Processing. The functions of SDP are clarified, and several examples are provided on SDP coding.

The discussions on SDP are based on RFC 2327 and Internet drafts. This chapter does not include every rule defined in this RFC; for this level of detail, you should study the RFC. I will cite the relevant Internet draft, where appropriate. You will find Appendices D and E helpful when reading this chapter.

SDP FUNCTIONS

SDP is designed to convey session information to recipients, as well as media information that pertain to the session, and it allows more than one media stream to be associated with a session. For example, one media stream could be for audio, and another might be for a white board media stream.

SDP is a format for a session description. It does not incorporate a transport protocol and is intended to use different kinds of port protocols as appropriate including the Session Initiation Protocol (SIP), Megaco, and the Hypertext Transfer Protocol (HTTP).

The conveyance of information about media streams (audio, video, etc.) in multimedia sessions allows the recipients of a session description to participate in the session, if they can support these streams. This concept also supports the negotiation of media stream parameters, such as a sampling rate of the signal, the size of packets, and so on.

Not only does SDP inform the receivers of its messages the existence of a session, it also conveys sufficient information to enable the joining and participating in the session. The SDP information includes: (a) the session name and its purpose, (b) the time the session is active, (c) the media pertaining to the session (video, audio, formats for the video/audio), (d) the pertinent IP addresses and port numbers for the session.

ATTRIBUTES

Attributes are the primary means for extending SDP. Attributes may be defined to be used as "session-level" attributes, "media-level" attributes, or both. They take the form:

a=<attribute> a=<attribute>:<value>.

A media description may have any number of attributes ("a=" fields), which are media specific. These are referred to as "media-level" attributes and add information about the media stream. Attribute fields can also be added before the first media field. These "session-level" attributes convey additional information that applies to the conference as a whole rather than to individual media; an example might be the conference's floor control policy.

Attribute fields may be of two forms:

- Property attributes. A property attribute is simply of the form **"a=<flag>"**. These are binary attributes, and the presence of the attribute conveys that the attribute is a property of the session. An example might be **"a=recvonly"** to connote a receive only stream.
- Value attributes. A value attribute is of the form **"a=<attribute>:<value>"**. An example might be that a whiteboard could have the value attribute **"a=orient:landscape"**.

TEXT-BASED VS. BINARY ENCODING

SDP session descriptions (the syntax of the SDP messages) are textually based, using the ISO 10646 character set in UTF-8 encoding. SDP field names and attributes names use only the US-ASCII subset of UTF-8, but textual fields and attribute values may use the full ISO 10646 character set. The textual form, as opposed to a binary encoding such as ASN/1 or XDR, was chosen to enhance portability to Web-based systems.

SDP DESCRIPTIONS

Each SDP session or media description is identified by using a standard ISP10646 character, called a 'type' letter. The set of 'type' letters is kept small, in order to keep the SDP operations simple and efficient. SDP parsers ignore any announcement that contains a 'type' letter that it does not understand. As mentioned earlier, the 'attribute' mechanism ('a=') can be used to extend SDP and tailor it to particular applications or media.

The attributes defined in RFC 2327 have a defined meaning but others may be added based on the specific needs of the SDP users. A session directory simply ignores any attribute it doesn't understand.

The connection ('c=') and "attribute" ('a=') information in the session-level section applies to all the media of that session unless overridden by connection information or an attribute of the same name in the media description.

Text records such as the session name and information are byte strings which may contain any byte with the exceptions of 0x00 (Nul), 0x0a (ASCII newline) and 0x0d (ASCII carriage return). The sequence CRLF (0x0d0a) is used to end a record. By default, these byte strings contain ISO- 10646 characters in UTF-8 encoding, but this default may be changed using the 'charset' attribute, discussed below.

SDP LINES OF TEXT

An SDP session description consists of a number of lines of text of the form: **<type>=<value>.** The following rules apply to this structure:

- <type> is always exactly one character and is case-significant.
- <value> is a structured text string whose format depends on <type>.

- The structure is case-significant unless a specific field defines otherwise.
- Whitespace is not permitted either side of the '=' sign.
- In general, <value> is either a number of fields delimited by a single space character or a free format string.

THE SDP INFORMATION

SDP uses these parts of the ISO and ASCII specifications. With some minor exceptions, these conventions are used also in Megaco, MGCP, and SIP.

Protocol Version

This field takes the form: **v= (protocol version)**. Currently, this field is 0.

Owner and/or Creator and Session Identifier

This field takes the form: **o= (owner/creator and session identifier)**. The field can also contain this information: **o=<username> <session id> <version> <network type> <address type> <address>**. The "o=" field gives the originator of the session (their username and the address of the user's host) plus a session id and session version number. The <username> is the user's login on the originating host, or it is "-" if the originating host does not support the concept of user ids. The <username> must not contain spaces.

The <session id> is a numeric string such that the tuple of <username>, <session id>, <network type>, <address type> and <address> form a globally unique identifier for the session. The method of <session id> allocation is up to the creating tool. For example, the Network Time Protocol (NTP) time-stamp can be used to ensure uniqueness.

The <version> is a version number for this announcement. It is needed for proxy announcements to detect which of several announcements for the same session is the most recent. Again, its usage is up to the creating tool, so long as <version> is increased when a modification is made to the session data.

The <network type> is a text string giving the type of network. Initially "IN" is defined to have the meaning "Internet." Since the Internet is the dominant network, there is little interest in using other type fields.

Although a mobile network, an AppleTalk network, an SNA network, etc. could be identified with the field.

The subfield <address type> is a text string giving the type of the address that follows. Initially "IP4" and "IP6" are defined. The subfield <address> is the globally unique address of the machine from which the session was created, such as IP.

Session Name

This field takes the form: **s= (session name).** There must be only one "s=" field per session description, and it must contain ISO 10646 characters.

Session Information

This field takes the form: **i=* (session information).** It identifies and session and media steams pertaining to the session. There is at most one session-level "i=" field per session description, and at most one "i=" field per media. A single "i=" field can also be used for each media definition. In media definitions, "i=" fields are primarily intended for labeling media streams. As such, they are most likely to be useful when a single session has more than one distinct media stream of the same media type. An example would be two different whiteboards, one for slides and one for a working board for feedback and questions.

URI

This field takes the form: **u=* (URI of description).** The URI should be a pointer to additional information about the conference. This field is optional, but if it is present it should be specified before the first media field. No more than one URI field is allowed per session description.

An Internet working draft [FUJI98][1] provides more detailed information on the use of URIs with SDP (and they are called URLs in this document). We will use this [draft to show some examples of how a SDP URL could be coded (bear in mind [FUJI98] in not a standard). The form: **sdp://[<address> [:ttl=<ttl>] [:noa=<noa>]] / [<sessionname>] [#<type>=<value> *[&<type>=<value>]]** is interpreted as follows.

The <address> is the connection address that will be either a unicast P address or a class-D IP multicast group address. The <ttl> (time-

---

[1][FUJI98] Fujikawa, Kenji, SDP URL Scheme, draft-fujikawa-sdp-url-01.txt, August, 1998.

to-live) defines the scope with which multicast packets sent in a session should be sent when the <address> is a multicast address. The <ttl> is ignored when the <address> is a unicast address. The value of <ttl> takes 1 when the <ttl> is omitted. The <noa> (number-of-addresses) is the number of multicast addresses contiguously allocated above the base address <address>.

The alterations to SDP rules for this notation are as follows: A whitespace is replaced by '+', a return by '&', and the characters reserved in RFC 1738 and a original '+' by ascii code described by %xx. The term "RTP/AVP" which specifies a transport protocol is replaced by the "RTP-AVP". The <type> of 'v', 'o', and 's', which cannot be omitted in the original SDP can be omitted. If 'v' is omitted, then the SDP version of an SDP URL is regarded as 1.

Here is an example of how the SDP URL can be coded. A multimedia session is on a multicast address 224.192.2.3, the session name "sdp test", TTL 16 and port 10000. The media type is audio, profile AVP and payload type PCM: **sdp://224.192.2.3:ttl=16/sdp+test#m=audio+10000 +RTP-AVP+0.**

E-mail Address and Phone Number

This field takes the form: **e=* (email address) p=* (phone number).** These fields specify contact information for the person responsible for the conference. This is not necessarily the same person that created the conference announcement. Either an e-mail field or a phone field must be specified. Additional e-mail and phone fields are allowed.

More than one e-mail or phone field can be given for a session description. Both e-mail addresses and phone numbers can have an optional free text string associated with them, normally giving the name of the person who may be contacted. This should be enclosed in parentheses if it is present. For example: e=mjh@isi.edu (Mark Handley). The alternative RFC 822 name quoting convention is also allowed for both email addresses and phone numbers. For example, e=Mark Handley <mjh@ isi.edu>.

Connection Information

This field takes the general form: **c=* (connection information)** and the specific form: **c=<network type> <address type> <connection address>.** A session announcement must contain one "c=" field in each media description, or a "c=" field at the session-level. It may contain a session-level "c=" field and one additional "c=" field per media description, in which case the per-media values override the session-level settings for the relevant media. The first sub-field is the network type, which is a text string giving the type of network. Initially "IN" is defined to have the meaning "Internet." The second sub-field is the address type. This allows SDP to be used for sessions that are not IP based. Currently only IP4 is defined. The third sub-field is the connection address.

For IP4 addresses, the connection address is defined as follows. Typically the connection address will be a class-D IP multicast group address. If the session is not multicast, then the connection address contains the fully-qualified domain name or the unicast IP address of the expected data source or data relay or data sink as determined by additional attribute fields. This field can also be used to support multicast pruning, a subject discussed in the multicasting section of this chapter.

Bandwidth Information

This field takes the form: **b=* (bandwidth information).** This field specifies the proposed bandwidth to be used by the session or media, and is optional. It can be coded in kbit/s, and as a single alphanumeric word It supports two modifiers.

The first is the CT Conference Total modifier is an implicit maximum bandwidth is associated with each TTL on the Mbone or within a particular multicast administrative scope region. If the bandwidth of a session or media in a session is different from the bandwidth implicit from the scope.

The second modifier is the AS Application-Specific Maximum modifier. With this modifier, the bandwidth is interpreted to be application-specific, i.e., will be the application's concept of maximum bandwidth. Normally this will coincide with what is set on the application's "maximum bandwidth" control if applicable.

CT gives a total bandwidth figure for all the media at all sites. AS gives a bandwidth figure for a single media at a single site, although there may be many sites sending simultaneously.

Time Description Information

The time description information takes the following forms: **t=<start time> <stop time> (time the session is active)** and **r=* (zero or more repeat times).** The "t=" fields specify the start and stop times for a conference session. Multiple "t=" fields may be used if a session is active at multiple and irregularly spaced times. Each additional "t=" field specifies an additional period of time for which the session will be active. If the session is active at regular times, an "r=" field (see below) should be used in addition to and following a "t=" field. In this situation, the "t=" field specifies the start and stop times of the repeat sequence.

The first and second subfields give the start and stop times for the conference respectively. These values are the decimal representation of Network Time Protocol (NTP) time values in seconds. To convert these values to UNIX time, subtract decimal 2208988800.

Permanent sessions may be shown to the user as never being active unless there are associated repeat times which state precisely when the session will be active. In general, permanent sessions should not be created for any session expected to have a duration of less than 2 months, and should be discouraged for sessions expected to have a duration of less than 6 months.

The time parameters can provide the following information: **r= <repeat interval> <active duration> <list of offsets from start-time>.** The "r=" fields specify repeat times for a session. For example, if a session is active at 10 A.M. on Monday and 11 A.M. on Tuesday for 1 hour each week for three months, then the <start time> in the corresponding "t=" field would be the NTP representation of 10 AM on the first Monday, the <repeat interval> would be 1 week, the <active duration> would be 1 hour, and the offsets would be zero and 25 hours. The corresponding "t=" field stop time would be the NTP representation of the end of the last session three months later. By default all fields are in seconds, so the "r=" and "t=" fields could be coded as: t= 3034423619 3042462419 r= 604800 3600 0 90000.

To make announcements more compact, times may also be given in units of days, hours or minutes. The syntax for these is a number immediately followed by a single case-sensitive character. Fractional units are not allowed—a smaller unit should be used instead. The following unit specification characters are allowed: d - days (86400 seconds) h - hours (3600 seconds) m - minutes (60 seconds) s - seconds (allowed for completeness but not recommended). Thus, the above announcement could also have been written: r=7d 1h 0 25h.

Monthly and yearly repeats cannot currently be directly specified with a single SDP repeat time. Instead separate "t" fields should be used to explicitly list the session times.

RFC 2327 also provides guidance on how to specify changes to daylight savings time, and vice-versa, as well as time zone information, and even seasonal times. I leave you to the RFC for this level of detail.

Encryption Key

This field takes the form: **k=* (encryption key)** and can be coded as: **k=<method> k=<method>:<encryption key>.** SDP can support the sending of encryption keys. A key field is permitted before the first media entry (in which case it applies to all media in the session), or for each media entry as required. The format of keys and their usage is outside the scope of SDP. The method indicates the mechanism to be used to obtain a usable key by external means, or from the encoded encryption key given.

The following methods are defined: **k=clear:<encryption key>.** The encryption key for RTP media streams under the AV profile (AVP) is included untransformed in this key field.

Another method is: **k=base64:<encoded encryption key>.** The encryption key for RTP media streams under the AV profile is included in this key field but has been base64 encoded because it includes characters that are prohibited in SDP.

Yet another method is: **k=uri:<URI to obtain key>.** A Universal Resource Identifier as used by Web clients is included in this key field. The URI refers to the data containing the key, and may require additional authentication before the key can be returned. When a request is made to the given URI, the MIME content-type of the reply specifies the encoding for the key in the reply. The key should not be obtained until the user wishes to join the session to reduce synchronization of requests to the Web server(s).

Another method is: **k=prompt.** No key is included in this SDP description, but the session or media stream referred to by this key field is encrypted.

Attributes

This field was introduced earlier. The field takes the form: **a=<attribute> a=<attribute>:<value>.** Recall that this field can be used for session-level or media-level attributes. Session-level attributes pertain to the conference, and media-level attributes pertain to a specific media stream. A media description can have any number of attributes ("a=" fields). Attribute values are byte strings. The only byte string values not allowed are those used for control information: (a) x00 (Nul), (b) x0A (LF), and (c) x0D (CR).

Unlike other text fields, attribute values are not affected by the 'charset' attribute. However, when an attribute is defined, it can be defined to be character set dependent (charset-dependent), in which case its value is interpreted in the session charset rather than in ISO-10646.

It is possible that attributes may not be registered with IANA. Unregistered attributes should begin with "X-" to prevent a conflict with registered attributes. If an attribute is received that is not understood, it is ignored by the receiver.

Media Announcements

Media announcements are quite important in unicast or mulitcast conferences, because they describe the nature of the session. They take the form: **m=<media> <port> <transport> <fmt list>.** A session description may contain a number of media descriptions. These subfields perform the following functions:

- *Media:* Currently defined media are "audio," "video," "application," "data," and "control."
- *Port:* This subfield identifies the transport port to which the media stream will be sent. The meaning of the transport port depends on the network being used as specified in the relevant "c" field and on the transport protocol defined in the third subfield. Other ports used by the media application (such as the RTCP port) should be derived algorithmically from the base media port. For applications where multiple streams are being sent to a unicast address, multiple transport ports can be specified using a similar notation to that used for IP multicast addresses in the "c=" field**: m=<media> <port>/<number of ports> <transport> <fmt list>**.

  In this situation, the ports used depend on the transport protocol. For RTP, only the even ports are used for data and the corresponding one-higher odd port is used for RTCP. For example, **m=video 49170/2 RTP/AVP 31** would specify that ports 49170 and 49171 form one RTP/RTCP pair and 49172 and 49173 form the second RTP/RTCP pair. RTP/AVP is the transport protocol and 31 is the format.

- *Transport:* The transport protocol values are dependent on the address-type field in the "c=" fields. Thus a "c=" field of IP4 defines that the transport protocol runs over IP4. Two transport protocols are defined: (a) RTP/AVP over UDP, and (b)UDP. The RTP AVP is described in Chapter 7.

  If an application uses a single combined proprietary media format and transport protocol over UDP, then simply specifying the transport protocol as UDP and using the format field to distinguish the combined protocol is recommended. If a transport protocol is used over UDP to carry several distinct media types that need to be distinguished by a session directory, then specifying the transport protocol and media format separately is required.

For RTP media streams operating under the RTP Audio/Video Profile, the protocol field is "RTP/AVP." Should other RTP profiles be defined in the future, their profiles will be specified in the same way. For example, the protocol field "RTP/XYZ" would specify RTP operating under a profile whose short name is "XYZ."

- *Media formats (fmt list):* For audio and video transmissions, these formats are usually in a media payload type as defined in the RTP Audio/Video Profile. It is possible that a list of formats may be coded. It so, all these formats can be used during the session. The first in the list becomes the default format.

  Two payload types are supported, static and dynamic. An example of a static payload type is u-law PCM coded single channel audio sampled at 8KHz. This is completely defined in the RTP Audio/Video profile (RTP AVP) as payload type 0, so the media field for such a stream sent to UDP port 49232 is **m=video 49232 RTP/AVP 0.** An example of a dynamic payload type is 16 bit linear encoded stereo audio at 16KHz. If we wish to use dynamic RTP/AVP payload type 98 for such a stream, additional information is required to decode it: **m=video 49232 RTP/AVP 98** and **a=rtpmap:98 L16/ 16000/2.**

Audio profiles used are those defined in RFC 1890, and others registered with IANA. For example, G.711 A-law is called PCMA in the SDP, and it is assigned profile 0. G.723 is profile 4, and H263 is profile 34. For more information on these profiles, go to http://www.isi.edu/in-notes/iana/assignments/rtp-parameters. RFC 1890 is an important reference, and is explained in Chapter 6.

RTP MAP

This last example introduces the rtpmap attribute. It takes the form: **a=rtpmap:<payload type> <encoding name>/<clock rate> [/<encoding parameters>].** For audio streams, **<encoding parameters>** may specify the number of audio channels. This parameter may be omitted if the number of channels is one, provided no additional parameters are needed. For video streams, no encoding parameters are currently specified.

No more than one rtpmap attribute can be defined for each media format specified. As an example: **m=audio 49230 RTP/AVP 96 97 98 a=rtpmap:96 L8/ 8000 a=rtpmap:97 L16/ 8000 a=rtpmap:98 L16/ 11025/2**.

RTP profiles that specify the use of dynamic payload types must define the set of valid encoding names and/or a means to register encoding names if that profile is to be used with SDP. Experimental and nonregistered encoding formats can also be specified using rtpmap, using the same rules described in the chapter for other SDP fields.

RTP audio formats typically do not include information about the number of samples per packet. If a nondefault (as defined in the RTP Audio/Video Profile) packetization is required, the "ptime" attribute is used, and explained shortly.

Suggested Attributes

RFC 2327 describes several "suggested" attributes. Each attribute is summarized in this part of the chapter.

- *Category:* The category attribute takes the form: **a=cat:<category>**. It gives the dot-separated hierarchical category of the session. This is to enable a receiver to filter unwanted sessions by category. It is a session-level attribute and is not dependent on charset.

- *Keywords:* This attribute takes the form **a=keywds:<keywords>**. It is similar to the cat attribute in that it is used to assist identifying wanted sessions at the receiver. This allows a receiver to select an interesting session based on keywords describing the purpose of the session.

- *Tool:* This attribute takes the form: **a=tool:<name and version of tool>**. This gives the name and version number of the tool used to create the session description.

- *Packet time:* This attribute takes the form: **a=ptime:<packet time>**. It gives the length of time in milliseconds represented by the media in a packet. Since most codec specifications state the length and time interval on a specific sample, it should not be necessary to know ptime to decode RTP or vat audio, and it is intended as a recommendation for the encoding/packetization of audio. It is a media attribute.

- *Receive only:* This attribute takes the form: **a=recvonly.** It specifies that the tools should be started in receive-only mode where applicable. It can be either a session or media attribute and is not dependent on charset.

- *Send and Receive:* This attribute takes the form: **a=sendrecv.** It specifies that the tools should be started in send and receive mode. This information is necessary for interactive conferences with tools that default to receive only mode. It can be either a session or media attribute.

- *Send Only:* This attribute takes the form: **a=sendonly.** It specifies that the tools should be started in send only mode. An example is where a different unicast address is to be used for a traffic destination than for a traffic source. In such a case, two media descriptions may be used, one sendonly and one recvonly. It can be either a session or media attribute, but it would normally only be used as a media attribute.

- *Whiteboard Orientation:* This attribute takes the form: **a=orient:<whiteboard orientation>.** It specifies the orientation of a the whiteboard on the screen. It is a media attribute. Permitted values are 'portrait', 'landscape', and 'seascape' (upside-down landscape).

- *Conference Type:* This attribute takes the form: **a=type:<conference type>.** It specifies the type of the conference. Suggested values are 'broadcast', 'meeting', 'moderated', 'test', and 'H332'. The 'recvonly' attribute should be the default for 'type:broadcast' sessions, 'type:meeting' should imply 'sendrecv' and 'type:moderated' should indicate the use of a floor control tool and that the media tools are started so as to "mute" new sites joining the conference. Specifying the attribute type:H 332 indicates that this loosely coupled session is part of a H. 332 session as defined in the ITU H. 332 specification. Media tools should be started 'recvonly'.

- *Character Set:* This attribute takes the form: **a=charset:<character set>.** It specifies the character set to be used to display the session name and information data. By default, the ISO-10646 character set in UTF-8 encoding is used.

- *Language:* This attribute takes the form: **a=sdplang:<language tag>.** This can be a session level attribute or a media level attribute. As a session level attribute, it specifies the language for the session description. As a media level attribute, it specifies the language for any media-level SDP information field associated with that media.

- *Frame Rate:* This attribute takes the form: **a=framerate:<frame rate>.** It gives the maximum video frame rate in frames/sec. It is a recommendation for the encoding of video data. It is a media attribute and is only defined for video media.

- *Quality:* This attribute takes the form: **a=quality:<quality>.** It gives a suggestion for the quality of the encoding as an integer value. The idea is to specify a nondefault trade-off between framerate and still-image quality. For video, the value in the range 0 to 10, with 10 representing the best still-image the compression scheme can give, a 5 representing a default behavior, given no quality suggestion, and a 0 representing the worst still-image quality that is considered usable (by the codec designer).

- *Format-specific:* The attribute takes the form: **a=fmtp:<format> <format specific parameters>.** It allows parameters that are specific to a particular format to be conveyed in a way that SDP doesn't have to understand them. The format must be one of the formats specified for the media. Format-specific parameters may be any set of parameters required to be conveyed by SDP and given unchanged to the media tool that will use this format.

EXAMPLES OF SDP CODING

As we proceed though the chapters on the Call Processing Protocols, there will be many examples of SDP coding. I defer showing more examples here, because they are better-shown in the context of a protocol's use of SDP.

SUMMARY

SDP is conveys session information to recipients, as well as media information that pertain to the session. The conveyance of information about media streams (audio, video, etc.) in multimedia sessions allows the recipients of a session description to participate in the session, if they can support these streams.

Attributes are the primary means for extending SDP. Attributes may be defined to be used as session-level attributes, media-level attributes, or both.

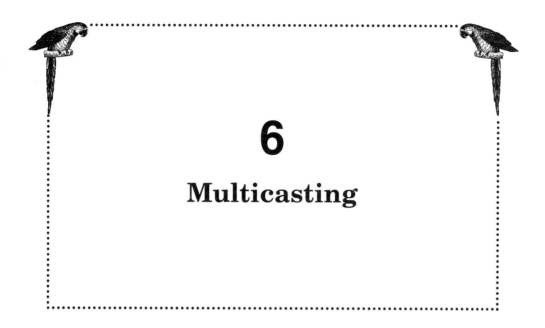

6
Multicasting

INTRODUCTION

This chapter examines multicasting operations in an internet. Multicasting is of keen interest to internet telephony and video users and designers because it paves the road for conference calls, a fundamental part of doing business in many companies.

We begin by defining multicasting in relation to unicasting and broadcasting, followed by an explanation of the IP multicasting address. Then the bulk of the chapter describes the Internet Multicasting Protocol (IGMP). The chapter concludes with a discussion of Small Group Multicast (SGM).

MULTICASTING CONCEPTS

Conventional Internet communications allows a host to send packets to another, single host, a concept called unicasting. A host may also send a packet to all hosts (within a routing domain), which is called broadcasting. A third way of sending traffic is multicasting, defined as the sending of packets from one host to a group of hosts.

The Internet has supported multicasting for a number of years with the Internet Group Management Protocol (IGMP). This protocol defines the procedures for a node (a host) to join a multicast group. It allows the

IP hosts to report their multicast group memberships to any neighboring multicast routers (and routers can act as hosts as well). Thereafter, the router is expected to forward to the hosts the relevant multicast traffic in which the hosts have expressed interest (that is, they are a member of a multicast group).

Once the host has joined the group, it can receive any multicasting traffic sent to this group. For example, the multicast session may be a quarterly conference of a special interest group, a meeting of a IETF Working group, a shot of a space shuttle, a concert, etc.

One of the attractive features of IGMP is that it does not require a host to know in advance about all the multicasting groups in an internet. Instead, the routers are knowledgeable of multicast groups and send advertisements to the hosts about their multicasting groups. For example, if an Internet task force is meeting and its proceedings are to be made available to the public, a user host will receive an advertisement from its router about the conference. In turn, the host can reply with a message stating whether it wishes to join the conference.

Since IP multicast system is a one-to-many operation, we know that the sender of the multicast traffic need only create one copy of the packet, which is sent to a multicast server (for example a router) which is then responsible for creating as many copies as needed to send to the router's outgoing interfaces to reach the receiving nodes.

MULTICASTING ADDRESSES

The format for the IP multicast address is shown in Figure 6–1. This address is also known as a class D address and the first four digits of the address are set to 1110. The remaining 28 bits are set aside for the multicast address.

The IP address can take the values ranging from 224.0.0.0 to 239.255.255.255.

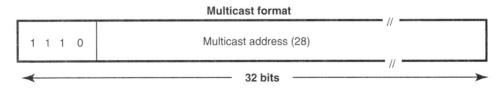

Figure 6–1   The Multicast Address

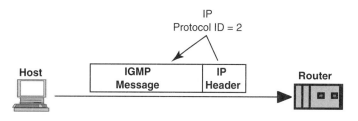

Figure 6–2   IP and IGMP

IGMP AND IP

IGMP operates directly with IP. That is, IGMP does not operate over the Internet transport layer. This idea was introduced in Chapter 3 with the discussion of the Internet Layered Model (see Figure 3–1). The IGMP message, residing in the IP Data field, is identified with IP Protocol ID of 2, as shown in Figure 6–2. Since the idea of IGMP is for adjacent hosts and routers to inform each other about their multicasting intents and capabilities, all IGMP messages have the IP TTL field set to 1.

THE IGMP MESSAGE

The IGMP message is depicted in Figure 6–3. The fields in this message are used to perform these functions. The Message Type field identifies the specific type of the IGMP message. As of this writing, these are the types of messages:

- *Membership Query:* The Membership Query message can be coded into a General Query or a Group-specific Query. The General Query message is used to determine which groups have members attached to specific network, and the Group-specific Query message is used to determine if a specific multicast group has any

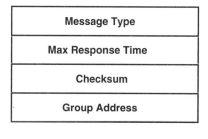

Figure 6–3   The IGMP Message

members on an attached network. IGMP is bootstrapped by starting operations with general queries, and as memberships are noted (and added) to a membership list, then Group-specific Query messages are used. However both can be used, and sent based on two independent timers.

- *Membership Report:* Periodically, a host sends this message to its group. A router that receives this report adds the group address in the message to a list of multicast addresses for the interface on which the report was received.
- *Leave Group:* This message is sent by a host if it wishes to be deleted from a multicast group. This message is sent with the destination address set to the all-routers multicast group (224.0.0.2).

The Max Response Time field is relevant in Membership Query messages, and specifies the maximum allowed time before sending a responding report in units of 1/10 second. In all other messages, it is set to zero by the sender and ignored by receivers.

The checksum is the 16-bit 1s complement of the 1s complement sum of the whole IGMP message (the entire IP payload). For computing the checksum, the checksum field is set to zero.

In a Membership Query message, the group address field is set to zero when sending a General Query, and set to the group address being queried when sending a Group-Specific Query. In a Membership Report or Leave Group message, the group address field holds the IP multicast group address of the group being reported or left.

IGMP OPERATIONS

In a multicasting environment, it is important that the multicasting routers add and drop group members in an efficient manner. As well, hosts should be able to dynamically join and leave groups. It is also important that the overhead messages to perform these operations do not consume a lot of resources. IGMP takes the approach of reducing the messages sent by routers attached to a physical network by having only one router query the hosts about multicasting memberships. To prevent each host in a group from sending a Membership Report back to this router, a host first checks to determine if another host has already sent the report. If this is the situation, it does not send a duplicate Membership Report.

It is also desirable for a router to have control of the multicast groups; that is, permitting or forbidding multicast memberships on each attached network. IGMP is designed to support all these services. In addition, IGMP Version 2 (V2) is backward compatible with IGMP Version 1 (V1).

Figure 6–4 is used to explain several aspects of IGMP operations. We assume routers 1 and 2 are both configured as multicast routers, and hosts A–F belong to at least one common multicast group. Routers 1 and 2 keep a list of multicast group memberships of each attached network, in this example, one Ethernet network. IGMP defines multicast group memberships as the presence of at least one member of a multicast group, and not a list of all members.

Initially, both routers 1 and 2 assume the role of a Querier, and send Query messages onto the network. If a router (say router 1) receives a Query message from a router with a lower IP address (say router 2), then router 1 becomes a Non-Querier for the network. Hereafter, router 2 is the Querier for the network, and router 1 assumes the role of backup. If router 1 does not hear a Query message from router 2 within a certain (configured) time, it assumes the role of Querier. This time is called the query timeout, and defaults to two times the query interval, explained next.

Based on a timer (called the query interval), router 2 sends a General Query message on to the network. The query interval is usually a default value, permitting one Query message to be sent per minute, but it can be over-ridden. The destination address in the IP header is set to all-systems multicast group (224.0.0.1), the Group Address field is set to 0, and the Max Response Time is set to a configured value.

Let's assume host A (and the other hosts) receive a General Query message from router 2. It sets a random timer, within a range of 0–Max

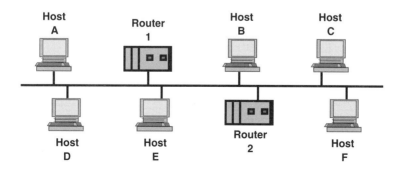

Figure 6–4   IGMP Operations Example

Response Time. When the timer expires, host A sends a Membership Report message on the network, with the IP TTL field set to 1. What do hosts B–F do? In this example, we assume host A's random timer expires before any of those in the other hosts. Consequently, hosts B–F, upon receiving a copy of A's Membership Report stop their timers, and they do not send duplicate reports.

Even though router 2 is the Querier, both routers process the Membership Report message. If this message indicates a new group, the routers add the group to their list of multicast group memberships for this network interface.

The hosts must respond (at least one of them, ideally). If the Querier router does not receive a response, it assumes there are no group members, and is not obligated to forward multicasts that it receives from another network.

A host is allowed to send an unsolicited Message Report, as soon as it joins a group. To help assure that the multicast router receives this message, this report is sent more than one time.

The rules for leaving a multicast group are a bit more involved than joining a group, and keeping the membership active. I summarize these rules form RFC 2236.

When a host leaves a multicast group, if it were the last host to reply to a Query with a Membership Report for that group, it sends a Leave Group message to the all-routers multicast group (224.0.0.2). If it were not the last host to reply to a Query, it need not send anything, as there must be another member on the physical network.

When a Querier receives a Leave Group message for a group that has group members on the network interface, it sends Group-Specific Queries to the group being left. These Group-Specific Queries have their Max Response time set to a time called the Last Member Query Interval. If no reports are received after the response time of the last query expires, the routers assume that the group has no local members.

RELATIONSHIPS OF MULTICASTING AND UNICASTING ADDRESSES

The multicast traffic can run inside the data field of the IP datagram. If this is the approach taken, it relies on the conventional IP header for delivery of the traffic through an internet. This concept is called multicast tunnels in the sense that the multicast traffic is tunneled through an Internet by riding inside the IP datagram.

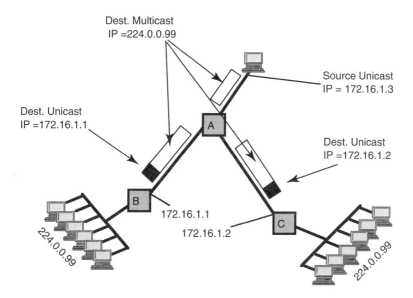

Figure 6–5 Multicasting Tunnels

Figure 6–5 shows that multicasting traffic is destined to the hosts residing on the networks attached to routers B and C. The traffic emanates from a host attached to router A. The figure shows that the destination multicast IP address is 224.0.0.99. The figure also shows the unicast IP addresses of the sending host (172.16.1.3) and router B (172.16.1.1.), and router C (172.16.1.2).

This double IP header set is not needed in some systems. For example, if an OSPF (Open Shortest Path First) router were trying to reach other OSPF-capable routers on an Ethernet segment, it need only create the single IP multicast address; the outer IP header is not used.

Certain restrictions are placed on using a multicast address in an internet, and therefore, a unicast outer header may be needed. For example, some firewalls don't like multicast addresses, and fill not allow them to pass-through.

MULTICASTING TABLES

Multicast routers use IGMP tables to learn which groups have members on each of their attached physical networks. A multicast router keeps a list of multicast group memberships for each attached network, and a timer for each membership, shown in Figure 6–6. Re-

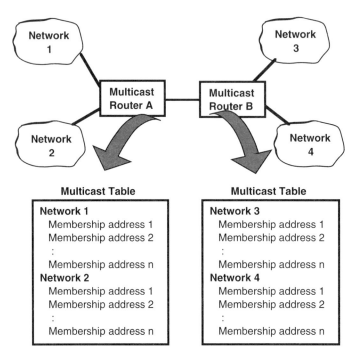

Figure 6–6   Multicast Tables

call that multicast group memberships means the presence of at least one member of a multicast group on a given attached network, not a list of all of the members.

IGMP STATE DIAGRAMS

To continue our analysis of IGMP, RFC 2236 defines the behavior of multicast hosts and routers with state diagrams. This section provides a summary of these state diagrams, based on Sections 6 and 7 of the RFC. The state diagrams are shown in Figures 6–7 through 6–10. Each state transition is labeled with the event that causes the transition. In parentheses are any actions taken during the transition. An action must always be triggered by an event.

Host State Diagram

Figure 6–7 shows the host state diagram. A host is in one of three possible states. Five events can cause a state transition. Seven possible

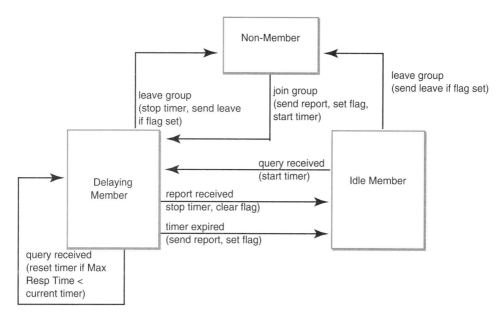

Figure 6–7   Host State Diagram

actions may be taken in response to the five events. These states, events, and actions are summarized in Table 6–1.

Router State Diagrams

Three state diagrams define the behavior of the multicast router. The first governs whether the router is a Querier or a Non-Quierer. The second governs its operations if it is a Querier, and the third governs its operations if it is a Non-Querier.

Querier and Non-Querier Determination.   Figure 6–8 shows the state diagram for Querier and Non-Querier determination. For this operation, a router is in one of two possible states. Three events can cause a state transition. Three possible actions may be taken in response to the three events. These states, events, and actions are summarized in Table 6–2. This table should be consulted as you study Figure 6–8.

Router Behavior in Querier State.   Figure 6–9 shows the state diagram for a router in Querier state. For this operation, a router is in one of four possible states. Six events can cause a state transition. Seven possible actions may be taken in response to the three events. These states,

Table 6–1   IGMP States, Events, and Transitions for Hosts

States

• Non-member: Host does not belong to the group on an interface.

• Delaying member: Host belongs to the group on interface and has a report delay timer running for the membership.

• Idle: Host belongs to a group but does not have a report delay timer running.

Events

• Join group: Host joins a group on an interface.

• Leave group: Host leaves group on an interface.

• Query received: Host receives a Query message.

• Report received: Host receives a Membership Report message.

• Timer expired: The report delay timer expires for a group on an interface.

Possible Actions

• Send report: Send a Report message for the group on the interface.

• Send leave: Send a Leave Message for the group on the interface.

• Set flag: Set a flag to indicate host was last host to send a report on this interface.

• Clear flag: Set a flag to indicate host was not last host to send a report on this interface.

• Start timer: Start timer between 0–Max Response Time.

• Reset timer: Set the timer to a new value.

• Stop timer: Stop the timer for this interface.

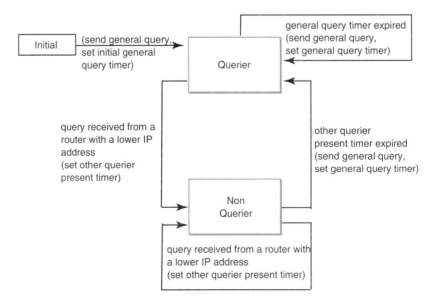

Figure 6–8   Router State Diagram to Determine Querier or Non-Querier Status

Table 6–2   IGMP States, Events, and Transitions for Routers (Querier or Non-Querier Status)

States

• Querier: Designated to send Membership Query Messages.

• Non-Querier: Not designated to send these messages.

Events

• Query timer expired: Timer set for query transmission expires.

• Lower IP address: Query received from a router with a lower IP address.

• Other Querier present timer expired: Occurs when timer set to note the presence of another querier with a lower IP address expires.

Possible Actions

• Start general query timer: Start this timer for this network interface.

• Start other querier present timer: Start a different timer for this interface (to provide more than one Querier present interval).

• Send general query: Send a General Query message to 224.0.0.1.

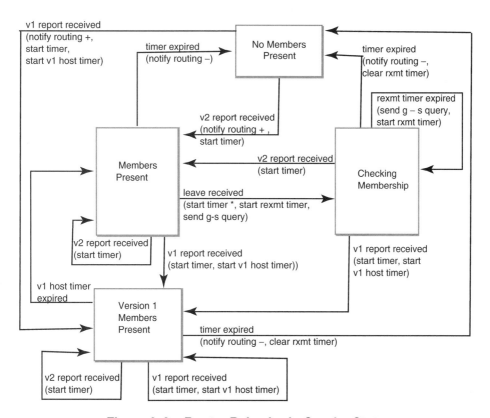

Figure 6–9   Router Behavior in Querier State

events, and actions are summarized in Table 6–3. This table should be
consulted as you study Figures 6–9 and 6–10.

Router Behavior in Non-Querier State. Figure 6–10 shows the
state diagram for a router in Non-Querier state. The difference between
this state diagram and the Querier state diagram is Non-Queriers do not
send any messages and are driven only by message reception.

**Table 6–3   IGMP States, Events, and Transitions for Routers in Querier
or Non-Querier State**

States

- No members present: No hosts on the network interface have sent reports (the initial
  stage of all groups on a router).
- Members present: A host on the network interface as sent a Membership Report.
- Version 1 members present: There is a IGMP Version 1 host on the network.
- Checking membership: Router has received a Leave Group Membership message, but
  has not yet heard a Membership Report message for the group.

Events

- V2 report received: Router has received a Version 2 Membership Report.
- V1 report received: Router has received a Version 1 Membership Report.
- Leave received: Router has received a Leave Membership message.
- Timer expired: Timer set for group membership expires.
- Retransmit timer expired: Timer set to send group-specific Membership Query expires.
- V1 host timer expired: Timer set to note the presence of a V1 host expires.

Possible Actions

- Start timer: Starts a timer for the group membership on the interface. If timer is run-
  ning, resets it to its initial value (Group Membership Interval).
- Start timer: An alternate action to coordinate information routers (see RFC 2236, Sec-
  tion 7 for details).
- Start retransmit timer: Start this timer for the group membership on the interface.
- Start V1 host timer: Starts a timer for the V1 group membership on the interface.
- Send group-specific (g-s) query: Send Group-specific Query message for a group on an
  interface.
- Notify routing +: Notify the routing protocol that there are members of this group on
  this interface.
- Notify routing –: Notify the routing protocol that there are no longer any members of
  this group on this interface.

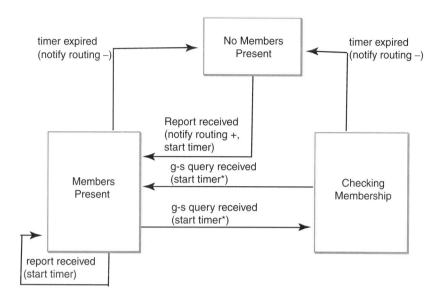

Figure 6–10   Router Behavior in Non-Querier State

IGMP TIMERS

We have looked at several of the IGMP timers, and Section 8, of RFC 2236 describes each of them, and their default values. I leave you to study this part of the specification if you need more details than provided in this overview.

OPTIONS FOR MULTICAST ADDRESSES IN A SESSION DESCRIPTION

Chapter 5 provides an explanation of the Session Description Protocol (SDP). In this section, we look at its use in multicasting.

Hierarchical or layered encoding schemes are data streams where the encoding from a single media source is split into a number of layers. The receiver can choose the desired quality (and hence bandwidth) by only subscribing to a subset of these layers. Such layered encodings are normally transmitted in multiple multicast groups to allow multicast pruning. This technique keeps unwanted traffic from sites only requiring certain levels of the hierarchy. For applications requiring multiple multicast groups, the following notation can be used for the connection address:

<base multicast address>/<ttl>/<number of addresses>

If the number of addresses is not given it is assumed to be one. Multicast addresses so assigned are contiguously allocated above the base address, so that, for example: **c=IN IP4 224.2.1.1/ 127/3** would state that addresses 224.2.1.1, 224.2.1.2, and 224.2.1.3 are to be used at a TTL (time-to-live) of 127. This is semantically identical to including multiple "c=" lines in a media description:

c=IN IP4 224.2.1.1/ 127 c=IN IP4 224.2.1.2/ 127 c=IN IP4 224.2.1.3/ 127.

Multiple addresses or "c=" lines can only be specified on a per-media basis, and not for a session-level "c=" field. It is illegal for the slash notation described above to be used for IP unicast addresses.

SMALL GROUP MULTICAST (SGM)

The Small Group Multicast (SGM) is explained in this section. The work on SGM is proceeding through [BOIV00],[1] and this explanation summarizes the major aspects of this working group.

The multicasting schemes described thus far in this chapter are designed to handle large groups of users and work well if one is trying to distribute a program to a large audience. They may have scalability problems when there is a very large number of groups. In some situations, information is sent to sites (groups) where it is not needed. If there are a large number of multicast groups, this creates overhead and scaling problems.

Some other schemes try to limit the amount of multicast routing information that needs to be disseminated, processed, and stored throughout the network. These schemes use a "shared distribution tree" that is shared by all the members of a multicast group and they try to limit the distribution of multicast routing information to just those nodes that need it. But these schemes also have problems. Because of the shared tree, they use less than optimal paths in routing packets to their destinations and they tend to concentrate traffic in small portions of a network. They also require that all of the routers in a multicast tree "signal," process, and store multicast routing information. In addition, they re-

---

[1][BOIV00]. Boivie, Rich and Feldman, Nancy. Small Group Multicast. draft-boivie-sgm-00.txt, March 2000.

quire that multicast routing information for the various multicast groups be communicated across inter-AS administrative boundaries. These requirements cause scalability problems and increase administrative complexity if there are a large number of multicast groups.

The Small Group Multicast (SGM) scheme attempts to eliminate these problems. In SGM, the source node keeps track of the destinations to which is wants to send traffic, and creates packet headers that contain the list of destination addresses. SGM-capable routers receive these packets, parse the SGM headers and use the ordinary unicast route table to determine how to route the packet to each destination.

This approach eliminates the need for network routers to store any state for the various multicast groups. This makes SGM very scaleable in terms of the number of groups that can be supported since the nodes in the network do not need to disseminate or store any multicast routing information for these groups. And since it doesn't use any multicast routing protocol, there are no inter-AS multicast routing "peering" issues to contend with.

SGM has the additional benefit that packets always take the "right" path as determined by the ordinary unicast route protocols. Unlike the shared tree schemes, SGM minimizes network latency and maximizes network "efficiency."

Thus, SGM makes multicast practical for very large numbers of small groups, which as suggested above is a very important case. Note that while SGM is not suitable for large multicast groups, such as the broadcast of an IETF meeting, it does provide an important complement to existing multicast schemes in that it can support very large numbers of small groups. I refer you to [BOIV00] for the rules of the SGM operations.

SUMMARY

The Internet Group Management Protocol (IGMP) defines the procedures for a node (a host) to join a multicast group, for routers to control the process. It allows the IP hosts to report their multicast group memberships to any neighboring multicast routers. Thereafter, the router is expected to forward to the hosts the relevant multicast traffic in which the hosts have expressed interest (that is, they are a member of a multicast group). Once the host has joined the group, it can receive any multicasting traffic sent to this group.

7

The Real Time Protocol (RTP)

INTRODUCTION

This chapter describes the operations of the Real Time Protocol (RTP), a key tool in IP Call Processing. First the attributes of RTP are explained, followed by a brief description of a companion protocol to RTP, the Real Time Control Protocol (RTCP). Next, translation and mixing operations are described. The remainder of the chapter provides more details on RTP operations, including it message formats, and the rules for running different types of payload in the RTP packet.

RTP and RTCP are documented in RFC 1889. Notwithstanding, RTP remains a work in progress and a variety of working drafts are expanding on the basic RTP operations published in this RFC. Appendix 7B, at the back of this chapter, provides a list of the RTP working papers and the URL where they can be found.

ATTRIBUTES OF THE REAL TIME PROTOCOL (RTP)

The Real Time Protocol (RTP) is designed to support real time traffic, that is to say traffic that requires playback at the receiving application in a time-sensitive mode, such as voice and video systems. RTP also operates with both unicast and multicast applications.

RTP provides services that include payload type identification, sequence numbering, time-stamping, and delivery monitoring. Applications usually run RTP on top of UDP to make use of its multiplexing and checksum services. RTP supports data transfer to multiple destinations using multicast distribution if provided by the underlying network (an IP multicast implementation).

RTP does not provide any mechanism to ensure timely delivery or provide other quality of service guarantees, but relies on lower-layer services to provide these services. It does not guarantee delivery or prevent out-of-order delivery, nor does it assume that the underlying network is reliable and delivers packets in sequence. The sequence numbers included in RTP allow the receiver to reconstruct the sender's packet sequence, but sequence numbers might also be used to determine the proper location of a packet.

THE REAL TIME CONTROL PROTOCOL (RTCP)

RTP also contains a control component, called the Real Time Control Protocol (RTCP) [ROSE98].[1] It is sent to the same multicast group as RTP, but on a different port number. Both data senders and receivers periodically multicast RTCP messages.

RTCP comes into the picture by providing the procedure for RTP nodes to keep each other informed about (a) the quality of services they think they are providing (if they are service providers), and/or (b) the quality of services they are receiving (if they are service clients).

RTCP packets provide many services, and their functions are described in Voice over IP, the prerequisite to this book. Summarizing [ROSE98], they are used to identify the users in a session. One RTCP packet type, the Source Descriptor (SDES) contains the name, email address, telephone number, fax, and location of the participant. Another, the receiver report, contains reception quality reporting. This information can be used by senders to adapt their transmission rates or encodings dynamically during a session. It can also be used by network administrators to monitor network quality.

---

[1][ROSE98]. Rosenberg, J. and Schulzrinne, H. Timer Reconsideration for Enhanced RTP Scalability, draft-ietf-avt-reconsider-00.txt, July, 1997.

TRANSLATION AND MIXING

Figures 7–1 and 7–2 show two major features of RTP and how it can support the traffic between RTP session senders and receivers, translation and mixing. These operations are not required of an RTP implementation. Rather, RTP is a good tool by which to implement them.

In Figure 7–1 the RTP system is acting as a translator. The RTP translator translates (encodes) from one payload syntax to a different syntax. This figure shows how the RTP translator operates. The user devices on the left side of the figure are set up to use a 512 kbit/s video stream for their video application. The user device on the right side of the figure uses a 384 kbit/s video stream. As another possibility, the transit network may not be able to support the 512 kbit/s rate. So, whether from the user station on the right or the network in the middle, the users cannot communicate with each other.

The RTP translator allows these user stations to interact with each other. The job of the translator is to accept the traffic of the stations on the left side of the figure, translate (encode) that traffic into a format that is (a) in consonance with the bandwidth limitations of the transit network, and/or (b) in consonance with the bandwidth limitations of the user station on the right side of the figure. The user's RTP packet shows that the user is the synchronization service.

Figure 7–2 shows an RTP server performing a mixer operation. Mixers combine multiple sources into one stream. Typically, mixers participate in audio operations and they do not decrease the quality of the

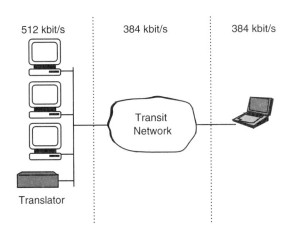

512 kbit/s   384 kbit/s   384 kbit/s

Transit Network

Translator

Figure 7–1   The RTP Translator

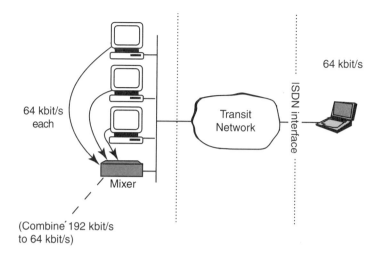

Figure 7–2   The RTP Mixer

signal to the recipients. They simply combine the signals into a consistent format.

RTP mixers do not translate each source payload into a different format. The original format is maintained, and the various source payloads are combined into one stream. The mixer is used for audio conferences, but not for video sessions, since mixing video streams is not yet a commercial reality. On the other hand, if the audio streams are uncomplicated pulse code modulation (PCM) traffic, it is possible to arithmetically sum the values of each source payload and combine them into a single stream.

THE RTP MESSAGE

Figure 7–3 shows the format of the RTP message. Before discussing the fields in the message, it should be noted that RTP's default port is 5004, if an application does not have a port setup. The reason for not having a well-known port is that RTP will be used with several-to-many applications which themselves are identified with ports. Part of the job of the IP Call Processing Protocols is to convey the port numbers between the communicating parties during a call set up operation.

The message format for RTP is designed to support different types of payloads (operating in the application layer, L_7), such as the ITU-T G.722 audio standard, and the JPEG video standard. The RTP protocol

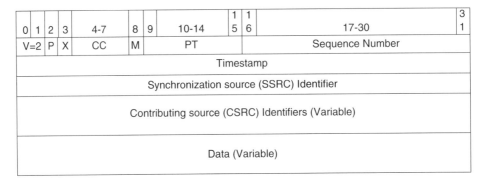

0	1	2	3	4-7	8	9	10-14	1 5	1 6	17-30	3 1
V=2	P	X		CC	M		PT			Sequence Number	
Timestamp											
Synchronization source (SSRC) Identifier											
Contributing source (CSRC) Identifiers (Variable)											
Data (Variable)											

Figure 7–3   RTP Message Format

data unit (PDU) is carried in the User Datagram Protocol (UDP) and Internet Protocol (IP) PDUs, with these protocols' headers as part of the complete data unit.

The fields are used in the following manner:

- *Version (v):* Version 2.
- *Padding (P):* Padding flag on, if padding bytes added to message. Padding at the end of the message payload may be needed for certain applications.
- *Extension (E):* To indicate a header after RTP header.
- *Contributor count (CC):* How many contributing source identifiers are in the message, which allows for 15 contributing sources.
- *Marker (M):* Specific to application, typically used set up demarcation boundaries in the data stream.
- *Payload type (PT):* Type of traffic in the data field (G.722 audio, GSM, etc.).
- *Sequence number (SN):* A number that increments by 1 for each RTP packet sent.
- *Time-stamp:* Reflects the sampling instant of the first octet in the RTP data packet. The sampling instant must be derived from a clock that increments monotonically and linearly in time to allow synchronization and jitter calculations. The resolution of the clock must be sufficient for the desired synchronization accuracy and for measuring packet arrival jitter. If RTP packets are generated periodically, the nominal sampling instant as determined from the sampling clock is to be used, not a reading of the system clock. For

example, for fixed-rate audio the time-stamp clock would likely increment by one for each sampling period. If an audio application reads blocks covering 160 sampling periods from the input device, the time-stamp would be increased by 160 for each such block, regardless of whether the block is transmitted in a packet or dropped as silent.

- *SSRC:* The SSRC field identifies the synchronization source. This identifier is chosen randomly, with the intent that no two synchronization sources within the same RTP session will have the same SSRC identifier.
- *CSRC:* The CSRC list identifies the contributing sources for the payload contained in this packet. The number of identifiers is given by the CC field. If there are more than 15 contributing sources, only 15 may be identified. CSRC identifiers are inserted by mixers, using the SSRC identifiers of contributing sources.

The sync source ID is the identifier of the original transmitter of the RTP message, which is responsible determining the values of the sequence number and the time-stamp in the message. This identifier is preserved by RTP translators, but an RTP mixer becomes the sync source and the other (original) sources become contributing sources, and are identified in the contributing source ID fields in the message.

The sequence number and time-stamp are used between the communicating parties to (a) make certain the traffic is in the proper sequential order, (b) to determine if any traffic is missing/lost, and (c) synchronize the traffic flow.

Note that RTP does not define the contents of the application data field which of course is left to the application. Thus, RTP can carry various types of application traffic.

RTP PROFILES FOR AUDIO AND VIDEO CONFERENCES (RFC 1890)

RFC 1890 is an important part of IP Call Processing because it sets forth the RTP audio/video profiles (RTP/AVPs) for unicast and multicast sessions.

Table 7–1 shows the various payload types (the AVP) that are carried in the data field of the RTP message. The right-most column in the

Table 7-1 RTP Payload Types

PT	encoding name	audio/video (A/V)	clock rate (Hz)	channels (audio)	
0	PCMU	A	8000	1	[RFC1890]
1	1016	A	8000	1	[RFC1890]
2	G721	A	8000	1	[RFC1890]
3	GSM	A	8000	1	[RFC1890]
4	G723	A	8000	1	[Kumar]
5	DVI4	A	8000	1	[RFC1890]
6	DVI4	A	16000	1	[RFC1890]
7	LPC	A	8000	1	[RFC1890]
8	PCMA	A	8000	1	[RFC1890]
9	G722	A	8000	1	[RFC1890]
10	L16	A	44100	2	[RFC1890]
11	L16	A	44100	1	[RFC1890]
12	reserved	A			
13	reserved	A			
14	MPA	A	90000		?[RFC1890,2250]
15	G728	A	8000	1	[RFC1890]
16	DVI4	A	11025	1	[DiPol]
17	DVI4	A	22050	1	[DiPol]
18–22	unassigned	A			
23	reserved	A			
24	reserved	V			
25	CelB	V	90000		[RFC2029]
26	JPEG	V	90000		[RFC2435]
27	reserved	V			
28	nv	V	90000		[RFC1890]
29	reserved	V			
30	reserved	V			
31	H261	V	90000		[RFC2032]
32	MPV	V	90000		[RFC2250]
33	MP2T	AV	90000		[RFC2250]
34	H263	V	90000		[Zhu]
35–71	unassigned	?			
72–76	reserved for RTCP conflict avoidance				[RFC1889]
77–95	unassigned	?			
97–127	dynamic	?			[RFC1890]

Source: www.ietf.org

table provides the reference for these payloads. Appendix 7A at the back of this chapter gives the details for these references.

As indicated by payload types 96–127, other payload types can be identified. For example, two parties may wish to communicate with proprietary codecs. They could agree on which of these dynamic numbers would be used to identify the codec payloads.

RFC 1890 also defines how multiple audio channels are carried in RTP packets, as well as a set of sampling frequencies for audio traffic. It defines these guidelines for default operating parameters (and be careful in using these guidelines, since they may not be the same as a specific codec specification):

> For packetized audio, the default packetization interval should have a duration of 20 ms, unless otherwise noted when describing the encoding. The packetization interval determines the minimum end-to-end delay; longer packets introduce less header overhead but higher delay and make packet loss more noticeable. For non-interactive applications such as lectures or links with severe bandwidth constraints, a higher packetization delay may be appropriate. A receiver should accept packets representing between 0 and 200 ms of audio data. This restriction allows reasonable buffer sizing for the receiver.

Audio profiles used are those defined in RFC 1890, and others registered with IANA. For example, G.711 A-law is called PCMA in the SDP, and is assigned profile 0. G.723 is profile 4, and H263 is profile 34. For more information on these profiles, go to http://www.isi.edu/in-notes/iana/assignments/rtp-parameters.

SAMPLE-BASED AND FRAME-BASED ENCODINGS

Some additional guidelines from RFC 1890 are worthy of mention here. They deal with sample-based encodings and frame-based encodings.

Sample-Based Encodings

In sample-based encodings, each audio sample is represented by a fixed number of bits. Within the compressed audio data, codes for individual samples may span octet boundaries. An RTP audio packet may contain any number of audio samples, subject to the constraint that the number of bits per sample times the number of samples per packet yields an integral octet count. Fractional encodings produce less than 1 octet per sample. The duration of an audio packet is determined by the number of samples in the packet.

For sample-based encodings producing one or more octets per sample, samples from different channels sampled at the same sampling instant are packed in consecutive octets. The packing of sample-based encodings producing less than 1 octet per sample is encoding-specific.

Frame-Based Encodings

Frame-based encodings encode a fixed-length block of audio into another block of compressed data, typically also of fixed length. For frame-based encodings, the sender may choose to combine several such frames into a single message. The receiver can tell the number of frames contained in a message since the frame duration is defined as part of the encoding.

All frame-oriented audio codecs should be able to encode and decode several consecutive frames within a single packet. Since the frame size for the frame-oriented codecs is given, there is no need to use a separate designation for the same encoding, but with different number of frames per packet.

RTP PAYLOAD FOR TELEPHONY TRAFFIC

In Chapter 4, I explained the importance of a data network being able to represent the telephone's signals (dialed digits), and events (off-hook, on-hook, etc.) correctly. By correctly, I mean the proper representation of the telephone signal, as well as how long it is transmitted (for example, how long we press a key on the telephone key pad).

Considerable work has been done in the past few years about how to represent the telephone's signals and events in a packet network. The Frame Relay Forum and the ATM Forum have published specifications on these operations, as has the IETF. For those of you who are interested in the work done by the Forums, I refer you to [BLAC99].[2] For this book, we concentrate on the Internet solutions being developed by the IETF. This part of the chapter is based on the work of Henning Schulzrinne and Scott Petrack [SCHU99].[3]

---

[2][BLAC99]. Black , Uyless. *Voice over IP*. Prentice Hall, 1999.
[3][SCHU99]. Schulzrinne, Henning, and Petrack, Scott. "RTP Payload for DTMF Digits, Telephony Tones, and Telephony Signals," Internet Draft, ietf-avt-tones-01.ps.

Payload Format

The payload format for these operations is shown in Figure 7–4. The events field identifies DTMF digits and line/trunk events, explained later in this chapter. The volume field expresses the power level of the DTMF digit, with a range of 0 to –63 dBm0. It is set to 0 for events other than DTMF digits. The duration field defines the duration of the digit. The digit begins at the instant of the value in the time-stamp field. The time-stamp in the header represents the measurement point for the current packet, and extends forward. The R field is reserved for future use.

The idea of capturing the caller's dialing signals and pattern is for the signaling gateway to begin sending event packets immediately upon recognizing an event and every 50 ms thereafter, until the event is finished; for example, until the caller stops pressing a button on the telephone key pad. If a person is a slow dialer, and presses a number for a while, the gateway sends a new event packet, but keeps the time-stamp the same value as the packet for the beginning of the digit, and increases the duration field accordingly.

In addition, if no new digit has been sent in the last interval, the gateway retransmits the digit three times or until the next digit is recognized.

One could ask why worry about the duration of the digit, and the time between the entry of the digits? Why not just accept the dialed digit stream, and send it out in a standard timing sequence (something like dialing from a PC). The answer is that some telephony components are aware of digit duration and digit delay, and the source gateway must go though the operations just described to emulate the duration and delay.

DTMF Events

Table 7–2 lists the DTMF events and the decimal representations in the RTP packet. Chapter 2 provides information on DTMF (see Table 2–2, and accompanying explanations).

0-7	8	9	10-15	1 6	17-30	3 1
Event	E	R	Volume		Duration	

Figure 7–4 RTP Payload Format for Telephony Events, Tones, and Signals

Table 7–2   DTMF Events

Event	Decimal Encoding
0–9	0–9
*	10
#	11
A–D	12–15
Flash	16

Data Modem and Fax Events

If a subscriber line is servicing a computer/modem or a fax machine, the gateway must be able to interface with these devices, accept their signals, and code them into the RTP payload. In so doing, the gateway must "understand" several international standards that deal with data communications over a telephone line. For the details on these specfications, see [BLAC95].[4] Here is general description:

> V.8: Describes the procedures for starting sessions of data communications over the Public Switched Telephone Network (PSTN).

> V.25: Describes the procedures automatic answering equipment and/or parallel automatic calling equipment on the PSTN, including procedures for disabling of echo control devices for both manually and automatically established calls.

> V.21: A very old modem specification for call-and-answer handshakes, and its use in IP call processing it so support Group 3 fax machines and their exchange of T.30 information. The calling fax modem sends on channel 1 and receives on channel 2; the answering fax modem sends on channel 2 and receives on channel 1. V.21 uses frequency shift keying (FSK), and four frequency tones to represent the binary 1s and 0s on the two channels.

Table 7–3 shows the data and fax events defined for transport in RTP packets. The ANS, /ANS, ANSam, and /ANSam codes represent frequency tones used to disable echo cancellers and or echo suppressors.

Listed below are these events and a summary of their functions, a more detailed explanation is available in [SCHU99].

---

[4][BLAC95]. Black, Uyless. *The V Series Recommendations,* McGraw Hill, 1995.

Table 7–3   Data and Fax Events

Event	Decimal Encoding
Answer tone (ANS)	32
/ANS	33
ANSam	34
/ANSam	35
Calling tone (CNG)	36
V.21 channel 1, "0" bit	37
V.21 channel 1, "1" bit	38
V.21 channel 2, "0" bit	39
V.21 channel 2, "1" bti	40
CRd	41
CRe	42
ESi	43
ESr	44
MRd	45
MRe	46

- ANS: This 2100 +/– 15 Hz tone is used to disable echo suppression for data transmission. For fax machines, Recommendation T.30 refers to this tone as terminal identification (CED) answer tone.
- /ANS: This signal is the same signal as ANS, except that it reverses phase at an interval of 450 +/– 25 ms. It disables both echo cancellers and echo suppressors.
- ANSam: The modified answer tone (ANSam) [3] is a signal at 2100 +/– 1 Hz without phase reversals, amplitude-modulated by a sinewave at 15 +/– 0.1 Hz. This tone is sent by modems if network echo canceller disabling is not required.
- /ANSam: The modified answer tone with phase reversals (ANSam) is a signal at 2100 +/– 1 Hz with phase reversals at intervals of 450 +/– 25 ms, amplitude-modulated by a sinewave at 15 +/– 0.1 Hz. This tone is sent to disable echo suppressors.
- CNG: After dialing the called fax machine's telephone number (and before it answers), the calling Group 3 fax machine (optionally) begins sending a Calling tone (CNG) consisting of an interrupted tone of 1100 Hz.

- CRdi: Capabilities Request (CRd), initiating side, is a dual-tone signal with tones at 1375 Hz and 2002 Hz for 400 ms, followed by a single tone at 1900 Hz for 100 ms. This signal requests the remote station transition from telephony mode to an information transfer mode and requests the transmission of a capabilities list message by the remote station.
- CRdr: CRdr is the response tone to CRdi. It consists of a dual-tone signal with tones at 1529 Hz and 2225 Hz for 400 ms, followed by a single tone at 1900 Hz for 100 ms.
- CRe: Capabilities Request (CRe) is a dual-tone signal with tones at 1375 by a single tone at 400 Hz for 100 ms. This signal requests the remote station transition from telephony mode to an information transfer mode and requests the transmission of a capabilities list message by the remote station.
- CT: The calling tone consists of a series of interrupted bursts of binary 1 signals or 1300 Hz, on for a duration of not less than 0.5 s and not more than 0.7 s and off for a duration of not less than 1.5 s and not more than 2.0 s.
- ESi: Escape Signal (ESi) is a dual-tone signal with tones at 1375 Hz and 2002 Hz for 400 ms, followed by a single tone at 980 Hz for 100 ms. This signal requests the remote station transition from telephony mode to an information transfer mode. Signal ESi is sent by the initiating station.
- ESr: Escape Signal (ESr) [12] is a dual-tone signal with tones at 1529 Hz and 2225 Hz for 400 ms, followed by a single tone at 1650 Hz for 100 ms. It is the same as ESi, but sent by the responding station.
- MRdi: Mode Request (MRd), initiating side, is a dual-tone signal with tones at 1375 Hz and 2002 Hz for 400 ms followed by a single tone at 1150 Hz for 100 ms. This signal requests the remote station transition from telephony mode to an information transfer mode and requests the transmission of a mode select message by the remote station.
- MRdr: MRdr is the response tone to MRdi. It consists of a dual-tone signal with tones at 1529 Hz and 2225 Hz for 400 ms, followed by a single tone at 1150 Hz for 100 ms.
- MRe: Mode Request (MRe) is a dual-tone signal with tones at 1375 Hz and 2002 Hz for 400 ms, followed by a single tone at 650 Hz for 100 ms. This signal requests the remote station transition from telephony mode to an information transfer mode and requests the transmission of a mode select message by the remote station.

RTP PAYLOAD FOR H.263 VIDEO

The IETF Audio-Video Transport (AVT) Working Group is in the process of defining the RTP payload format for ITU-T's H.263 Recommendation.[5] Our approach is to describe the RTP header usage and the video packet. The Internet draft cited in footnote 5 has a wealth of information on this subject, which is beyond the summary explanations in this book.

Each RTP packet starts with a fixed RTP header. The following fields of the RTP fixed header are used for H.263 video streams:

- *Marker bit (Mbit):* The Marker bit of the RTP header is set to 1 when the current packet carries the end of current frame, and is 0 otherwise.
- *Payload Type (PT):* The Payload Type shall specify the H.263 video payload format.
- *Time-stamp:* The RTP time-stamp encodes the sampling instance of the first video frame data contained in the RTP data packet. The RTP time-stamp shall be the same on successive packets if a video frame occupies more than one packet. In a multilayer scenario, all pictures corresponding to the same temporal reference should use the same time-stamp. For an H.263 video stream, the RTP time-stamp is based on a 90 kHz clock, the same as that of the RTP payload for H.261 stream information, it is required that those timing information run synchronously. That is, both the RTP time-stamp and the temporal reference (TR in the picture header of H.263) should carry the same relative timing information.

A section of an H.263 compressed bit stream is carried as a payload within each RTP packet. For each RTP packet, the RTP header is followed by an H.263 payload header, which is followed by a number of bytes of a standard H.263 compressed bit stream. The size of the H.263 payload header is variable depending on the payload involved as detailed in the section 4. The layout of the RTP H.263 video packet is shown in Figure 7–5.

RTP Multiplexing Operations

RTP multiplexing is provided by the destination transport address.[6] For example, a teleconference consisting of audio and video streams can

---

[5]See draft-ietf-avt-rtp-h263-video-02.txt

[6]Don't forget, the term transport address is an ITU-T term and refers to a network layer address and a port number. In the Internet, this is known as a socket.

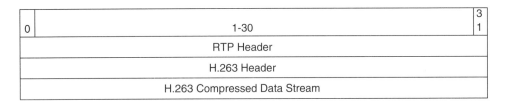

0	1-30	3 1
RTP Header		
H.263 Header		
H.263 Compressed Data Stream		

Figure 7–5   RTP H.263 Video Packet

use two connections, each with a transport address (and different SSRCs). The use of separate RTP sessions is recommended by H.225.0 (see Sections A.5.2) for the following reasons:

- If one payload type were switched during a session, there would be no means to identify which of the old values the new one replaced.
- An SSRC is defined to identify a single timing and sequence number space. Interleaving multiple payload types would require different timing spaces if the media clock rates differ and would require different sequence number spaces to tell which payload type suffered packet loss.
- The RTCP sender and recur reports can only describe one timing and sequence number space per SSRC and do not carry a payload type field.

Rosenberg and Schulzrinne have proposed an RTP payload format for multiplexing traffic from multiple users into a single RTP packet.[7] These authors cite the following inefficiencies with separate RTP sessions.

The audio payloads carried in each RTP packet are generally small. For example, the ITU-G.729 speech coder generates a rate of 8 kbit/s in frames of 10-ms duration. If packed three frames per packet, the resulting RTP payloads are 30 bytes long. The IP, UDP, and RTP headers add up to 40 bytes, resulting in a packet efficiency of only 43%.

On the other hand, suppose the payloads from two users are multiplexed into the same RTP session and packet. A multiplexing protocol is now required to delineate the packets. The protocol defined (by the authors and explained next) typically adds 16 bits of overhead per multiplexed user. In the two-subscriber example, this allows an RTP packet to be constructed with 60 bytes of useful payload and 41 bytes of header, the efficiency improves to 59%.

---

[7]From the AVT (Audio Visual Transport) Working Group, J. Rosenberg and H. Schulzrinne. See draft-ietf-avt-aggregation-00.txt © The Internet Society.

A further benefit of multiplexing is a potential reduction in packetization delays. Most Internet telephony applications use fairly large packetization delays, mainly for the purpose of raising the size of the payloads to increase efficiency. However, if multiplexing is performed, the packet payload increases. This allows smaller packetization delays to be used as the number of multiplexed users increases.

This section of the chapter summarizes the Rosenberg/Schulzrinne draft pertaining to the RTP multiplexing packets. I refer you to their draft for more details as well as a discussion on these issues and operations: (a) QOS considerations, (b) security, (c) use of multiple packets, and (d) open issues, such as H.323 and MPEG-4 interworking.

Multiplexing Packet Formats. All fields of the RTP header except the time-stamp, marker bit, and SSRC maintain their current definition. This format for the multiplexing packet is shown in Figure 7–6.

- *Payload Type:* The payload type field designates the RTP packet as a multiplexed payload. The payload type value is chosen dynamically and the binding to this format is conveyed via non-RTP means.

- *Time-stamp:* This protocol requires that all multiplexed streams in one packet have the same clock rate (i.e., sampling rate for audio) and generate media frames at integer multiples of a common frame duration. It is possible, for example, that a set of users generates a packet every 10 ms, while others generate packets at intervals of 20 and 30 ms, but all frame generation instants must be multiples of this 10 ms interval.

- *Marker Bit:* This field is not used for multiplexing and always has a value of zero. A marker bit is included for each user in the multiplexing header.

- *SSRC:* This field is used to identify groups of users (instead of a single user) whose frames are time synchronized.

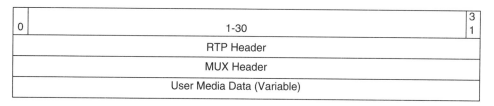

Figure 7–6   The RTP Multiplexing Packet

The multiplexing (MUX) header contains information about each user that is part of the multiplexing operation. It contains information on the type of payload and an identifier value for each user payload.

SUMMARY

RTP is designed to support real time traffic. RTP supports both unicast and multicast applications. RTP provides services that include payload type identification, sequence numbering, time-stamping, and delivery monitoring. Applications usually run RTP on top of UDP to make use of its multiplexing and checksum services.

APPENDIX 7A   REFERENCES FOR RTP PAYLOAD TYPES

References

[RFC1889] Schulzrinne, H., S. Casner, R. Frederick, V. Jacobson, "RTP: A Transport Protocol for Real-Time Applications," RFC 1889, GMD Fokus, Precept Software, Xerox Palo Alto Research Center, Lawrence Berkeley National Laboratory, October 1996.
[RFC1890] Schulzrinne, H., "RTP Profile for Audio and Video Conferences with Minimal Control," RFC 1890, GMD Fokus, January 1996.
[RFC2029] Speer, M., and D. Hoffman, "RTP Payload Format of Sun's Cell B Video Encoding," RFC 2029, Sun Microsystems, October 1996.
[RFC2032] Turletti, T., and C. Huitema, "RTP Payload Format for H.261 Video Streams," RFC 2032, MIT, Bellcore, October 1996.
[RFC2435] Berc, L., W. Fenner, R. Frederick, S. McCanne, and P. Stewart, "RTP Payload Format for JPEG-Compressed Video," RFC 2435, DEC, PARC, LBL, October 1998.
[RFC2250] Hoffman, D., Fernando, G., Goyal, V., and M. Civanlar, "RTP Payload Format for MPEG1/MPEG2 Video," RFC 2250, Sun Microsystems, Precept Spftware, AT&T Labs—Research, January 1998.

People

[DiPol] Joseph Di Pol, <Joe.Dipol@eng.sun.com>, May 1996.
[Hoffman] Don Hoffman, <hoffman@eng.sun.com>, January 1996.
[Kumar] Vineet Kumar, <Vineet_Kumar@ccm.jf.intel.com>, January 1997.
[McCanne] Steve McCanne, <mccanne@ee.lbl.gov>, January 1996.
[Schulzrinne] Henning Schulzrinne, <schulzrinne@fokus.gmd.de>, May 1996.
[Speer] Michael Speer, <michael.speer@eng.sun.com>, January 1996.
[Turletti] Thierry Turletti, January 1996.
[Zhu] Chunrong Zhu, <Chunrong_Zhu@ccm.jf.intel.com>, June 1996.

APPENDIX 7B   OTHER REFERENCES ON CURRENT RTP ACTIVITY

1. *http URL:*draft-jonsson-robust-hc-04.txt
   Title: RObust Checksum-based header COmpression (ROCCO)
2. *http URL:*draft-crossman-avt-rtp-g7221-00.txt
   Title: RTP Payload Format for ITU-T Recommendation G.722.1
3. *http URL:*draft-ietf-rohc-rtp-rocco-video-00.txt
   Title: ROCCO Conversational Video Profiles
4. *http URL:*draft-degermark-crtp-cellular-01.txt
   Title: CRTP over cellular radio links
5. *http URL:*draft-ietf-avt-rtp-g7221-00.txt
   Title: RTP Payload Format for ITU-T Recommendation G.722.1
6. *http URL:*draft-rgcc-avt-mpeg4flexmux-00.txt
   Title: RTP Payload Format for MPEG-4 Streams
7. *http URL:*draft-berger-mpls-hdr-comp-00.txt
   Title: MPLS/IP Header Compression
8. *http URL:*draft-ietf-avt-dv-video-03.txt
   Title: RTP Payload Format for DV Format Video
9. *http URL:*draft-ietf-avt-profile-new-08.txt
   Title: RTP Profile for Audio and Video Conferences with Minimal Control
10. *http URL:*draft-ietf-rohc-rtp-ace-00.txt
    Title: Adaptive Header ComprEssion (ACE) for Real-Time Multimedia
11. *http URL:*draft-miyazaki-rohc-kwhc-01.txt
    Title: Robust Header Compression using Keyword-Packets
12. *http URL:*draft-ietf-avt-dv-audio-02.txt
    Title: RTP Payload Format for 12-bit DAT, 20- and 24-bit Linear Sampled Audio
13. *http URL:*draft-ietf-avt-rtp-mp3-01.txt
    Title: A More Loss-Tolerant RTP Payload Format for MP3 Audio
14. *http URL:*draft-gharai-ac3-00.txt
    Title: RTP Payload Format for AC-3 Audio
15. *http URL:*draft-gc-avt-mpeg4visual-00.txt
    Title: RTP payload format for MPEG-4 Visual Advanced Profiles

16. *http URL*:draft-ietf-rohc-rtp-rocco-01.txt
    Title: RObust Checksum-based header COmpression (ROCCO)

17. *http URL*:draft-mauve-rtpi-00.txt
    Title: RTP/I: An Application Level Real-Time Protocol for Distributed Information

18. *http URL*:draft-koren-avt-crtp-enhance-01.txt
    Title: Enhancements to IP/UDP/RTP Header Compression

19. *http URL*:draft-ietf-rohc-rtp-requirements-02.txt
    Title: Requirements for robust IP/UDP/RTP header compression

20. *http URL*:draft-lakaniemi-avt-mime-amr-00.txt
    Title: MIME Type Registration of AMR Speech Codec

21. *http URL*:draft-gharai-hdtv-video-00.txt
    Title: RTP Payload Format for Uncompressed HDTV Video Streams

22. *http URL*:draft-ietf-avt-mpeg4streams-00.txt
    Title: RTP Payload Format for MPEG-4 with Flexible Error Resiliency

23. *http URL*:draft-ietf-avt-rtptest-02.txt
    Title: RTP Testing Strategies

24. *http URL*:draft-ietf-rohc-rtp-rocco-performance-00.txt
    Title: ROCCO Performance Evaluation

25. *http URL*:draft-friedman-avt-rtcp-report-extns-00.txt

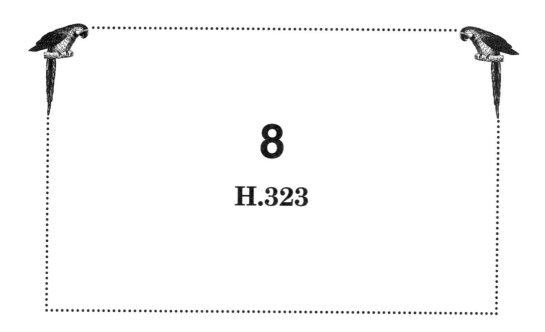

8

H.323

INTRODUCTION

This chapter explains H.323, currently the most widely used Call Processing Protocol in the industry. We begin by an examination of the design intent of H.323, followed by a description of the H.323 Gatekeepers, Gateways, Multipoint Control Units (MCUs), and user endpoints (workstations). The message structure of H.323 is explained, and several message protocol flows are provided to help convey how H.323 supports call processing and many other operations. Also, this chapter explains the relationship of H.323 with its supporting protocols, principally H.225 and H.245.

DESIGN INTENT OF H.323

H.323 was originally designed to support multimedia services over a LAN (a network with no QOS guarantees). As it has evolved, it has been expanded to support WAN and Internet telephony.

H.323 is not a stand-alone protocol (but then, few protocols are). The full H.323 system includes H.245 for control operations, H.332 for managing large conferences, H.225 for connection management, H.235 for security support, T.120 for document support for conferences, and H.246 for circuit-switch interworking. All totaled, it is a complex protocol stack.

H.323 also borrows heavily on the ITU-T ISDN signaling protocol, Q.931. It also borrows from several ITU-T multimedia protocols: H.324 for telephony terminals, H.320 for ISDN, and H.321 for ISDN B channels.

With the "legacy" of all these protocols, H.323 is an amalgamation of a variety of procedures, borrowed from these other systems. It defines many messages and hundreds of information elements (fields) for these messages. As one would expect from a procedure that has fused together other procedures, the fusion is not very clean. As examples, a call forwarding operation requires the invocation of components from H.225, and H.245 [SCHU].[1] Furthermore, H.245 and H.225 can be used together in three different ways: (a) as separate connections, (b) tunneling H.245 through H.225, and (c) the FastStart in version 2 of H.323 (I will discuss these operations later).

One more point: H.323 uses a binary syntax for its messages, as defined in several ITU-T and ISO standards (ASN.1 and Basic Encoding Rules). As such, it requires rather elaborate code-generators.

The point of my last few comments is that H.323 is rich in function and complexity.

H.323 ARCHITECTURE

The H.323 Recommendation is now being deployed in a number of voice over packet products. The H.323 Recommendation assumes the transmission path between the telephony users passes through at least one local area network (LAN), such as an Ethernet or a token ring. It is further assumed that the LAN may not provide a guaranteed quality-of-service (QOS) need to support the telephony traffic. As shown in Figure 8–1, the H.323 encompasses end-to-end connection between H.323 terminals and other terminals and through different kinds of networks.

The H.323 terminal provides real-time, two-way audio, video, or data communications with another H.323 terminal. The terminal can also communicate with an H.323 Gateway or a Multipoint Control Unit (MCU). While I cite the ability to support voice, video, and data, the terminal need not be configured for all those services, and H.323 does not require the terminal to be multiservice-capable.

---

[1][SCHU] Schulzrinne, Henning and Rosenberg, Jonathan, "A Comparison of SIP and H.323 for Internet Telephony," a white paper, to go hgs@cs.comumbia.edu and jdrosen@bell-labs.com, date not given.

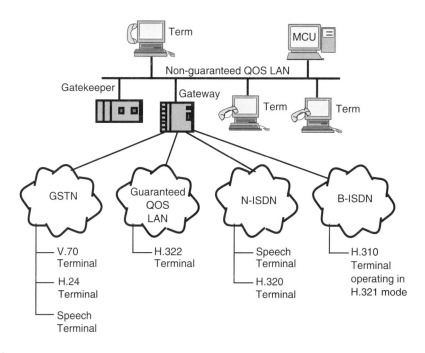

Where:
  MCU   Multipoint control units
  GSTN   General switched telephone network
  QOS   Quality of service
  ISDN   Integrated Services Digital Network (N: narrowband; G=B: broadband)

Figure 8–1   The H.323 Architecture

The H.323 Gateway is a node on a LAN that communicates with the H.323 terminal or other ITU-T terminals attached to other networks. If one of the terminals is not an H.323 terminal, the Gateway performs translation of the transmission formats between the terminals. One H.323 Gateway can interwork with another H.323 Gateway. In addition, the Gateway can operate with other ITU switched circuit networks (SCNs); (a) the General Switched Telephone Network (GSTN), (b) the narrowband-ISDN (N-ISDN), and (c) the broadband-ISDN (B-ISDN, an ATM-based network). Also, the Gateway can operate as an H.323 Multi-point Control Unit (MCU), discussed next.

The Gateway can setup and clear calls on the LAN and SCN. In ef-fect, it reflects the LAN characteristics to the H.323 terminal on the LAN video and the SCN terminal characteristics on the SCN side. Under cer-tain conditions, the Gateway can be used to bypass a LAN router or a low bandwidth communications link.

The Multipoint Control Unit (MCU) supports multiconferencing between three or more terminals and Gateways. A two-terminal point-to-point conference can be expanded to a multipoint conference.

ZONES

The H.323 nodes are organized by (and into) zones, illustrated in Figure 8–2. The zone is a collection of terminals, Gateways, MCUs, and one Gatekeeper. This Gatekeeper is in charge of the zone, and any node that wants the services of the Gateway must go through a process of "discovering" an appropriate Gatekeeper, then "registering" with that Gate-

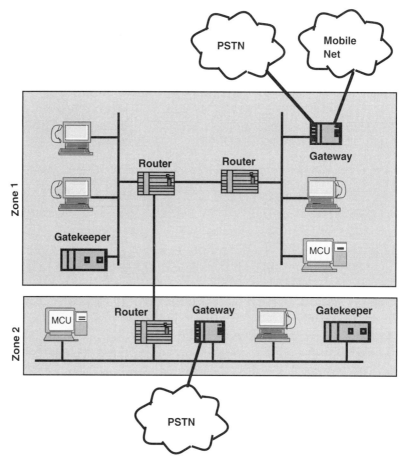

Figure 8–2   H.323 Zones

keeper. Thereafter, when an H.323 endpoint (such as a terminal, an MCU, a Gateway) wishes to establish a session with another endpoint, it will send some preliminary messages to the Gatekeeper. In turn, the Gatekeeper will receive these messages and make decisions about how to support the endpoint sessions. A zone must have at least one terminal and only one Gatekeeper. It is not required to have Gateways or MCUs.

THE H.323 PROTOCOL STACK

H.323 consists of several standards, and cites the use of others, as shown in Figure 8–3. For audio applications, G.711 is required, and other G Series recommendations are options. However, the preference in recent commercial products is not G.711, because of its 64 kbit/s bandwidth requirement.

The video standards are H.261 and H.263. Data support is though T.120, and the various control, signaling, and maintenance operations are provided by H.245, and Q.931.

The audio and video packets must be encapsulated into the Real Time Protocol (RTP) and carried on a UDP socket pair between the

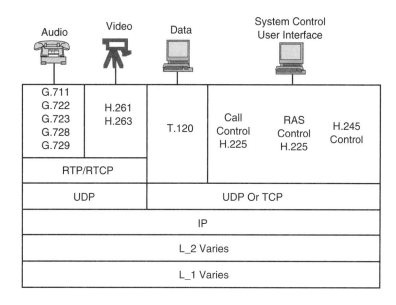

Where:
  RAS   Registration, admission, and status

Figure 8–3   The H.323 Protocol Stack

sender and the receiver. The Real Time Control Protocol (RTCP) is used to assess the quality of the sessions and connections as well as to provide feedback information among the communicating parties. The data and support packets can operate over TCP or UDP.

RELATIONSHIP TO MEGACO AND MGCP

The relationship of Megaco/MGCP to H.323 is shown in Figure 8–4. Be aware that Megaco/MGCP does not have to be a part of H.323, but if it is, the Megaco/MGCP Media Gateway Controller/Call Agent (hereafter in Figure 8–4, called a Controller) acts as an H.323 Gatekeeper. This approach is in keeping with the functions of the H.323 Gatekeeper, who provides address translation and call control services to H.323 endpoints.

The Controller in this example has signaling operations with four networks. Some of these placements will depend on many factors, such as marketplace acceptance of IP-based protocols in the local loop.

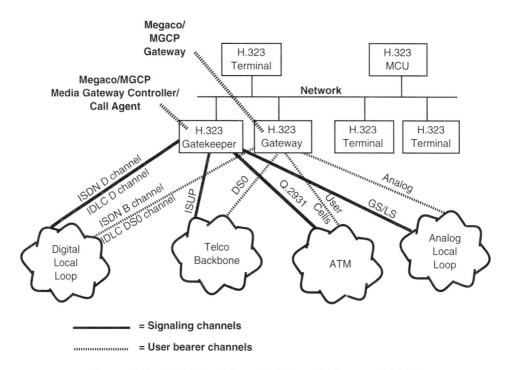

Figure 8–4   Relationship of H.323 and Megaco/MGCP

The solid lines indicate signaling links and the dashed lines indicate links for user traffic. In some of the network interfaces, the signaling traffic and user traffic can be transmitted on the same physical link. I separate them in this figure for purposes of discussion.

We examine the signaling interfaces first (the solid lines in the figure). For a digital local loop to a remote digital terminal (RDT) into a residential neighborhood or an industrial park, the Controller uses ISDN D channels (and Q.931 operating inside the D channel) for digital local links. If the loop is configured with Bellcore's GR-303 (a very common interface in North America), IDLC messages (Integrated Digital Loop Carrier System) are exchanged, or (not shown here) conventional ABCD signals in accordance with GR-303. The Controller exchanges SS7 ISUP messages with the telco network, Q.2931 messages with the ATM network, and a variety of ground start/loop start (GS/LS) signals on analog local links.

Next, let's consider user traffic (the dashed lines in the figure). The Controller handles the user traffic, and provides signal translations as necessary: DS0 signals with the telco network, ATM user cells with the ATM network, and either conventional analog signals on analog local links, or B channels on digital local links.

These four interfaces are not exhaustive. I have not included mobile wireless, fixed wireless, or coaxial systems.

THE MULTIPOINT CONTROL UNIT (MCU)

The Multipoint Control Unit (MCU), depicted in Figure 8–5, supports multiconferencing between three or more terminals and Gateways. A two-terminal point-to-point conference can be expanded to a multipoint conference. The MCU consists of a mandatory multipoint controller (MC) and optional multipoint processor (MP).

The MC supports the negotiation of capabilities with all terminals in order to insure a common level of communications. It can also control the resources in the multicast operation. The MC is not capable of the mixing or switching of voice, video, or data traffic. However, the MP can perform these services (under the control of the MC). The MP is the central processor of the voice, video, and data streams for a multipoint conference.

The MCU may (or may not) control three types of multipoint conferences:

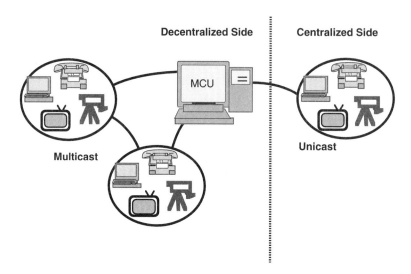

Figure 8–5   The Multipoint Control Unit (MCU)

- *Centralized Multipoint Conference:* All participating terminals communicate with the MCU point-to-point. The MC manages the conference, and the MP receives, processes, and sends the voice, video, or data streams to and from the participating terminals.
- *Decentralized Multipoint Conference:* The MCU is not involved in this operation. Rather, the terminals communicate directly with each other through their own MCs. If necessary, the terminals assume the responsibility for summing the received audio streams and selecting the received video signals for display.
- *Mixed Multipoint Conference:* As the name suggests, this conference is a mix of the centralized and decentralized modes. The MCU keeps the operations transparent to the terminals.

THE MAJOR OPERATIONS

H.323 invokes several operations (and protocols) to support an end user's communications. These are called phases in some parts of the H.323 literature. Figure 8–6 shows the major phases, and others may be invoked, depending upon specific implementations.

Event 1: The discovery phase entails an endpoint, such as a user workstation, finding with which Gatekeeper it should register. Dur-

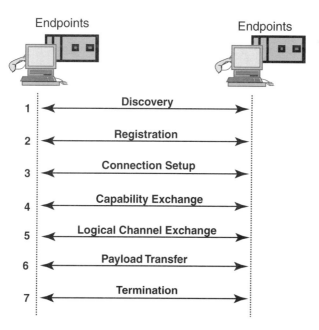

Figure 8–6   The Major Operations

ing this phase, the endpoint and the Gatekeeper exchange addresses.

Event 2: The registration operations define how an endpoint registers with a Gatekeeper. The addresses established during the discovery process are used during this phase, as well as some optional addresses. Also, the terminal type is identified, such as an end-user terminal, a Gateway, an MCU, or an MC.

Event 3: The connection setup phase is used to set up a connection between to endpoints for the end-to-end call.

Event 4: Next the capability exchange is executed. Its purpose is to ensure that any multimedia traffic sent by one endpoint can be received correctly by the receiving endpoint. Information, such as bit rates and codec types are exchanged during this exchange.

Event 5: H.323 permits the transmittal of different types of media streams over logical channels. The next phase is used to open one or more logical channels to carry the traffic.

Events 6 and 7: After all these procedures have been completed, user traffic can be exchanged. Eventually, after the user session is complete, termination operations take place.

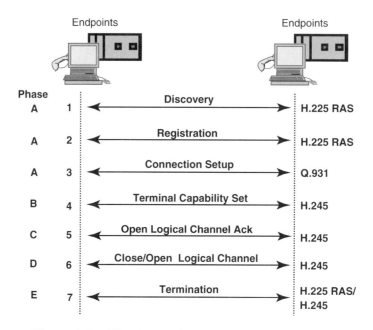

Figure 8–7   The Major Operations and the Phases

Figure 8–7 provides more information about the H.323 control protocols in relation to the H.323 "phases." On the left side of the figure the phases (A–E) are shown in relation to the major operations. On the right side of the figure, the H.225 RAS, Q.931, and H.245 notations indicate which protocol or protocols are invoked during the phases.

Notice in phase E that the figure shows the invocation of H.225 RAS and H.245 for the call termination operations. H.245 is used by the endpoints to terminate a call. If a Gatekeeper is involved in the operations between the endpoints, then H.225 RAS is invoked to release the bandwidth. If a Gatekeeper is not involved, H.225 RAS need not be invoked for the termination operations.

THE H.323 MESSAGE CODING CONVENTIONS

H.323 defines the messages exchanged between the various nodes in a general way. It is left to the H.225.0 to define the contents of these messages using Abstract Syntax Notation.1 (ASN.1). The ASN.1 coding for some of these three messages are listed below and Table 8–1 describes a few simple rules to help you understand the code.

Table 8–1   Rules for Reading ASN.1 Code

::=	Means defined as.
SEQUENCE	Means a sequence of ASN.1 elements. H.325 uses the SEQUENCE statement to explain the fields in the packet.
Words beginning with an upper case	This word describes a field in the packet and somewhere in the code, it must be defined by another ASN.1 descriptor called the "type". A type could be integer, Boolean, etc.
Word beginning with a lower case	This word is supposed to be a "user friendly" description of the associated upper case word. An ASN.1 compiler does not act upon these words.
OPTIONAL	The entry is not required in a message.
CHOICE	One and only one of the fields is present in the message.
NULL	A type stating that information may not be available.
—	Comments in the code.
{	Proclaims the start and end of a part of the code.
}	
, after the field	Signifies the continuance of the code.
Words all in CAPS	These are ASN.1 reserved words.

ASN.1 Code for the H.323 Addresses and Identifiers

Figure 8–8 shows some examples of ASN.1 code (available in H.245) that defines the key H.323 addresses and identifiers. The transport address (**TransportAddress**) is a **CHOICE** type, allowing the selection of a unicast address (**UnicastAddress**), or a multicast address (**Multicast-Address**).

The unicast address is also a **CHOICE** type, with the IP address (**iPAddress**) defined as a **SEQUENCE** type. Notice that the sequence objects are a **network** and **tsapIdentifier.** These object are the conventional IP address, and an Internet port number respectively.

Thus, the H.323 transport address is analogous to an Internet socket number; that is, the concatenation of the IP address and the port number.

Below the ASN.1 code is information on the Internet port numbers that have been reserved for H.323 and H.225. The specific port selected depends on the nature of the operation. For example, port 1718 is used

```
-Begin ASN.1 Code


TransportAddress ::=CHOICE

{
            unicastAddress                      UnicastAddress,
            mullticastAddress                   MulticastAddress,
            ...
}
UnicastAddress                                  ::=CHOICE
            iPAddress                           SEQUENCE
            {
                  network                       OCTETSTRING (SIZE(4)),
                  tsapIdentifier                INTEGER(0..65535),
                  ...
            },
-and others, such as IPX, IPv6, Netbios, OSI NSAP, nonstandard
-End ASN.1 Code

H.323:
            Well-known port numbers: 1300, 1718, 1719, 1720,
            2517, and 11720

H.225:
            Well-known port numbers: 2099
```

Figure 8–8   ASN.1 Code for H.323 Addresses and Identifiers

only for discovery operations, and port 1720 is used for a conventional host (endpoint) calling operation.

GATEKEEPER DISCOVERY

The Gatekeeper discovery is a straightforward procedure used by an endpoint to determine with which Gatekeeper it should register. The process is automatic and does not require manual configuration, and allows the association between the endpoint and its Gatekeeper to change over time.

Figure 8–9 shows the messages exchanged for the Gatekeeper discovery operation, which starts in event 1 with endpoint 1 sending a Gate-

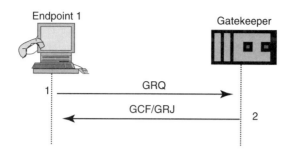

Figure 8–9   Gatekeeper Discovery Operations

keeper Request (GRQ) message on the LAN. This message is examined by one or more Gatekeepers who may (or may not, depending on the implementation) respond with a Gatekeeper Confirmation (GCF) message. This message contains the transport address of the Gatekeeper's RAS channel.

The transport address is implemented with a Transport Service Access Point (TSAP), and allows the multiplexing of multiple connections on a TSAP. The transport address is a LAN MAC address and a TSAP.

An alias address can be used as an alternate method for identifying an endpoint. An example of an alias address is E.164 (the ISDN telephony address). If alias addresses are used, they must be unique within a zone, also Gatekeepers, MCs, and MCUs cannot use alias addresses.

The endpoint starts a timer upon issuing the GRQ message. If it does not receive a response, the time expires and another GRQ can be issued. If auto discovery fails, the network administrator must troubleshoot to determine the problem. Alternatively, the Gatekeeper may return a Gatekeeper Reject (GRJ) message if it chooses not to be the endpoint's Gatekeeper.

The contents of these messages are used primarily for identification purposes and contain the following information:

- *requestSeqNum:* A number unique to the sender, returned by the receiver in any messages associated with this message.
- *protocolIdentifier:* Used to determine version/vintage of implementation.
- *nonStandardData:* An optional parameter whose contents are not defined.
- *rasAddress:* The transport address that this endpoint uses for registration and status messages.
- *endpointType:* Specifies the type(s) of the terminal that is registering.

- *GatekeeperIdentifier:* Identifies the Gatekeeper that the terminal would like to receive permission to register from a missing or null string *GatekeeperIdentifier* indicates that the terminal is interested in any available Gatekeeper.
- *callServices:* Provides information on support of optional Q-Series protocols to the Gatekeeper and called terminal.
- *endpointAlias:* Contains external address (if used), such as E.164.
- *rejectReason:* Codes for why the GRQ was rejected by this Gatekeeper.

Here is the ASN.1 Code for the Discovery Messages

```
GatekeeperRequest               ::=SEQUENCE-- (GRQ)
{
    requestSeqNum               RequestSeqNum,
    protocolIdentifier          ProtocolIdentifier,
    nonStandardData             NonStandardParameter OPTIONAL,
    rasAddress                  TransportAddress,
    endpointType                EndpointType,
    gatekeeperIdentifier        GatekeeperIdentifier OPTIONAL,
    callServices                QseriesOptions OPTIONAL,
    endpointAlias               SEQUENCE OF AliasAddress OPTIONAL,
}
GatekeeperReject                ::=SEQUENCE-- (GRJ)
{
    requestSeqNum               RequestSeqNum,
    protocolIdentifier          ProtocolIdentifier,
    nonStandardData             NonStandardParameter OPTIONAL,
    gatekeeperIdentifier        GatekeeperIdentifier OPTIONAL,
    rejectReason                GatekeeperRejectReason,
}
GatekeeperRejectReason          ::=CHOICE
{
    resourceUnavailable         NULL,
    terminalExcluded            NULL,--permission failure, not a re-
                                    source failure
    invalidRevision             NULL,
    undefinedReason             NULL,
}
GatekeeperConfirm               ::=SEQUENCE-- (GCF)
{
    requestSeqNum               RequestSeqNum,
    protocolIdentifier          ProtocolIdentifier,
    nonStandardData             NonStandardParameter OPTIONAL,
    gatekeeperIdentifier        GatekeeperIdentifier OPTIONAL,
    rasAddress                  TransportAddress,
}
```

REGISTRATION PROCEDURES

Once the discovery process has taken place, registration procedures are undertaken. These administrative operations define how an endpoint joins a zone and provides the Gatekeeper with its transport (and alias) address(es). Figure 8–10 shows the message exchange, with an endpoint 1 sending the Registration Request (RRQ) message to the Gatekeeper, who was discovered with the auto-discovery operation. Of course, the connect transport address is used in the RRQ message. In event 2, the Gatekeeper responds with the Registration Confirmation (RCF) message or the Registration Reject (RRJ) message.

Either the endpoint or the Gateway can cancel the registration, and end the association between the two entities. The operations in events 3 and 4 show the registration cancellation emanating from the endpoint with the Unregister Request (URQ) message. The Gatekeeper can respond with the Unregister Confirm (UCF) message or the Unregister Reject (URJ) message. The Gatekeeper starts the registration cancellation process with the URQ message and the endpoint must respond with the UCF message.

The contents of registration messages are summarized here:

- *requestSeqNum:* A number unique to the sender. It is returned by the receiver in any response associated with this specific message.

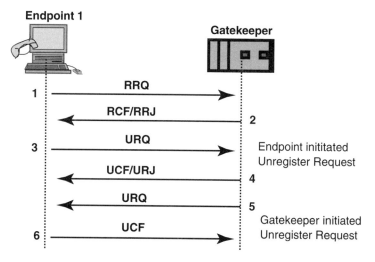

Figure 8–10   Registration Procedures

- *protocolIdentifier:* Identifies the H.225.0 vintage of the sending terminal.

- *discoveryComplete:* Set to TRUE if the requesting endpoint has preceded this message with the Gatekeeper discovery procedure; set to FALSE if registering only.

- *callSignalAddress:* The call control transport address for this endpoint. If multiple transports are supported, they must be registered all at once.

- *rasAddress:* The registration and status transport address for this endpoint.

- *terminalType:* Specifies the type(s) of the terminal that is registering.

- *terminalAlias:* A list of external addresses.

- *gatekeeperIdentifier:* Identifies the Gatekeeper that the terminal wishes to register with.

- *endpointVendor:* Information about the endpoint vendor.

- *callSignalAddress:* An array of transport addresses for H.225.0 call control messages: one for each transport that the Gatekeeper will respond to. This address includes the TSAP identifier.

- *endpointIdentifier:* A Gatekeeper assigned terminal identity string: which is echoed in subsequent RAS messages.

- *callServices:* Provides information on support of optional Q-Series protocols to Gatekeeper and called terminal.

- *endpointAlias:* Contains external address (if used), such as E.164.

- *rejectReason:* Codes for why the GRQ was rejected by this Gatekeeper.

Here is the ASN.1 code for the registration messages:

```
RegistrationrRequest              ::=SEQUENCE-- (RRQ)
{
    requestSeqNum                 RequestSeqNum,
    protocolIdentifier            ProtocolIdentifier,
    nonStandardData               NonStandardParameter OPTIONAL,
    discoveryComplete             BOOLEAN,
    callSignalAddress             SEQUENCE OF TransportAddress,
    rasAddress                    SEQUENCE OF TransportAddress,
    terminalType                  EndpointType,
    terminalAlias                 SEQUENCE OF AliasAddress OPTIONAL,
    terminalIdentifier            GatekeeperIdentifier OPTIONAL,
    endpointVendor                VendorIdentifier,
}
```

```
RegistrationConfirm              ::=SEQUENCE-- (RCF)
{
    requestSeqNum                RequestSeqNum,
    protocolIdentifier           ProtocolIdentifier,
    nonStandardData              NonStandardParameter OPTIONAL,
    callSignalAddress            SEQUENCE OF TransportAddress,
    terminalAlias                SEQUENCE OF AliasAddress OPTIONAL,
    gatekeeperIdentifier         GatekeeperIdentifier OPTIONAL,
    endpointVendor               VendorIdentifier,
}


RegistrationReject               ::=SEQUENCE-- (RRJ)
{
    requestSeqNum                RequestSeqNum,
    protocolIdentifier           ProtocolIdentifier,
    nonStandardData              NonStandardParameter OPTIONAL,
    rejectReason                 RegistrationRejectReason,
    gatekeeperIdentifier         GatekeeperIdentifier OPTIONAL,
}


RegistrationRejectReason         ::=CHOICE
{
    discovery required           NULL,-- registration permission
                                  has aged
    invalidRevision              NULL,
    invalidCallSignalAddress     NULL
    invalidRASAddress            NULL,-- supplied address is invalid
    duplicateAlias               SEQUENCE OF AliasAddress,
    invalidTerminalType          NULL,
    undefinedReason              NULL,
    transportNotSupported        NULL,--permission failure, not a
                                  resource failure
}
UnregistrationRequest            ::=SEQUENCE-- (URQ)
{
    requestSeqNum                RequestSeqNum,
    callSignalAddress            SEQUENCE OF TransportAddress,
    endpointAlias                SEQUENCE OF AliasAddress OPTIONAL,
    nonStandardData              NonStandardParameter OPTIONAL,
    endpointIdentifier           EndpointIdentifier OPTIONAL,
}
UnregistrationConfirm            ::=SEQUENCE-- (UCF)
{
    requestSeqNum                RequestSeqNum,
    nonStandardData              NonStandardParameter OPTIONAL,
}
UnregistrationReject             ::=SEQUENCE-- (URJ)
```

```
{
    requestSeqNum                 RequestSeqNum,
    rejectReason                  UnregRejectReason,
    nonStandardData               NonStandardParameter OPTIONAL,
}
UnregRejectReason                 ::=CHOICE
{
    notCurrentlyRegistered    NULL,
    callInProgress            NULL,
    undefinedReason           NULL,
}
```

ADMISSION PROCEDURES

H.323 defines the use of a modified Q.931 signaling protocol. An example of how Q.931 is used with RAS is shown in Figure 8–11 to support the Admission procedures. Notice that the RAS messages are used between the terminals (Endpoint 1 and Endpoint 2) and the Gatekeeper—which of course is the purpose of RAS. The Q.931 messages are exchanged between the H.323 terminals.

In events 1/2 and 5/6, the terminals and the Gatekeeper exchange these messages:

- *ARQ:*   The Admission Request message

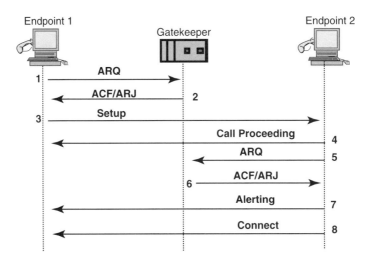

Figure 8–11   Admission Procedures

- *ACF:*   The Admission Confirmation message
- *ARJ:*   The Admission Reject message (perhaps)

Let us examine the content of these messages first and then look at the Q.931 messages. Keep in mind: to this point, the RAS operations have been concerned with discovery and registration procedures. Thus far, there have been no requests for bandwidth or other services.

Figure 8–12 illustrates another possibility for a call setup, one in which neither endpoint is registered with a Gatekeeper. The two endpoints use H.323's version of Q.931 to communicate directly with each other.

In event 1, endpoint 1 sends the setup message to endpoint 2. This message contains the TSAP ID of endpoint 2. The messaging proceeds as usual. In event 4, the Connect message contains an H.245 Control Channel Transport Address that will be used in H.245 operations (shown later).

The contents of these messages are as follows:

- *requestSeqNum:* A number unique to the sender. It shall be returned by the receiver in any response associated with this specific message.
- *callType:* The Gatekeeper uses this parameter to determine bandwidth usage. The default value if *pointToPoint* for all calls.
- *callModel:* If direct, the endpoint is requesting the direct terminal to terminal call model.
- *endpointIdentifier:* An endpoint identifier that was assigned to the terminal by RCF, probably the E.164 address or H323_ID. It is used as a security measure to help ensure that this is a registered terminal within its zone.

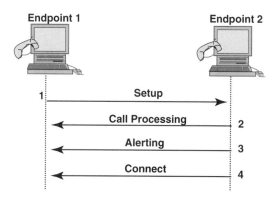

Figure 8–12   **Admission Operations without a Gatekeeper**

- *destinationInfo:* Sequence of external addresses for the destination terminal, such as E.164 addresses or H323_IDs.
- *destCallSignalAddress:* Transport address used at the destination.
- *destExtraCallInfo:* Contains external addresses for multiple calls.
- *srcInfo:* Sequence of external addresses for the source terminal, such as E.164 address or H323_IDs.
- *srcCallSignalAddress:* Transport address used at the source for call signaling.
- *bandWidth:* The number of 100 bit/s requested for the bi-directional call. For example, a 128 kbit/s call would be signaled as a request for 256 kbit/s. The value refers only to the audio and video bit rate excluding headers and overhead.
- *callReferenceValue:* The CRV from Q.931 for this call; used by a Gatekeeper to associate the ARQ with a particular call.
- *nonStandardData:* An optional value whose contents are not defined.
- *irrFrequency:* The frequency, in seconds, that the endpoint shall send information request response (IRR) messages to the Gatekeeper while on a call.
- *requestSeqNum:* the same value that was passed in the ARQ.
- *rejectReason:* Reason the bandwidth request was denied.
- *callServices:* Information on support of optional Q-Series protocols.
- *conferenceID:* Unique conference identifier.
- *activeMC:* If TRUE, the calling party has an active MC; otherwise FALSE.
- *answerCall:* Used to indicate to a Gatekeeper that a call is incoming.

Here is the ASN.1 coding for these messages.

```
AdmissionRequest      ::=SEQUENCE-- (ARQ)
{
    requestSeqNum               RequestSeqNum,
    callType                    CallType,
    callModel                   CallModel OPTIONAL,
    endpointIdentifier          EndpointIdentifier,
    destinationInfo             SEQUENCE OF AliasAddress OPTIONAL,
    destCallSignalAddress       TransportAddress OPTIONAL,
    destExtraCallInfo           SEQUENCE OF AliasAddress OPTIONAL,
    srcInfo                         SEQUENCE OF AliasAddress,
    srcCallSignalAddress        TransportAddress OPTIONAL,
```

```
        bandWidth                      BandWdith,
        callReferenceValue             CallReferenceValue,
        nonStandardData                NonStandardParameter OPTIONAL,
        callServices                   QseriesOptions OPTIONAL,
        conferenceID                   ConferenceIdentifier,
        activeMC                       BOOLEAN,
        answerCall                     BOOLEAN, —answering a call
}
CallType                               ::=CHOICE
{
        pointToPoint                   NULL, —Point-to-point
        oneToN                         NULL, —no interaction (FFS)
        nToOne                         NULL, — no interaction (FFS)
        nToN                           NULL, —interactive (multipoint)
}
CallModel                              ::=CHOICE
{
        direct                         NULL,
        GatekeeperRouted               NULL,
}
AdmissionConfirm                       ::=SEQUENCE-- (AFC)
{
        requestSeqNum                  RequestSeqNum,
        bandWidth                      BandWdith,
        callModel                      CallModel,
        destCallSignalAddress          TransportAddress,
        irrFrequency                   INTEGER (1..65535) OPTIONAL
        nonStandardData                NonStandardParameter OPTIONAL,
        ...
        AdmissionReject                ::=SEQUENCE-- (ARJ)
{
        requestSeqNum                  RequestSeqNum,
        reject Reason                  AdmissionRejectReason,
        nonStandardData                NonStandardParameter OPTIONAL,
        ...
}
AdmissionRejectReason                  ::=CHOICE
{
        calledPartyNotRegistered       NULL, —cannot translate address
        invalidPermission              NULL, —permission has expired)
        requestDenied                  NULL, — no bandwidth available
        undefinedReason                NULL,
        callerNotRegistered            NULL,
        routeCallToGatekeeper          NULL,
        invalidEndointIdentifer        NULL,
        resourceUnavailable            NULL,
        ...
}
```

The contents of the Setup message are as follows:

- *protocolIdentifier:* Set by the calling endpoint to the version of H.225.0 supported.
- *h245Address:* A specific transport address on which the calling endpoint or Gatekeeper handling the call would like to establish H.245 signaling.
- *sourceAddress:* Contains the H323_IDs for the source; the E.164 number of the source is in the Q.931 part of SETUP.
- *sourceInfo:* Contains an EndpointType to allow the called party to determine whether the call involved a Gateway.
- *destinationAddress:* The address the endpoint wishes to be connected to.
- *destCallSignalAddress:* Informs the Gatekeeper of the destination terminal's call signaling transport address.
- *destExtraCallInfo:* Needed to make possible additional channel calls, i.e. for 2 x 64 kbit/s call on the WAN side.
- *destExtraCRV:* CRVs for the additional SCN calls specified by *destExtraCallInfo*. Their use is for further study.
- *activeMC:* Indicates that the calling endpoint is under the influence of an active MC.
- *conferenceID:* Unique conference identifier.
- *conferenceGoal:* Indicates a desire to join an existing conference, start a new conference, or to invite a party to join an existing conference.
- *callServices:* Provides information on support of optional Q-Series protocols to Gatekeeper and called terminal.
- *callType:* The Gatekeeper uses this parameter to determine bandwidth usage. The default value if pointToPoint for all calls.

Here is the coding for the setup messages.

```
Setup_UUIE                      ::=SEQUENCE
{
    protocolIdentifier          ProtocolIdentifier,
    h245Address                 TransportAddress OPTIONAL,
    sourceAddress               SEQUENCE OF AliasAddress OPTIONAL,
    sourceInfo                  EndpointType,
    destinationAddress          SEQUENCE OF AliasAddress OPTIONAL,
    destCallSignalAddress       TransportAddress OPTIONAL,
    destExtraCallInfo           SEQUENCE OF AliasAddress OPTIONAL,
    destExtraCRV                SEQUENCE OF CallReferenceValue OPTIONAL,
```

```
    activeMC                    BOOLEAN,
    conferenceID                ConferenceIdentifier,
    conferenceGoal              CHOICE
    activeMC                    CHOICE
{
    create                      NULL,
    join                        NULL,
    invite                      NULL,
    ...
}
    callServices                QseriesOptions OPTIONAL,
    callType                    CallType,
    ...
}
```

GATEKEEPER ROUTED CALL SIGNALING

Now that some of the basic H.225 and Q.931 operations have been explained, it is a good idea to show some more scenarios for H.323 channel operations, and to bring H.245 into the discussion. We will dispense

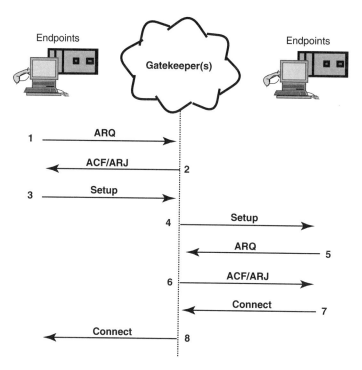

Figure 8–13   Routed Call Routing

with showing examples of the message contents and the ASN.1 code, with the expectation that you have a grasp of these subjects.

Figure 8–13 shows Gatekeeper Routed Call Signaling. The call signaling messages are relayed through one or more Gatekeepers between the endpoints. The Gatekeeper is allowed to close the call signaling channel after the call set up is completed, since it is no longer needed. Remember that the conventional Q.931 termination messages are not used, so the call signaling channel serves no further purpose.

DIRECT ENDPOINT CALL SIGNALING

Figure 8–14 shows a second method for managing the call signaling; it is called Direct Endpoint Call Signaling. As the figure shows, the call signaling messages are passed directly between the endpoints. These two methods use the same procedures and the same messages. In both cases, after the operations are complete, the H.245 Control Channel operations occur. The method actually employed is determined by the Gatekeeper.

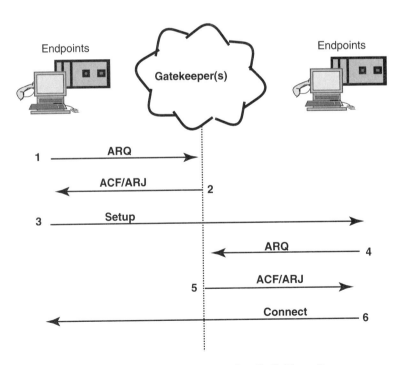

Figure 8–14   Direct Endpoint Call Signaling

OTHER GATEKEEPER ROUTED CALL OPERATIONS

There are also two methods to handle the Gatekeeper Routed Call operation in relation to H.245. Figure 8–15 shows a direct H.245 Control Channel connection between the endpoints. It is not yet approved (for further study), so we will not examine it any further.

Figure 8–16 shows the approved procedure for the H.245 Control Channel operations. The Gatekeeper routes the H.245 messages between the endpoints. In so doing, the Gatekeeper can redirect the H.245 Control Channel to an MC if an ad hoc conference switches from a point-to-point conference to multipoint conference.

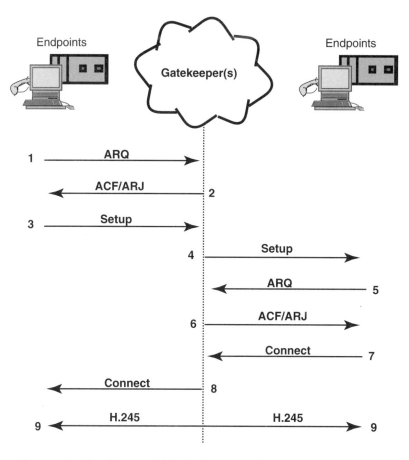

Figure 8–15 Direct H.245 Control Channel Connection (Under Study)

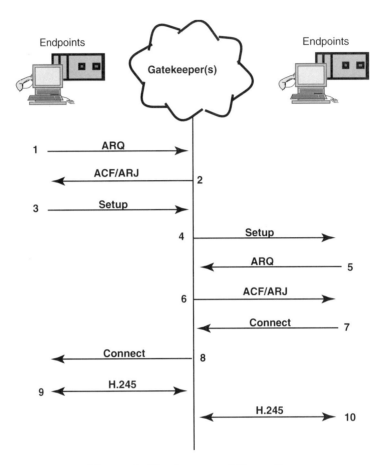

Figure 8–16   Approved Operation

ENDPOINTS REGISTERED TO DIFFERENT GATEWAYS

Endpoints may not be registered with the same Gatekeeper, yet they are allowed to engage in direct and routed call signaling. This operation is shown in Figure 8–17. The labeled events are similar to those described in previous examples, but a few further explanations are in order.

The calling endpoint's Gatekeeper chooses direct call signaling, and called endpoint's Gatekeeper chooses routed call signaling. The operations begin with the conventional exchange of ARQ and ACF messages between endpoint A and Gatekeeper 1, depicted as events 1 and 2. In this initial operation, if the two Gatekeepers have a relationship with each

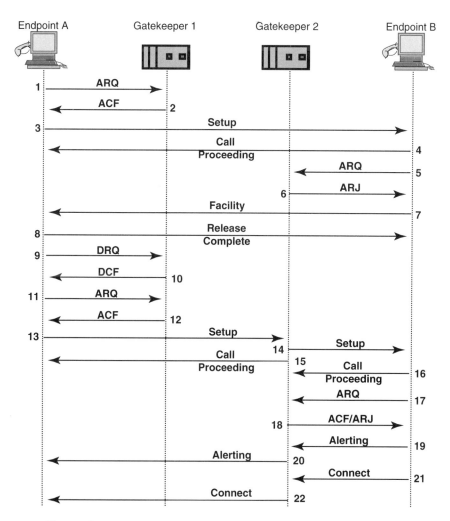

Figure 8–17   Endpoints Registered to Different Gateways

other, Gatekeeper 1 can exchange the call signaling channel transport address of endpoint B in the ACF message.

Next, endpoint A sends a setup message to endpoint B. This message has one of two addresses: (a) the transport address returned by the Gatekeeper, or (b) the call signaling channel transport address of endpoint B. A call proceeding message is returned, as shown in events 3 and 4.

In either case, if endpoint B desires to accept this call, it exchanges the ARQ and ARJ messages shown in events 5 and 6 in the figure. The Gatekeeper sends a call signaling channel transport address in the ARJ (in the cause code **routeCallToGatekeeper**). This information is relayed to endpoint A in event 7 with the Facility message. In event 8, endpoint A sends the Release Complete message to endpoint B.

Next, in events 9–12, endpoint 1 and Gatekeeper A disengage the RAS and set it up again. After these events, the set up is executed between endpoint A and Gatekeeper 2, and endpoint B, shown in events 13–16. The ARQ/ACF operations then take place again (events 17 and 18). Finally, the set up exchanges in events 19–22 (a) allow endpoint 2 to send its H.245 Control Channel transport address, and (b) allows Gatekeeper 2 to send this H.245 address or its own H.245 address to endpoint A.

MULTIPOINT CONFERENCES

For multipoint conferences, all endpoints in the conference must exchange call signaling with the MCU. The procedures for these message exchanges are the same in all the examples shown thus far in this chapter, and the MCU can be a calling or a called endpoint. MCU-endpoint signaling is governed also by the following rules.

Centralized Multipoint Conference:

- The H.245 Control Channel is open between endpoints and the MC within the MCU.
- The audio, video, and data channels are open between the endpoints and the MP within the MCU.

Decentralized Multipoint Conference:

- The H.245 Control Channel is open between the endpoint and the MC (one Control Channel for each call).
- The audio and video channels are multicast to all endpoints in the conference. The data channel is open with the data MP.

Ad hoc Multipoint Conference:

- Used no MC exists within the endpoints and the H.245 Control Channel is routed through the Gatekeeper. Initially, the H.245 Control Channel is routed between the endpoints through the Gatekeeper. When the conference switches to multipoint, the MC at the Gatekeeper can be activated by the Gatekeeper for subsequent operations.

- If one or both of the endpoints have an MC, normal set up procedures occur.

OTHER RAS PROCEDURES

As mentioned earlier, all the RAS procedures are not discussed in this overview. So, here is a brief description of the others.

Terminal Gatekeeper Requests for Changes in Bandwidth

These messages are exchanged for this procedure:

- *BRQ:* Bandwidth Change Request, contains the bandwidth parameter.
- *BCF:* Bandwidth Change Confirmation, confirms the change request.
- *BRJ:* Bandwidth Change Reject, rejects the request and provides the reason.

Location Requests

This procedure is not an actual location request, but a service that the Gatekeeper provides a requester. The service translates an address (say E.104) to transport address (a port or socket).

The location request procedure uses two messages:

- *LRQ:* Location Request, contains the endpoint identifier and destination info parameters.
- *LCF:* Location Confirm, contains the call signal address and the RAS address.

Disengage Procedures

This procedure is invoked by an endpoint to notify the Gatekeeper that an endpoint is being dropped. If the Gatekeeper invokes the procedure, it forces a call to be dropped. These messages are exchanged for this procedure:

- *DRQ:* Disengage Request, contains the identifiers associated with this endpoint, the ID of the call (endpoint ID, conference ID), and the reason for the disengage.
- *DCF:* Disengage Confirmation.
- *DRJ:* Disengage Reject.

Status Request Procedures

These procedures are used to obtain status information.

- *IRQ:* Information Request, contains the call reference value.
- *IRR:* Information Request Response, contains information about the terminal or Gatekeeper as well as information about the call. The call information provides fields for identifying (a) RTP data, (b) type of call (video, voice), (c) bandwidth usage, etc.

MAJOR H.245 SERVICES

H.245 is responsible for defining the syntax and semantics of the messages and their functions, principally for the exchange of information about overall audiovisual and data capabilities, and specific modes within those capabilities. It is used also to manage the logical channels on which the multimedia traffic is carried. The following explanation describes the major services offered by H.245. Several message types may be associated with each of these services.

- *Master slave determination:* Resolves overlapping message exchanges if only one message permitted. It is possible that two terminals involved in a call with each other initiate similar events, but only one such event is permitted. For example, both terminals ask for resources for a session, but only one resource is available. To avoid this problem, the terminals set up which acts as a master, and which acts as a slave, and rules state how precedence is established for a potential conflict.
- *Terminal capability:* These messages identify a terminal's multimedia capabilities. Examples are (a) video, audio, data, encryption, conference capabilities. Within those capabilities are (b) receive, send, or send and receive. ATM capabilities are defined such as (c) clocking options, size of payload, AAL type, etc. Within

the video capability information is included more detailed facts such as (d) H.261, H.262, samples per line, frames per second, still image transmission, etc. Within the audio capability information is included more detailed facts such as (e) G.711, G.728, G.729, etc. Within the data capabilities information is included more detailed facts such as the use of (f) V.14, LAPM, V.42 bis, V.120, etc.

- *Logical channel:* Sets up and tears down logical channels and identifies each logical channel with a channel number, port number, the traffic on the channel, and other parameters associated with each channel and port.
- *Multiplex entry:* Identifies each multiplexed byte in a logical channel and associates each byte with a specific logical channel.
- *Request mode:* Identifies modes of transmission, such as video, audio, data, encryption.
- *Round-trip delay:* This operation measures round-trip delay between sending and receiving node. Its use is implementation-specific.
- *Maintenance loop:* Defines loopback operations between two nodes.
- *Communication mode:* Used in conferences to define unicast, multicast, centralized, and decentralized modes of operation. It also supports these types of services: (a) lists of terminals in the conference, (b) establishes a chair for a conference, and (c) password authentication.
- *Nonstandard:* Message not defined in H.323.

BANDWIDTH CHANGE REQUEST

Figure 8–18 shows another example of an H.323 operation: a bandwidth change request from the transmitter. Prior to the operation, the initial bandwidth is set up by the Gatekeeper during the admission of an endpoint into a session. It is the responsibility of the endpoint to determine that sufficient bandwidth is requested from the Gatekeeper for all sent/received audio and video channels. This bandwidth does not include the headers of the PDUs that support these channels.

Bandwidth requirements may change during an endpoint connection in a session. For example, users in a conference (let's say doctors) may not need a lot of bandwidth for most of the conference time. But one doctor may wish to share an x-ray image with the others. It makes little

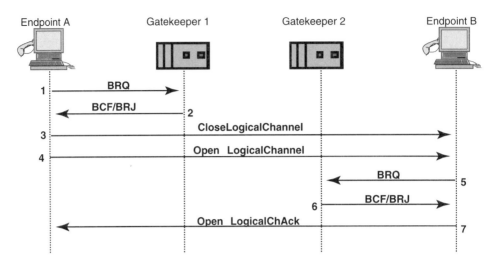

Figure 8–18   Bandwidth Change Request

sense to reserve bandwidth for this one transmission for the entire session, so H.323 permits the session bandwidth to be changed during the session.

It may turn out that the x-ray transmission does not result in a bandwidth change request. If all the send and receive channels (in aggregate) can support the transmission, the operations shown in this figure need not occur.

Assuming they do occur, in event 1, the endpoint sends a Bandwidth Change Request (BRQ) message to the Gatekeeper. In event 2, the Gatekeeper responds with a Bandwidth Change Confirm (BCF), or a Bandwidth Change Reject (BRJ). How the Gatekeeper decides on the granting or denial of the bandwidth change is not defined in H.323. Obviously, the Gatekeeper must keep a record of the ongoing sessions and their respective bandwidth consumption, and make decisions based on this knowledge.

The purpose of events 3 and 4, the exchange of the close and open logical channel operations, is to reset the parameters for the bandwidth change. In turn the BRQ and BCF/BRJ messages are exchanged between endpoint B and Gatekeeper 2 to get the other end of the session coordinated (shown in events 5 and 6). The result of this message exchange is the sending of the ACK of the open logical channel message from endpoint B to endpoint A. This final action ensures that all nodes are aware of the bandwidth change and can support it.

CONFERENCE CREATION OPERATION

Figure 8–19 shows an example of a direct endpoint call signaling operation for a conference create scenario. The events unfold as follows:

- 1: Endpoint 1 sends a setup message to endpoint 2. This message contains a globally unique CID of N, and a **conferenceGoal** of create.
- 2a: If endpoint 2 wishes to join the conference, it returns a Connect message with the same CID value of N. This operation means the endpoint is not participating in another conference or if it is another conference (say with CID = M), but it is capable of participating in more than one conference.

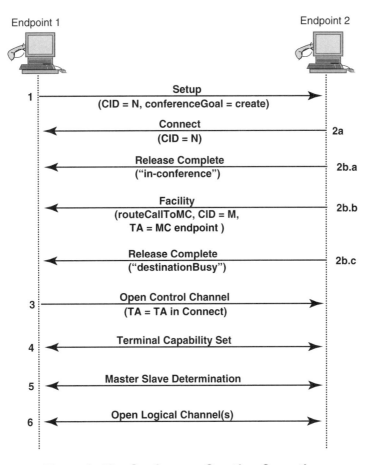

Figure 8–19   Conference Creation Operation

- 2b.a: If it can participate in only conference at a time, and sends a Release Complete message, indicating it is "in-conference."
- 2b.b: Alternately, it can ask endpoint 1 to join the conference (with CID = M) with a Facility message. In the message is **routeCall-ToMC** with the call signaling channel transport address of the endpoint containing the MC and CID = M of the conference.
- 2b.c: Alternately, it rejects the call because it does not wish to join the conference. It sends a Release Complete message with "destination busy."
- 3: Assuming endpoint 2 wishes to participate in the conference, endpoint 1 opens the Control Channel by using the transport address of the Control Channel that was provided in the Connect Message.
- 4: The two endpoints exchange **TerminalCapabilitySet** messages.
- 5: The endpoints then determine who is the master and who is the slave. In the routed operation, the master might be in the Gatekeeper's MC. During this operation, the master may assign the endpoints a terminal number from the low-order 8 bits of the SSRC field in the RTP header. This procedure supports the identification of each stream from an endpoint.
- 6: The transmitter of the streams can now open the logical channels. The capabilities of the receiver are known now, because of the exchange of information in the terminal capability set operations.

THE T.120 SPECIFICATIONS

The T.120 specifications define the data (document) conferencing part of a multimedia conference. IMTC,[2] describes T.120 as a protocol that distributes files and graphical information in real-time during a multipoint multimedia meeting. The objective is to assure interoperability between terminals without either participant assuming prior knowledge of the other system. T.120 permits data sharing among participants in a multimedia teleconference; including, whiteboard image sharing,

---

[2]International Teleconferencing Corsortium, Inc. (IMTC). HTTP://www.imtc.org/main.html

graphic display information, image exchange, and protocols for audio-graphic or audiovisual applications.

The T.120 series governs the audiographic portion of the H.320, H.323, and H.324 series and operates either within these or by itself. The T.120 suite consists of a series of recommendations, which are summarized in Table 8–2.

Table 8–2   ITU T.120 Recommendations

Recommendation	Description
T.120	Data protocols for multimedia conferencing: This provides an overview of the T.120 series.
T.121	Generic Application Template: This provides a guide for development of T.120 application protocols.
T.122	Multipoint Communication Service (MCS) Description: This describes the multiport services available to developers.
T.123	Protocol stacks for audiographic and audiovisual teleconference applications: This specifies transport protocols for a range of networks.
T.124	Generic Conference Control (GCC): This defines the application protocol supporting reservations and basic conference control services for multipoint teleconferences.
T.125	Multipoint Communication Service (MCS) Protocol specification: This specifies the data transmission protocol for multipoint services.
T.126	Multipoint still image and annotation protocol: This defines collaborative data sharing, including white board & image sharing, graphic display information, and image exchange in a multipoint conference.
T.127	Multipoint Binary File Transfer Protocol: This defines a method for applications to transmit files in a multipoint conference.
T.130	Real-time architecture for multimedia conferencing: Provides an overview description of how T.120 data conferencing works in conjunction with H.320 videoconferencing.
T.131	Network-specific mappings: Defines how real-time audio and video streams should be transported across different networks (i.e. ISDN, LAN, ATM) when used in conjunction with T.120 data conferencing.
T.132	Real-time link management: Defines how real-time audio and video streams may be created and routed between various multimedia conferencing endpoints.
T.133	Audiovisual control services: Defines how to control the source and link devices associated with real time information streams.
T.RES	Reservation Services: This is an overview document which specifies how terminals, MCUs, and reservation systems need to interact, and defines the interfaces between each of these elements.

EXTENSIBILITY

One of the attractive aspects of conventional telephony is the ability of the customer to obtain service features from the service provider, such as call screening, caller ID, etc. Recently, the ITU-T Intelligent Network (IN) and Bellcore Advanced Intelligent Network (AIN) standards have established architectures that enable a service provider to add service features in a more efficient and cost-effective manner than in the past. This issue adding revenue-producing features is really dependent upon the "extensibility" of the system. If a system is not easily extended to support changes it is at a decided disadvantage.

H.323 supports extensibility through the ASN.1 **NonStandard-Parameter** field. This field is for a nonstandard data field. It is intended for a vendor-specific function. As you can see, as you read the ASN.1 examples in this part of the material, a vendor must place vendor-specific fields where the **NonStandardParameter** field is placed. The vendor cannot add a new field outside the definition of the ASN.1 coding.

Moreover, H.323 has no mechanism for allowing terminals to inform each other about the extensions supported or not supported. So, what you see is what you get—a rather rigid approach.

One other point on extensions and new versions: A new H.323 version must be fully backward compatible with the old version(s). With all the features and the many headers of H.323, this requirement will likely create major maintenance problems as H.323 changes and has extensions added.

OTHER THOUGHTS

We have learned that H.323 uses a mix of H.225 and H.245 for its signaling operations. [MA98][3] and [SCHU] describe why and how these protocols are used. In a telephony-based network, the call signaling (i.e., setup and teardown) and bearer capability control are processed in two protocols, Q.931 for ISDN and ISUP for SS7 network. However, since different H.323 terminals in VoIP may have different logical channel capabilities, ITU H.323 specifies the call signaling and bearer capability control in two separate protocols, H.225 and H.245.

---

[3][MA99] Ma, Gene, "H.323 Signaling and SS7 ISUP Gateway: Procedure Interworking," draft-ma-h323-isup-Gateway-00.txt, October, 1998.

The call signaling specified in H.225 begins by exchanging the RAS information on the unreliable channel. This processing is followed by the call setup sequence through a reliable channel, which is based on the ISDN Q.931 protocol with modifications. One modification is the bearer capability information element in the SETUP message can be ignored if the call is bounded in the packet-based network, in which case the bearer is set up by H.245. Another difference is that closing the H.225 call signaling channel does not end the call unless the H.245 channel is also closed. The RELEASE and DISCONNET messages in Q.931 are forbidden in H.225 for H.323 systems.

H.245 uses the reliable H.225 call signaling channel to perform H.245 control functions, such as master/slave determination, terminal capability exchange, open/closing logical channels, and others. During the terminal capability exchange procedure, the parties use their own terminal capability to set up the mutual acceptable bearer service to the network. Then logical channel(s) are opened to handle the bearer capability, for example, two channels for video and one for audio. This procedure is very similar to the bearer capability request in the ISDN Q.931 and SS7 ISUP.

The original version of H.323 had H.225 and H.245 set up separate connections: (a) first the signaling channel, (b) then the H.245 Control Channel, and (c) then the user (media) channels. The revised version permits H.245 to be tunneled through H.224. Also, version 2 defines a Fast-Start capability, in order to reduce the overhead of the other two approaches.

SUMMARY

H.323 is a Call Processing Protocol, with a wide variety of other features, such as registration, and zone administration. H.323 was originally designed to support multimedia services over a LAN (a network with no QOS guarantees). As it has evolved, it has been expanded to support WAN and Internet telephony.

The "full" H.323 fuses a number of other ITU-T protocols, borrowing heavily from H.235 and Q.931. I think you will agree that it is a complex protocol stack, but it does have very powerful conferencing capacities. From the technical stand point, I prefer the other Call Processing Protocols, discussed in the next three chapters.

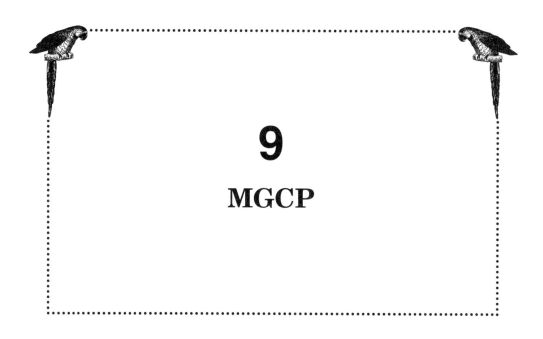

9
MGCP

INTRODUCTION

We now focus on the Media Gateway Control Protocol (MGCP). It is published as RFC 2705, and integrates the Simple Gateway Control Protocol (SGMP) and the Internet Protocol Device Control (IPDC) specification. It is quite similar to SGMP, but provides several features beyond that offered by SGMP. The pertinent aspects of SGMP and IPDC are included in our discussion of MGCP. For those readers who wish more detail on these specifications, I refer you to the appropriate RFCs and working documents available at www.ietf.org. Go to this page, and click on RFCs and/or working drafts.

MGCP CONCEPTS

MGMP describes an application programming interface (API), and a complementary protocol (MGCP). Its purpose is to define the operations of telephony Gateways, as directed by a controller, known as *Call Agents* or *Media Gateway Controllers* (MGC). The telephony Gateway provides conversion and internetworking operations between the audio signals used on telephone circuits and data packets used by the Internet or other packet oriented networks. The Call Agent directs the operations of the Gateway.

MGCP is concerned with several types of Gateways, some are shown in Figure 9–1. The trunking Gateway operates between a conventional telephone network and a voice over IP network. The residential Gateway operates between a traditional telephony end user (analog RJ11 interfaces) and the voice over IP network. The ATM Gateway operates the same way as a trunking, except the interface it between an ATM networks and a voice over IP network. The access Gateway provides an analog or digital interface of a PBX into an IP over internet network.

THE CALL AGENT

MGCP assumes the bulk of the intelligence for call control operations resides in the Call Agent. This statement does not mean that the Gateways are completely unintelligent. Rather, it means that the most of the control operations are performed by the Call Agent. In essence, signaling and Gateway "behavior" is the responsibility of a Call Agent. The Call Agents act as masters to the slave Gateways, and the Gateways receive commands that define their operations from the Call Agents. In

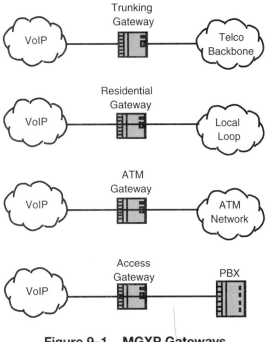

Figure 9–1   MGXP Gateways

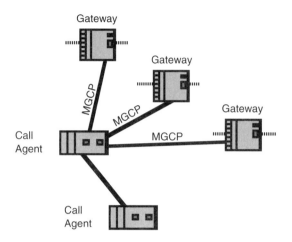

Figure 9–2   Call Agents and Gateways

Figure 9–2, one Call Agent is in control of three Gateways, but the actual configurations depend upon specific installations. The figure also shows that two Call Agents are communicating with each other. MGCP defines the operations between the Call Agents and the Gateways, but does not define the operations between the Call Agents.

MGCP GATEWAY COMPONENTS

MGCP supports the conventional telephony operations, such as dial tone, offhook, etc. It also supports telephony-based links, such as DS1. All these components are identified with names. We describe them here, but will not go into the rules for the syntax of each name, which are quite detailed and beyond the general explanation.

Figure 9–3 shows the concepts of endpoints, connections, and calls. Endpoints in MGCP are sources and sinks of data. Endpoints can be physical links, like a T1 trunk. They may be traffic that operates over the physical links, such as an RTP media flow.

Endpoints are identified by names. The name is in two parts. The first part is the domain name of the Gateway that is at the endpoint, and the second part is a local name in the Gateway. The syntax of the local name is dependent upon the type of endpoint, but a hierarchical name is required, forming a naming path from the Gateway name to the individual endpoint.

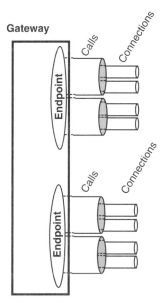

Figure 9–3 MGCP Gateway Components

Endpoints in MGCP must be correlated with comparable entities in SS7. In an SS7 network, endpoints are trunks connecting switches, or a switch to a MGCP Gateway. In ISUP, trunks are grouped into trunk groups, and are identified by an SS7 point code. Circuits within a trunk group are identified by a circuit identification code (CIC). It is the job of MGCP to map SS7 identifiers to MGCP names.

Connections are managed at the endpoints (for example, on a trunk [T1, etc.]). Connections can be grouped into calls. Connections are created by the Gateway, and each connection has a unique connection identifier associated with it. The connection identifier is within the context of its endpoint. MGCP uses an unstructured octet string for the identifier.

Several connections, that may or may not belong to the same call, can terminate in the same endpoint. Calls also have identifiers and are created by the Call Agent. They are also unstructured octet strings. Call identifiers must be unique within the system. A Call Agent may build several connections pertaining to the same call, and the connections must be associated with the same call.

When a Call Agent builds several connections that pertain to the same call, either on the same Gateway or in different Gateways, the connections that belong to the same call share the same call-ID. This identifier can then be used by accounting or management procedures, which are outside the scope of MGCP.

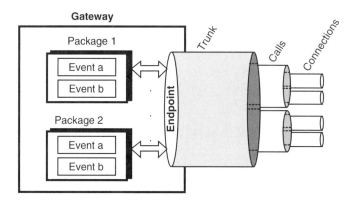

Figure 9–4   Events and Packages

EVENTS AND PACKAGES

In order to manage connections, other identifiers and their associated entities are needed, specifically *events* and *packages*. Figure 9–4 depicts the concepts of events and packages. An event is an occurrence in an endpoint. Examples of events are off-hook and on-hook events. Events correspond to associated signals, which are grouped into packages. Examples of signals are (a) dual tone multiple frequency, and (b) dial tone. A package is the grouping of events and signals that are supported by a specific type of endpoint. Event names and package names are used to identify each event and package. Both names are strings of letters.

Events and signals are grouped into packages within which they share the same namespace. The package must be supported by a particular type of endpoint. As examples, one package may contain a group of signals and events for an analog endpoint, and another package may contain a group of signals and events for a digital endpoint.

THE TEN PACKAGES

The final RFC defines ten packages. They are listed in Table 9–1, and explained in this section of the chapter.

Generic Media Package

The generic media package groups the events and signals that can be observed on several types of endpoints, such as trunking Gateways,

Table 9–1   The MGCP Packages

Package	Name
Generic Media	G
DTMF	D
MF	M
Trunk	T
Line	L
Handset	H
RTP	R
Network Access Server	N
Announcement Server	A
Script	Script

access Gateways, or residential Gateways. Examples (not all-inclusive) are ringback tone, modem detected, fax tone detected, network congestion tone, and ring back on connection.

DTMF package

The DTMF package describes the telephone DTMF signals, such as DTMF 0, 1, etc. Chapter 2 explains DTMF.

MF Package

The MF package describes the trunk MF signals, and is also described in Chapter 2. In addition to the description of digits, the package also describes events such as:

- *Wink:* A transition from unseized to seized to unseized trunk states within a specified period. Typical seizure period is 100–350 msec.
- *Incoming seizure:* Incoming indication of call attempt.
- *Return seizure:* Seizure in response to outgoing seizure.
- *Unseize circuit:* Unseizure of a circuit at the end of a call.
- *Wink off:* A signal used in operator services trunks. A transition from seized to unseized to seized trunk states within a specified period of 100–350 ms.

Trunk Package

The Trunk package defines events that occur on a trunk circuit. Prevalent examples, (again, not all-inclusive) are:

- *Continuity Test (co2):* A tone at the 1780 + or – 30 Hz.
- *Milliwatt Tones:* Old Milliwatt Tone (1000 Hz), New Milliwatt Tone (1004 Hz).
- *Line Test:* 105 Test Line test progress tone (2225 Hz + or – 25 Hz at –10 dBm0 + or – 0.5dB).
- *No circuit:* The tri-tone, low to high.

Line Package

The Line package defines common line tones, such as: (a) dial tone, (b) message waiting indicator, (c) alerting tone, (d) call waiting tone, (e) caller ID, and others.

Handset Emulation Package

The handset emulation package is an extension of the line package, to be used when the Gateway is capable of emulating a handset. The difference with the line package is that events such as off-hook can be signaled as well as detected. Some examples are: on-hook transition, flash hook, answer tone, busy tone, ringing tone, and network busy tone.

RTP Package

The RTP package defines several event pertaining to RTP payload transmission such as:

- *Codec Changed:* Codec changed to a different algorithm.
- *Sampling Rate Changed:* Sampling rate changed, perhaps on the direction of the Call Agent.
- *Jitter Buffer Size Changed:* When the Media Gateway has the ability to automatically adjust the depth of the jitter buffer for received RTP streams, it is useful for the Media Gateway Controller to receive notification that the Media Gateway has automatically increased its jitter buffer size to accommodate increased or decreased variability in network latency.
- *Packet Loss Exceeded:* Packet loss rate exceed the threshold of the specified number of packets per 100,000 packets.

- *Quality Alert:* The packet loss rate or the combination of delay and jitter exceed a specified quality threshold.

Network Access Server Package

This package deals with several status and diagnostic events. Examples are carrier lost, authorization succeeded/denied, call back has been requested, and packet arrival (at least one packet was recently sent to an Internet address that is observed by an endpoint).

Announcement Server Package

This package defines three events that pertain to a server: (a) play an announcement, (b) report on completion of an event, and (c) report failure.

Script Package

The package defines how to direct a node to load (and report of success or failure) the following scripts: (a) Java, (b) Pearl, (c) TCL, (d) and XML.

ENDPOINTS

In a commercial product, endpoints may be implemented in a variety of ways. For example, a vendor may package an endpoint product in a hardware interface that includes T1, T3, and fractional T1 capabilities. MGCP assumes that Media Gateways support collections of endpoints. The type of the endpoint determines its capabilities and functions. Thus far, these types of endpoints are defined:

- *Digital channel (DS0):* Conventional 64 kbit/s PCM voice channel.
- *Analog line:* Conventional voice line.
- *Announcement server access point:* Node with announcement service.
- *Interactive Voice Response access point:* Conventional telco interactive unit, that plays announcements and listens for responses.
- *Conference bridge access point:* Component for multimedia audio/video conferencing; provides access to a specific conference.
- *Packet relay:* Interface supporting two connections.

- *Wiretap access point:* Access to a recording, or live playback.
- *ATM "trunk side" interface:* Conventional ATM user network interface (UNI).

In this section, the eight endpoints are examined in more detail. Keep in mind that these specified endpoints are not meant to be the final set of endpoints. In the future, it is expected that other endpoints will be added. Figure 9–5 will be helpful during this discussion.

Digital Channels

Digital channels provide the conventional 64 kbit/s PCM capabilities, such as those found in T1 and ISDN systems. They use TDM interfaces. The Gateway must be capable of translating the digital signals (encoded according to A or μ-law, using either the complete set of 8 bits or only 7 of these bits), into audio packets.

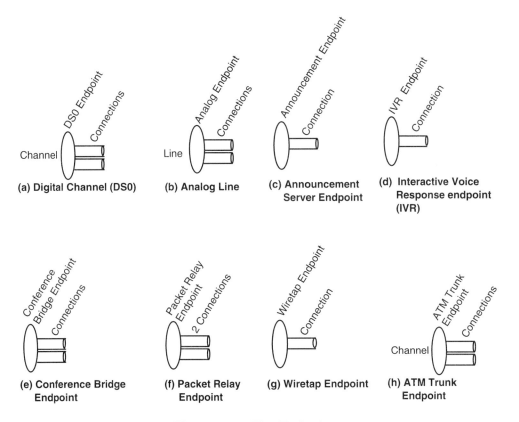

Figure 9–5   The Endpoints

When the Media Gateway also supports a Network Access Server (NAS) service, the Gateway must be capable of receiving either audio-encoded data (modem connection) or binary data ISDN connection) and convert them into IP data packets.

Media Gateways should be able to establish several connections between the endpoint and the packet networks, or between the endpoint and other endpoints in the same Gateway. The signals originating from these connections shall be mixed according to the connection "mode," as explained later in this material.

If the digital systems are sending signaling traffic, such as SS7 or ISDN connection control messages, the Media Gateways must be able to pass this traffic to a call agent.

Analog Channels

Analog lines can are typically supported to an end user terminal (telephone, PBX, etc.). MGCP requires that a Media Gateway be able to support several connections between the endpoint and the packet network, or between the endpoint and other endpoints in the same Gateway. The audio signals originating from these connections can be mixed according to the connection "mode," as defined by MGCP and discussed later.

Announcement Server Endpoint

An announcement server endpoint provides access to an announcement service. Under the direction of the call agent, the announcement server plays back a specified announcement. The announcement server endpoint supports one connection at a time. If several connections were established to the same endpoint, the same announcements would be played simultaneously over all the connections.

Connections to an announcement server are typically one-way, or "half duplex"; the announcement server is not expected to listen the to audio signals from the connection.

Interactive Voice Response (IVR) Endpoint

An IVR endpoint, under the direction of the call agent, plays back announcements as well as other information, such as tones. In turn, it is capable of listening to responses from the user. As with the announcement server endpoint, the IVR endpoint also is not supposed to support more than one connection at time in order to preclude playing the same tones and announcements over all connections.

Conference Bridge Endpoint

The conference bridge endpoint provides access to a voice or video conference. A Media Gateway supports multiple connections between the bridge endpoint and one or more packet networks, or between the endpoint and several endpoints in the same Gateway. The signals that originate from these connections are mixed according to the connection mode, explained later.

Packet Relay Endpoint

The packet relay endpoint is similar to the conference bridge, but supports only two connections. Examples of packet relays are firewalls between a trusted and an untrusted network, or transcoding servers used to provide interoperation between incompatible Gateways, such as those that do not support compatible compression algorithms, or Gateways that operate over different transmission networks such as Frame Relay and ATM.

Wiretap Access Endpoint

The wiretap access endpoint provides access to a recording or a live play-back of a connection. This endpoint supports only one connection at a time, and operates in half-duplex mode. This means the wiretap device does not signal its presence.

ATM Trunk Side Endpoint

The ATM trunk side endpoint is used when one or several ATM permanent virtual circuits are used as a replacement for the legacy T1 TDM switches. When ATM/AAL2 is used, several trunks or channels are multiplexed on a single virtual circuit; each of these trunks correspond to a single endpoint.

Media Gateways can establish several connections between the endpoint and the packet networks, or between the endpoint and other endpoints in the same Gateway. The signals originating from these connections shall be mixed according to the connection mode, described later.

CONNECTION STATES

Figure 9–6 shows the behavior of the Gateway with regards to the connection setup and the exchange of the session description parameters. It also shows how the half open (wait) and the open (wait) state are en-

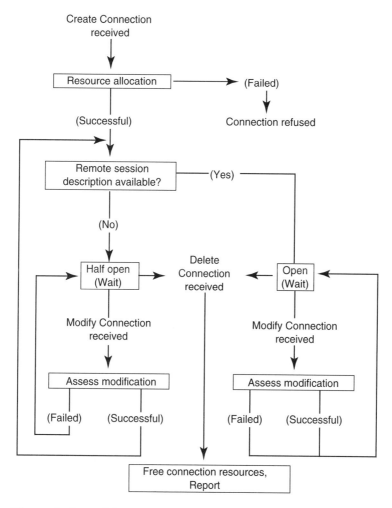

Figure 9–6   MGCP Connection States, as Seen by the Gateway

tered and exited. You may wish to refer to this flowchart as you read about the messages and protocol flows covered later in the chapter.

LOCAL DIRECTIVES AND SESSION DESCRIPTIONS

Many types of resources will be associated with a connection, such as specific signal processing functions and compression operations. The resources allocated to a connection are chosen by the Gateway under instructions from the call agent. The call agent will provide these instructions by sending two sets of parameters to the Gateway:

- The local directives instruct the Gateway on the choice of resources that should be used for a connection.
- When available, the "session description" provided by the other end of the connection.

Figure 9–7 shows the relationships of the session descriptions and the local directives. The local directives specify such parameters as the

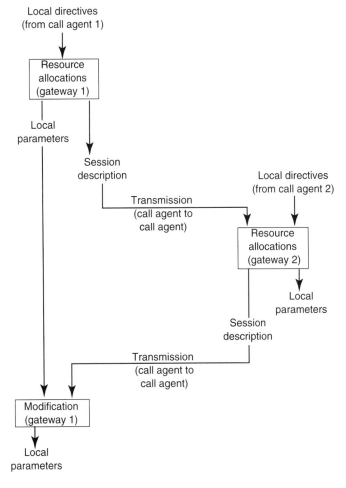

Figure 9–7   Information Flow of Local Directives and Session Descriptions

mode of the connection (e.g., send only, send-receive), preferred coding methods, usage of echo cancellation or silence suppression, etc. For each of these parameters, the call agent can either specify a value, a range of values, or no value at all. This allows the implementation of various levels of control, from a very tight control where the call agent specifies minute details of the connection handling to a very loose control where the call agent only specifies broad guidelines, and lets the Gateway choose the detailed values.

Based on the value of the local directives, the Gateway will determine the resources allocated to the connection. When this is possible, the Gateway will choose values that are in line with the remote session description—but there is no absolute requirement that the parameters be exactly the same.

After the resources have been allocated, the Gateway will compose a session description that describes the way it intends to receive packets.

MGCP MODES

Before we examine the messages that are exchanged between the Call Agent and the Gateway, we need one more piece of information. Each connection is defined by the following modes: (a) send only, (b) receive only, (c) send/receive, (d) conference, (e) data, (f) inactive, (g) loopback, (h) continuity test, (i) network loop test, or (j) network continuity test. The mode of the connection determines how voice signals are handled. The MGCP sets forth the following rules for these modes, and I quote (with amplifying comments) from RFC 2705.

Voice signals received in data packets through connections in receive, conference, or send/receive mode are mixed and sent to the endpoint. Voice signals originating from the endpoint are transmitted over all the connections whose mode is send, conference, or send/receive. In addition to being sent to the endpoint, voice signals received in data packets through connections in conference mode are replicated to all the other connections whose mode is conference.

The loopback and continuity test modes are used during ISUP maintenance and continuity test operations on telephony circuits. They are invoked during a call setup to ensure that the source and sink endpoints are fully connected and exchanging signals correctly. The rules for these tests vary between the SS7 ISUP specifications published by the standards groups.

There are two implementations of the continuity test (COT), one as specified by ITU-T, and one (used in the US), as specified by Bellcore and ANSI. In the ITU-T case, the test is a loopback test. The source switch sends a tone (the go tone) on the bearer circuit and expects the sink switch to loopback the circuit. If the source switch sees the same tone returned (the return tone), the COT has passed. If not, the COT has failed.

In the Bellcore/ANSI case, the go and return tones are different. The source switch sends a certain go tone. The sink switch detects the go tone, it then asserts a different return tone to the source. When the source switch detects the return tone, the COT is passed. If the source switch never detects the return tone, the COT has failed.

In either the ITU-T or Bellcore/ANSI cases, the COT must be performed correctly, or the call setup operations are suspended.

If the mode is set to loopback, the Gateway is expected to return the incoming signal from the endpoint back into that same endpoint. This procedure will be used, typically, for testing the continuity of trunk circuits according to the ITU specifications.

If the mode is set to continuity test, the Gateway is informed that the other end of the circuit has initiated a continuity test procedure according to the Bellcore specification. The Gateway will place the circuit in the transponder mode required for dual-tone continuity tests.

If the mode is set to network loopback, the voice signals received from the connection will be echoed back on the same connection.

If the mode is set to network continuity test, the Gateway will process the packets received from the connection according to the transponder mode required for dual-tone continuity test, and send the processed signal back on the connection.

THE APPLICATIONS PROGRAMMING INTERFACE (API)

The gist of MGCP is the issuance of commands to the Gateway and the Gateway acting on these commands and sending back responses. The purpose of the commands is to control the operations of the Gateway in regard to the creation and termination of connections, and to keep the Call Agent informed of events occurring at the Gateway's endpoints.

Nine commands are defined in the MGCP. These commands are described in two ways: (a) as an application programming interface (API) between a user application and the MGCP software in the Call Agent and Gateway, (b) as messages exchanged between the Call Agent and the Gateway. See Figure 9–8. This concept is in keeping with layered proto-

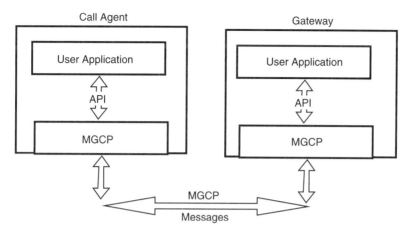

Figure 9–8   The Applications Programming Interface (API)

col concepts where the user application at the sending node invokes a command at the API to the MGCP, which uses the command to construct a message and send to the receiving node. At this node, the message is parsed and the information is passed to the receiving applications by MGCP via the API.

Here is a summary of the MGCP API primitives and the resulting messages:

- The Call Agent can issue an *EndpointConfiguration* command to a Gateway, instructing the Gateway about the coding characteristics expected by the "line-side" of the endpoint.
- The Call Agent issues a *NotificationRequest* command to instruct the Gateway to watch for specific events such on a specified endpoint.
- The Gateway responds with the *Notify* command to inform the Call Agent when the specific events occur.
- The Call Agent issues the *CreateConnection* command to create a connection that terminates on a specified endpoint in the Gateway.
- The Call Agent issues the *ModifyConnection* command to change the parameters associated with a previously established connection.
- The Call Agent issues the *DeleteConnection* command to delete an existing connection. This command is also used by a Gateway to

inform the Call Agent that a connection can no longer be sustained.

- The Call Agent issues the *AuditEndpoint* and *AuditConnection* commands to check on the status of an endpoint and any associated connections and calls.
- The Gateway issues the *RestartInProgress* command to notify the Call Agent that the Gateway (or a group of endpoints) is being taken out of service or is being placed back in service.

RULES ON CONNECTION IDENTIFIERS

Before we examine the parameters that are coded in the messages, we need to pause and examine some characteristics of the connection creation operation, and some of the identifiers and other parameters that are exchanged during the create operation. This explanation is a summary of parts of Section 2.3.3 of RFC 2705.

A RemoteConnectionDescriptor parameter is the connection identifier for the remote side of a connection, on the other side of the IP-based network. It contains the same fields as those found in the LocalConnectionDescriptor parameter. These fields describe the session according to the Session Description Protocol (SDP) RFC.

This parameter may have a null value when the information for the remote end is not yet known. This situation can occur because the entity that builds a connection starts by sending a CreateConnection to one of the two Gateways involved in the session, and not to the final receiving endpoint.

Consequently, for the first CreateConnection issued, no information is available about the other side of the connection. This information may be provided later by a ModifyConnection call.

A second ID, called the SecondEndPointId can be used instead of the RemoteConnectionDescriptor to establish a connection between two endpoints located on the same Gateway. The SecondEndPointId can be fully specified by assigning a value to the parameter SecondEndPointId in the function call or it may be "under-specified" by using an "anyone" wildcard convention. If the SecondEndPoint is underspecified, the second endpoint identifier will be assigned by the Gateway and its complete value returned in the SecondEndPointId parameter of the response.

The Gateway returns a ConnectionId, that uniquely identifies the connection within one endpoint, and a LocalConnectionDescriptor, which is a session description that contains information about addresses and RTP ports, as defined in SDP. The LocalConnectionDescriptor is not returned in the case of data connections.

The SpecificEndPointId is an optional parameter that identifies the responding endpoint. It can be used when the EndpointId argument referred to a "any of" wildcard name. When a SpecificEndPointId is returned, the Call Agent should use it as the EndpointId value in successive commands referring to this call.

When a SecondEndpointId is specified, the command creates two connections that can be manipulated separately through ModifyConnection and DeleteConnection commands. The response to the creation provides a SecondConnectionId parameter that identifies the second connection.

THE MESSAGE PARAMETERS

These parameters are present in the API and/or an MGCP message. A suggested approach to this analysis is for you to review this section and refer back to it in the next sections. I think you will recognize some of these parameters as a result of our previous discussions on MGCP. Table 9–2 shows the relationship of the parameters to the MGCP messages. The parameters for the MGCP messages have changed from the working drafts, so you need to be very careful if you are making changes to an ongoing system that relied on the earlier specifications. Table 9–2 is a summary of the relationships of the MGCP messages and the MGCP parameters.

- *CallID:* A globally unique parameter that identifies the call to which the connection belongs.
- *ConnectionID:* Value returned by the Gateway during a connection creation. It uniquely identifies the connection within the endpoint.
- *Connection-parameters:* A general term to describe a list of parameters about a connection.
- *DetectEvents:* During the quarantine period, a list of events that are currently detected. The quarantine period is discussed later.
- *DigitMap:* A method to collect digits according to a dial plan.
- *SpecificEndPointId:* The name of the endpoint in a Gateway.
- *LocalConnectionDescriptor:* A descriptor of the connection assigned by the Gateway, and returned to the Call Agent during the connection creation. It contains addresses and RTP ports, as defined in SDP.

Table 9–2   MGCP Message Parameters

Parameter name	EP CF	CR CX	MD CX	DL CX	RQ NT	NT FY	AU EP	AU CX	RS IP
ResponseACK	O	O	O	O	O	O	O	O	O
BearerInformation	M	O	O	O	O	F	F	F	F
CallId	F	M	M	O	F	F	F	F	F
ConnectionId	F	F	M	O	F	F	F	M	F
RequestIdentifier	F	O+	O+	O+	M	M	F	F	F
LocalConnection Options	F	O	O	F	F	F	F	F	F
ConnectionMode	F	M	M	F	F	F	F	F	F
RequestedEvents	F	O	O	O	O*	F	F	F	F
SignalRequests	F	O	O	O	O*	F	F	F	F
NotifiedEntity	F	O	O	O	O	O	F	F	F
ReasonCode	F	F	F	O	F	F	F	F	O
ObservedEvents	F	F	F	F	F	M	F	F	F
DigitMap	F	O	O	O	O	F	F	F	F
Connection parameters	F	F	F	O	F	F	F	F	F
SpecificEndpointID	F	F	F	F	F	F	F	F	F
SecondEndpointID	F	O	F	F	F	F	F	F	F
RequestedInfo	F	F	F	F	F	F	M	M	F
QuarantineHandling	F	O	O	O	O	F	F	F	F
DetectEvents	F	O	O	O	O	F	F	F	F
EventStates	F	F	F	F	F	F	F	F	F
RestartMethod	F	F	F	F	F	F	F	F	M
RestartDelay	F	F	F	F	F	F	F	F	O
SecondConnectionID	F	F	F	F	F	F	F	F	F
Capabilities	F	F	F	F	F	F	F	F	F
RemoteConnection Descriptor	F	O	O	F	F	F	F	F	F
LocalConnection Descriptor	F	F	F	F	F	F	F	F	F

- *LocalConnectionOptions:* Used by the Call Agent to direct the Gateway as to how the connection is to be handled. A wide variety of fields can be contained in this parameter. Some of them are defined in the SDP standard. The fields are discussed along with the CreateConnection command.

- *ConnectionMode:* Defines the mode of operation for this side of the connection.

- *NotifiedEntity:* Specifies where Notify or DeleteConnection commands are to be sent; defaults to the originator of the CreateConnection command.

- *ObservedEvents:* A list of events that the Gateway has detected.

- *QuarantineHandling:* In notification messages, Gateways can receive a list of events that they should watch for and monitor. The Call Agent uses this operation to keep track of the calls, and the state of the endpoint. The events are examined as they occur, and the controlled Gateway accumulates information about the event, and some point may send a notification to the Call Agent.

- *ReasonCode:* The value indicates the reason for the disconnection.

- *RemoteConnectionDescriptor:* A descriptor of the connection assigned to the Gateway.

- *RequestedEvents:* List of events that the Gateway is requested to direct and report to the Call Agent. Detailed rules stipulate how the events are handled in the Gateway and how/when/if they are reported to the Call Agent. Examples of parameters here are: (a) accumulate dialed digits according to the Digit Map, (b) ignore the event, (c) notify Call Agent immediately of the event (of delay notification), (d) keep signal active, and so on.

- *RequestedInfo:* Information that is requested with a ConnectionID within an endpoint. This field can contain: CallId, NotifiedEntity, LocalConnectionOptions, Mode, RemoteConnectionDescriptor, LocalConnectionDescriptor, and ConnectionParameters.

- *RequestIdentifier:* A unique value to identify a request.

- *RestartDelay:* The number of seconds before a restart operation is attempted. The number is randomly generated to reduce chances of multiple machines restarting at same time.

- *RestartMethod:* Coded as graceful, forced, or restart.

- *SignalRequests:* Set of signals that the Gateway must apply to the endpoint, such as ringing, off-hook, continuity tones, etc.

- *ResponseACK:* This parameter is used in a hand shake, to allow Gateways to delete copies of old responses, without waiting for a 30-second timer.
- *BearerInfromation:* Defines the coding of the data received from the line side. It is coded as a list of subparameters. Thus far, only an encoding value has been defined for A-law or μ-law compression of the digitized voice signal.
- *SecondEndPointId:* An optional parameter. It can be used in place of the RemoteConnectionDescriptor to establish a connection between two endpoints of the same Gateway.
- *EventStates:* Describes the state the endpoint is in, such as off-hook, on-hook, etc.
- *SecondConnectionId:* As discussed earlier, this parameter is used instead of the RemoteConnectionDescriptor to establish a connection between two endpoints located on the same Gateway.
- *Capabilities:* Used during an audit operation to inform the Call Agent about an endpoint's capabilities. Examples of capabilities are supported codecs, time range of packetization operations, support or nonsupport of echo cancellation, support or nonsupport of encryption, packages supported by the endpoint, etc.

THE MGCP MESSAGE FORMAT

We learned earlier that the Call Agent and the Gateway exchange eight types of MGCP messages, and we discussed them in a general way. The messages are called commands when sent to the Gateway, and responses when sent from the Gateway.

Figure 9–9 shows the format for the MGCP message. The messages are coded as lines of text consisting of a command header, followed by a session description. The command header is composed of a command line, and a set of parameter lines. Text lines are separated by line feed character. The items in the message are simply strings of ASCII printable characters, separated by an ASCII space (0×20) or tabulation characters (0×09).

The command line contains four fields: (a) the identifier of the message (called a verb), (b) a transaction number, (c) the endpoint towards which the command is requested, and (d) the protocol version number.

The parameter lines are made up of a parameter name, a colon, a space, and the parameter value. Several parameter names have a re-

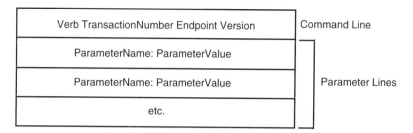

Figure 9–9   The Message Format

served code (ASCII character) reserved for them. For example, the code "N" is reserved for the NotifiedEntity, and it means the parameter value is coded according to RFC 822. As another example, the code "D" is used for a digit map, and is coded in accordance with the digit map rules cited earlier.

The IETF drafts that were referenced earlier have many examples of how to code the GMCP commands, and the many rules for them are beyond this text.

Example of a Message

Figure 9–10 shows an example of a coded message. Line 1 is the command line. RQNT is the verb for a NotificationRequest command; the transaction number is 4561; the directed endpoint is endpoint 44@tgw-21.infoinst.com; and the MGCP version is 0.1.

Line 2 is the NotifiedEntity of: abc@cal.infoinst.com:5777. Line 3 is a hexadecimal string for the RequestIdentifier. Line 4 is code for an event name, and the "hd" code is for offhook transition.

This command is sent by the Call Agent to the Gateway to direct the Gateway to monitor for an offhook transition on endpoint-44 at the trunking Gateway with a domain name suffix of cal.infoinst. The 5777 is the port number.

Each message verb is coded a four character ASCII field, as shown in the table in Figure 9–10.

Line 1   RQNT 4561   endpoint-44@tgw-21.infoinst.com MGCP 0.1
Line 2   N: abc@cal.infoinst.com:5777
Line 3   X: 45848484
Line 4   R: hd

Verb	Code
CreateConnection	CRCX
EndpointConfiguration	EPCF
ModifyConnection	MDCX
DeleteConnection	DLCX
NotificationRequest	RQNT
Notify	NTFY
AuditEndpoint	AUEP
AuditConnection	AUCX
RestartInProgress	RSIP

Figure 9–10   Example of the Coding of the Message

SECURITY SERVICES

The final RFC now contains information on security services. The idea is that if unauthorized entities could use the MGCP, they would be able to setup unauthorized calls, or to interfere with authorized calls. The RFC authors expect that MGCP messages will always be carried over secure Internet connections, as defined in the IP security architecture in RFC 2401, using either the IP Authentication Header (AH), defined in RFC 2402, or the IP Encapsulating Security Payload (ESP), defined in RFC 2406. The complete MGCP protocol stack would thus include the layers shown in Figure 9–11.

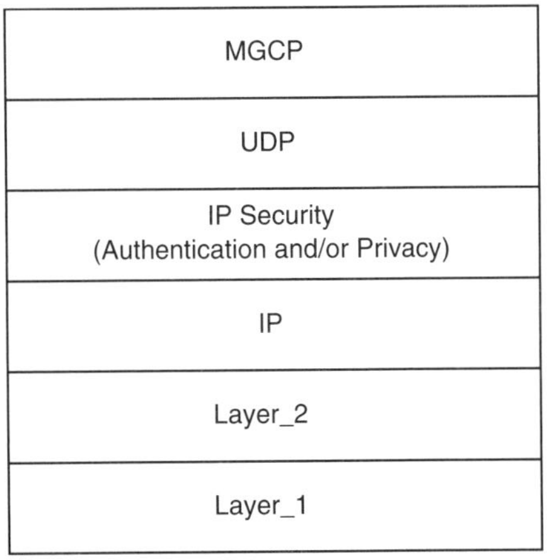

MGCP
UDP
IP Security (Authentication and/or Privacy)
IP
Layer_2
Layer_1

Figure 9–11 The Security Stack for MGCP

EXAMPLE OF MGCP PROTOCOL EXCHANGES

Figures 9–12 and 9–13 present an example of MGCP in action. For those readers who wish more detail on the MGCP and these examples, I refer you to [ARAN98], [ARAN98a], and [TAYL98].[1] Figure 9–12 shows events 1–24, and Figure 9–13 shows events 25–37. Two Gateways are involved, a residential Gateway and a trunking Gateway. In addition, the common database is shown, as well as an accounting Gateway. Here is a description of each event:

Event 1: The NotificationRequest command must be sent to the residential Gateway before the Gateway can handle a connection. Be aware that this command is not a crafting (configuration) command. The Call Agents and Gateways must be preconfigured. Let us assume that this command is directing the Gateway to monitor for an off-hook condition on a specific endpoint connection.

Event 2: The Gateway acknowledges the command. It uses the same transaction number that was in the command in event 1.

Event 3: Thereafter, the Gateway monitors for this transition, and eventually the user goes off-hook to make a call.

Event 4: The Gateway sends a NotificationRequest to the Call Agent, with the message coded to show the off-hook event for the monitored endpoint.

Event 5: The Call Agent must acknowledge the Gateway's transmission.

Event 6: The Call Agent's decisions on what to tell the Gateway next will depend on the type of line being monitored. Assuming it is a conventional dialup (nondirect) line, it sends a NotificationRequest command directing the Gateway to play a dial tone, and to collect digits.

Event 7: The Gateway responds with an ACK, and gives dialtone to the user. The exact sequence of these two events vary, depending on the specific implementation.

---

[1][ARAN98] Arango, Mauricio and Huitema, Christian. Simple Gateway Control Protocol (SGCP), Internet Engineering Task Force draft-huitema-sgcp-va-o2.txt.

[ARAN98a] Arango, Mauricio, Dugan, Andrew, Elliott, Isacc, Huitema, Christian, and Pickett, Scott. Media Gateway Control Protocol (MGCP). Internet Engineering Task Force draft-huitema-MGCP-v0r1-01.txt.

[TAYL98] Taylor, P., Calhoun, Pat R., and Rubens, Allan C. IPDC Base Protocol. Internet Engineering Task Force. Draft-taylor-Ipdc-99.txt.

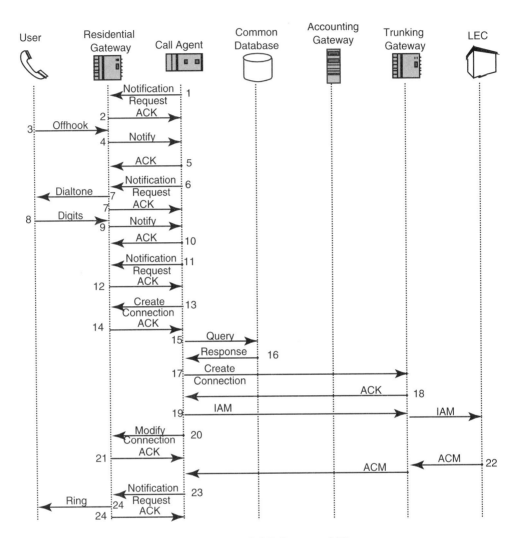

Figure 9–12   MGCP Protocol Flows

Event 8: Based on the digit map sent to it in event 7, the Gateway accumulates digits.

Event 9: And based on this digit map, the Gateway notifies the Call Agent with a message containing an ObservedEvent parameter. This parameter contains the collected digits.

Event 10: The Call Agent ACKs the message.

Event 11: Next, the Call Agent sends a NotificationRequest command to direct the Gateway to stop collecting digits, and to monitor for an onhook transition.

Event 12: The Gateway ACKs the command.

Event 13: The CreateConnection command is sent by the Call Agent to seize the incoming circuit. This message contains the CallId, LocalConnectionOptions, and the ConnectionMode parameters. Recall that the LocalConnectionOptions are: (a) packetization period in milliseconds, (b) compression algorithm (G.711, G.729, etc.), (c) bandwidth for the connection, and (d) user of nonuse of echo cancellation. The ConnectionMode is set to receive only.

Event 14: The Gateway ACKs the command. In this message is the identification of the new connection (ConnectionId), and the session description (an SDP announcement) that is used to receive the audio traffic. This description may contain the IP address at which the Gateway is ready to receive the audio data, the protocol used to transport the packets (RTP), the RTP port (3456), the audio profile (AVP, in accordance with RFC 1890). The AVP defines the payload type, such as G.711. This message can also be used to inform the Call Agent that the Gateway is ready to use other audio profiles. For example, G.726 for 32 kbit/s ADPCM may also be stipulated.

Event 15: The Call Agent now must determine where to route the call and to which egress Gateway the connection should be established. It sends a query to the common database to obtain this information.

Event 16: The needed information is returned to the Call Agent.

Event 17: The Call Agent has sufficient information to send a CreateConnection command to the egress Gateway, in this example, a trunking Gateway. The parameters in this message mirror the parameters exchanged in events 13 and 14 between the residential Gateway and the Call Agent, and the session description in this message is the same as the description given to the Call Agent by the residential Gateway. There are two differences: (a) the EndPointId identifies the endpoint at the outgoing at the trunking Gateway, and (b) the mode parameter is set to send/receive. The CallId is the same in this message since the two endpoint connections belong to the same call.

Event 18: The trunking Gateway responds with an ACK. In this message is this Gateway's session description such as its IP address, its port, and its RTP profile.

Event 19: Based on the information obtained in event 18, the Call Agent now builds an SS7 ISUP Initial Address Message (IAM) and sends it to the trunking Gateway. This Gateway relays this message to a designated local exchange carrier (LEC). It is the job of the Call

Agent to correlate the MGCP endpoints to the SS7's CIC. Some of the information gathered in events 1–18 are used to help build the IAM. For example, calling and called party numbers, echo cancellation, international call, ISUP used end-to-end, and other fields are placed in this message.

Event 20: The information obtained in event 18 is used to create the ModifyConnection command that is sent to the residential Gateway. The parameters in this command reflect the parameters in the ACK in event 18.

Event 21: The Gateway ACKs the command.

Event 22: The LEC returns an SS7 ISUP Address Complete Message (ACM) to the Call Agent. This message contains fields (backward call indicators) to aid the Call Agent in directing the residential Gateway, as explained in the next event.

Event 23: The receipt of the ACM at the Call Agent precipitates the sending of a NotificationRequest command to the residential Gateway. This message directs the Gateway to place ringing tones on the line.

Event 24: The Gateway ACKs the commands and places ringing tones on the line to the user telephone.

Event 25: When the called party answers the call at the remote end, the offhook condition will result in an ISUP answer message (ANM) being returned to the Call Agent.

Event 26: The Call Agent sends a NotificationRequest command to the residential Gateway to instruct it to remove the ring tone from the line.

Event 27: The Gateway removes the ring tone and ACKs the command.

Event 28: To this point, the connection at the local end has been in a receive only mode. To change connection to full duplex mode, the Call Agent sends a ModifyConnection command to the Gateway.

Event 29: The Gateway responds, and sends back an ACK. The connection is now established.

Event 30: In this example, the called party hangs-up, and the offhook condition precipitates the ISUP Release message (REL), that is conveyed to the Call Agent.

Event 31: The Call Agent sends a DeleteConnection command to both Gateways. Each message contains the respective EndPointId, and ConnectionID at each Gateway as well as the global CallId.

Event 32: The Gateways respond with the performance data fields in the response.

Event 33: The local line is placed in an onhook state by the local party hanging up.

Event 34: The onhook event is relayed to the Call Agent with a NotificationRequest message.

Event 35: The Call Agent ACKs the message.

Event 36: The Call Agent then "resets" the endpoint by informing the Gateway to monitor for an offhook condition.

Event 37: The Gateway ACKs the command.

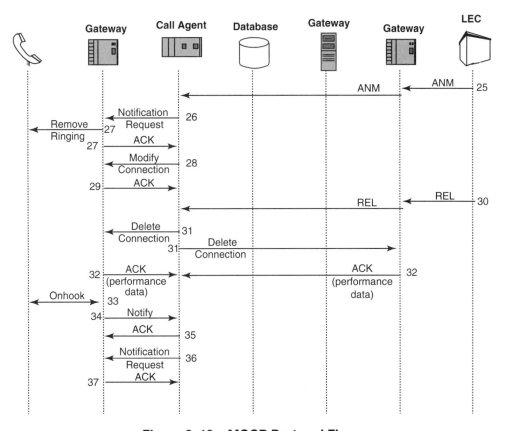

Figure 9–13   MGCP Protocol Flows

SUMMARY

MGCP is another IP Call Processing Protocol. Its purpose is to define the operations of telephony Gateways. This control comes from external call control elements, known as Call Agents. The Gateway provides conversion and internetworking operations between the audio signals used on telephone circuits and data packets used by the Internet or other packet oriented networks. The Call Agent directs the operations of the Gateway.

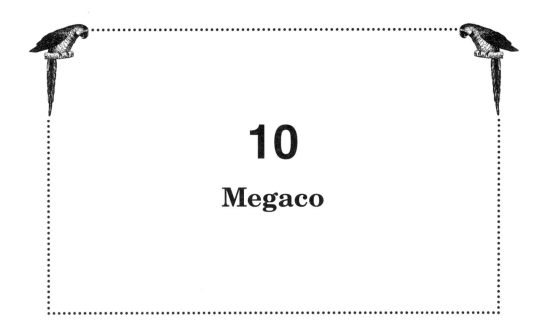

10

Megaco

INTRODUCTION

This chapter explains Megaco, predicted by many to become a widely used Call Processing Protocol. We begin by an examination of the status of the Megaco specification, followed by a review of the structure of the Megaco architecture. The message structure of Megaco is explained, and several message protocol flows are provided to help convey how Megaco provides call processing and many other operations. We conclude the chapter with a review of the Megaco Management Information Base (MIB)

STATUS OF MEGACO

It is expected that the Megaco protocol will be published as a final RFC soon. In the meantime, your best reference is the working draft: <draft-ietf-megaco-protocol-08.txt>. Another working draft deals with an IP phone Media Gateway, and can be found in <draft-ietf-megaco-ipphone-01.txt>. A draft discussing packages for MGEGACO/H.428 is <draft-ietf-megaco-basicpkg-00.txt>. The Megaco MIB is available in <draft-ietf-megaco-mib-00.txt>.

STRUCTURE OF MEGACO

The Megaco Protocol (Megaco) is yet another Gateway Control Protocol. As we will see, it is similar to MGCP. Megaco architecture is based on two concepts, called abstractions in the specifications. First, Terminations (T) are entities representing entries such as a DS1 link, a DS0 channel on the D1 link, an individual party in a telephone call, etc. Terminations can also take other forms such as an RTP traffic flow, and voice over IP streams. A termination sources and/or sinks one or more media streams.

Second, Contexts (C) are collections of terminations. For example, audio connections are modeled by viewing the Context as a mixing bridge. Another example is a gateway that interfaces a telco DS1 trunk and DS0 voice channels to a VOIP network. A Context can contain multiple Terminations. For example, one for the DS0 Termination, and one for the VOIP RTP stream.

Megaco defines how to add and subtract Terminations to a Context, and how to move Terminations between two Contexts. It defines how Terminations can be programmed to detect events, and how to add or subtract events from Terminations. Terminations can also be modified, such as changing a Termination from "idle" to "send/receive." Gateways can send notification messages to Media Gateway Controllers about the status of Terminations, or events that occur at Terminations.

Megaco requires that a Context have at least one Termination. Also, a Termination may belong to only one Context at a time, but it is possible for a Termination to exist outside of a Context. A Context is created by the addition of its first Termination, and is destroyed a the subtraction of its last remaining Termination.

Introduction to the Megaco Packages

IP-based telephony Gateways are expected to support a wide array of operations, from simple local access to a telephone, to ATM interfaces. Therefore, Terminations will have different characteristics. Megaco supports these different systems by allowing a Termination to have different optional "profiles" that are grouped into packages. The options have parameters associated with them and are classified as follows, and depicted in Figure 10–1.

Properties. Properties define the characteristics of the Termination, and they can take many forms. Here are some examples (and only a

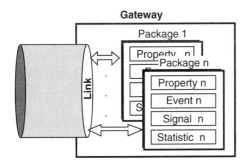

Figure 10–1   Parts of the Package

few of many). The service status of a termination may have the properties of: (a) test, (b) in-service, or (c) out-of-service. It may have a property that sets rules on how traffic flows into and out of it, such as: (a) send only, (b) receive only, (c) send and receive, or (d) loop-back the traffic. Termination properties can describe a type of modem, a version of IP, response/execution timers, size of a jitter buffer, even the maximum number of Terminations that may be associated with a Context. As stated, they take many forms.

Events.   The Gateway is programmed to monitor, detect, and report on events. Some examples of events are: (a) a fax tone, (b) on-hook, (b) off-hook, (c) results of a continuity test, (d) result of the collection of dialed digits, based on a digit map, etc.

Signals.   Signals are generated and detected by the Gateway. For example, the package may stipulate that upon detecting a off-hook, the Gateway must generate a dial-tone signal. Megaco defines how long audio tones are placed on a line, the parameters for DTMF signals, and on.

Statistics.   Statistics are the last part of a package. They contain performance information about the Termination's traffic. Examples of statistics are: (a) octets sent and received during a defined time, (b) packets send and received, (c) packets lost, (d) RTP jitter data, etc.

Identifiers (IDs)

All these aspects of Megaco are noted by IDs. Therefore, there are: (a) PropertyIds, EventIds, SignalIds, StatisticsIds, (and ParameterIds for all). They are associated with a package, which has a PackageName.

All have unique name spaces, and the same identifier may be used with each of them. The same identifier can be used in different packages.

Rules for Package Use

Megaco defines other rules for Package use. Events and signals are grouped in packages within which they share the same namespace which are called event names. Packages are groupings of the events that are related. For instance, one package may support a certain group of events and signals for analog access lines, and another package may support another group of events and signals for video lines. One or more packages may be applicable for a given Termination class, and part of the description of the Termination class consists of a list of supported packages.

Signals may happen as a result of an event, or as a result of the reception of a message. Signals are used to alert the Termination's users to inform them that they are expected to perform a specific action. Additional examples of signals are an on/off signal that stays the same until directed to change, a signal that times-out automatically, and a brief signal that stops on its own.

THE MEGACO CONNECTION MODEL

The connection model for Megaco describes the logical entities, or objects, within the Media Gateway that can be controlled by the Media Gateway Controller. As introduced earlier, the main abstractions used in the connection model are Terminations and Contexts, introduced earlier.

Recall that a Termination sends (sources) and/or receives (sinks) one or more media streams. In a multimedia conference, a Termination can be multimedia and can source or sink multiple media streams. The media stream parameters, as well as modem and bearer parameters, are encapsulated within the Termination.

A Context is an association between a collection of Terminations. There is a special type of Context, the null Context, which contains all Terminations that are not associated to any other Termination. For instance, in a decomposed access gateway, all idle lines are represented by Terminations in the null Context.

Figure 10–2 graphically depicts these concepts. The diagram gives several examples and is not meant to be an all-inclusive illustration. The

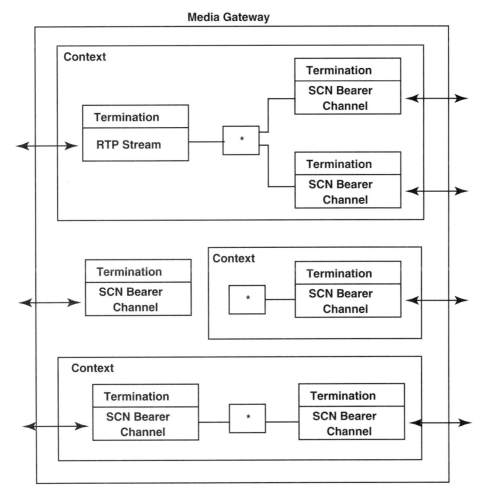

Figure 10-2   The Megaco Connection Model

asterisk box in each of the Contexts represents the logical association of Terminations implied by the Context.

The example in Figure 10–3 shows an example of one way to accomplish a call-waiting scenario in a decomposed access gateway, illustrating the relocation of a Termination between Contexts. Terminations T1 and T2 belong to Context C1 in a two-way audio call. A second audio call is waiting for T1 from Termination T3. T3 is alone in Context C2.

Next, in Figure 10–4, T1 accepts the call from T3, placing T2 on hold. This action results in T1 moving into Context C2.

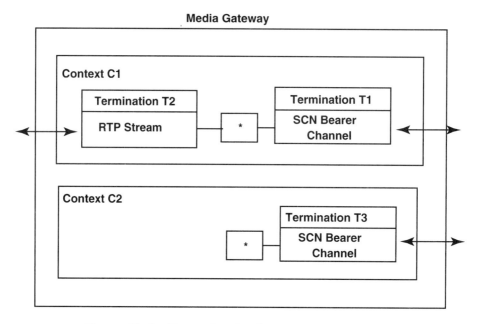

Figure 10–3   Example of a Call Waiting Operation

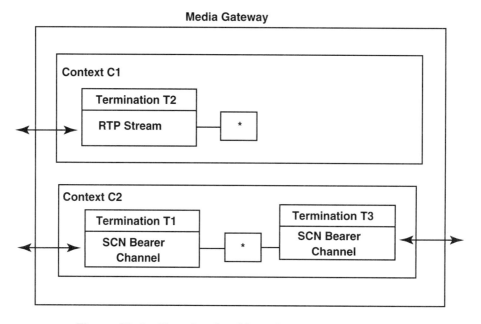

Figure 10–4   Termination Moved to Another Context

MEGACO PACKAGES IN MORE DETAIL

Annex E of the Megaco specification defines the Megaco "Basic" Packages. As Megaco evolves, and as it is deployed, other packages will be added. This part of the chapter provides an overview of these Packages, which are listed in Table 10–1. Recall that the Packages are described with Properties, Events, Signals, and Statistics.

- *Generic Package:* This package contains commonly encountered items, including error events, common signals, and signal interruptions.
- *Base Root Package:* This package defines Gateway wide properties. It includes properties establishing a bound on the maximum number of Contexts and Terminations per Context that can exist at any time. It also includes timers that establish when the MG should respond to the MGC's transaction, and vise-versa.
- *Tone Generator Package:* This package defines signals to generate audio tones. It is somewhat generic, and refers to other parts of the Megaco specification for the specific parameter values.
- *Tone Detection Package:* This package defines the events for audio tone detection, which can vary from country to country. Once again, it is somewhat generic. In a general way, it defines these events: (a) start tone detected, (b) end tone detected, and (c) long tone detected.

Table 10–1   The Megaco Basic Packages

Generic

Base root

Tone generator

Tone detection

Basic DTMF generator

DTMF detection

Call progress tones generator

Call progress tones detection

Analog line supervision

Basic continuity

Network

RTP

TDM circuit

- *Basic DTMF Generator Package:* This package defines the basic
  generated DTMF tones (see Chapter 2, Table 2–2 for an explanation of DTMF tones). The DTMF tones are identified by a signal ID
  as follows:

```
Signal Name            Signal ID
dtmf character 0       d1 (0x0010)
dtmf character 1       d1 (0x0011)
dtmf character 2       d2 (0x0012)
dtmf character 3       d3 (0x0013)
dtmf character 4       d4 (0x0014)
dtmf character 5       d5 (0x0015)
dtmf character 6       d6 (0x0016)
dtmf character 7       d7 (0x0017)
dtmf character 8       d8 (0x0018)
dtmf character 9       d9 (0x0019)
dtmf character *       ds (0x0020)
dtmf character #       do (0x0021)
dtmf character A       da (0x001a)
dtmf character B       db (0x001b)
dtmf character C       dc (0x001c)
dtmf character D       dd (0x001d)
```

- *DTMF Detection Package:* This package defines the basic DTMF
  tones detection. The mapping of DTMF events to digit map symbols is performed as follows:

```
DTMF Event                 Symbol
    d0                      "0"
    d1                      "1"
    d2                      "2"
    d3                      "3"
    d4                      "4"
    d5                      "5"
    d6                      "6"
    d7                      "7"
    d8                      "8"
    d9                      "9"
    da                      "A" or "a"
    db                      "B" or "b"
    dc                      "C" or "c"
    dd                      "D" or "d"
    ds                      "E" or "e"
    do                      "F" or "f"
```

- *Call Progress Tones Generator Package:* This package defines the basic call progress tones as signals. The definition includes a signal name and a signal ID. Each tone is defined as both a signal and a tone ID for the following signals: (a) dial tone, (b) ringing tone, (c) busy tone, (d) congestion tone, (e) special information tone, (f) warning tone, (g) payphone recognition tone, (h) call waiting tone, and (i) caller waiting tone.

- *Call Progress Tones Detection Package:* This package the basic call progress detection tones, and defines the tone just listed in the previous Package.

- *Analog Line Supervision Package:* This package defines events and signals for an analog line: (a) on-hook, (b) off-hook, (c) flash hook, and (d) ring.

- *Basic Continuity Package:* This package defines events and signals for continuity testing.

- *Network Package:* This package defines several properties of network terminations independent of network type: (a) jitter buffer, (b) network failure, and (c) quality alert (loss of quality of a connection).

- *RTP Package:* This package defines RTP packet transfers: (a) indication when there is a transition in the RTP payload from one format to another, (b) statistics on packets sent/received, (c) statistics of jitter (variation in interarrival time), and (d) statistics on delay.

- *TDM Circuit Package:* This package defines TDM (time division multiplexed Terminations). Two properties are defined: (a) echo cancellation (yes or no), and (b) gain control (adapting the level of the signal, yes or no).

As stated earlier, these basic packages are just that, basic. Additional Internet documentation will extend these packages.

MEGACO COMMANDS

Like other IP Call Processing Protocols, Megaco exchanges messages between the gateway controller and gateways. These messages, called Commands, are defined to provide the operations described below, and summarized in Table 10–2. Multiple Commands can be placed into a single transaction (a TransactionRequest). Responses are sent back in a TransactionAccept or a TransactionReject. In turn, multiple transactions can be placed into a single message.

Table 10–2   Megaco Commands

- Add
- Modify
- Subtract
- Move
- AuditValue
- AuditCapabilities
- Notify
- ServiceChange

- *Add:* Adds a Termination to a Context. The command on the first termination in a context is used to create a Context.
- *Modify:* Modifies the characteristics of a Termination (properties, events, and signals).
- *Subtract:* Disconnects a Termination from a Context, and returns statistics on the Termination's participation in the Context.
- *Move:* Moves a Termination to another Context.
- *AuditValue:* Returns current state of properties, events, signals and statistics are implemented at a Termination.
- *AuditCapabilities:* Returns all possible values for Termination properties, events, and signals allowed by the Media Gateway.
- *Notify:* Provides information to the MGC about pre-defined "observed events," such as offhook, onhook, digit collection, etc.
- *ServiceChange:* Signals that a Termination or a group of Terminations (or even a gateway) is about to be taken out of service, or has been brought back into service. This command is also used by the MG to announce its availability to an MGC (a registration procedure).

Command Parameters (Descriptors)

Megaco Commands contain several parameters, and are called Descriptors. A Descriptor consists of a name and a list of associated items. Each of these Descriptors is described below. To aid in your reading about these parameters, see Figure 10–5.

Descriptors

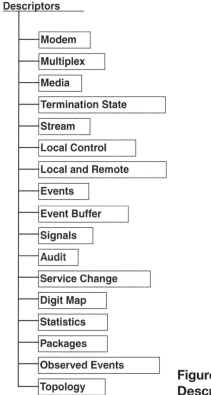

Modem

Multiplex

Media

Termination State

Stream

Local Control

Local and Remote

Events

Event Buffer

Signals

Audit

Service Change

Digit Map

Statistics

Packages

Observed Events

Topology

Figure 10–5   Command Descriptors

Modem Descriptor.   Specifies the modem type (and maybe parameters) that are to be used in H.324 and text transmissions. The following modems are stipulated: V.18, V.22, V.22bis, V.32, V.32bis, V.34, V.90, V.91, as well as synchronous ISDN.

Multiplex Descriptor.   A number of media streams can be carried on one or more bearer channels. This descriptor associates the media and the bearers, and includes the following multiplex types: H.221, H.223, H.226, and V.76.

Media Descriptor.   This descriptor specifies the parameters for the media streams. Each stream is identified by a StreamID. It is used to link the streams in a Context that belong together. The stream descriptor may contain up to three other (subsidiary) descriptors: LocalControl, Local, and Remote (discussed below).

Termination State Descriptor. This descriptor contains the ServiceStates and EventBufferControl properties, and properties of a Termination that are not stream-specific. The ServiceStates property describes the overall state of the Termination: test, out of service, or in service. The EventBufferControl property is explained shortly.

Stream Descriptor. The Stream Descriptor identifies the parameters associated with one bi-directional media stream. These parameters are used with this descriptor: one contains termination properties specific to a stream and one each for local and remote flows. The Stream Descriptor also includes a StreamID.

Streams are created by specifying a new StreamID on one of the terminations in a Context. A stream is deleted by setting empty Local and Remote descriptors for the stream with ReserveGroup and ReserveValue in LocalControl set to "false" on all terminations in the context that previously supported that stream. StreamIDs are of local significance between MGC and MG and they are assigned by the MGC. Within a context, the StreamID is used to indicate which media flows are interconnected. Streams with the same StreamID are connected.

LocalControl Descriptor. The LocalControl Descriptor contains the Mode property, the ReserveGroup and ReserveValue properties and properties of a termination (defined in Packages) that are stream specific, and are of interest between the MG and the MGC.

The allowed values for the mode property are send-only, receive-only, send/receive, inactive and loop-back. "Send" and "receive" are with respect to the exterior of the Context. For example, a stream set to mode=sendonly does not pass received media into the Context.

Signals and Events are not affected by mode. The boolean-valued Reserve properties, ReserveValue and ReserveGroup, of a Termination indicate what the MG is expected to do when it receives a local and/or remote descriptor, described next.

If the value of a Reserve property is True, the MG must reserve resources for all alternatives specified in the local and/or remote descriptors for which it currently has resources available. It then responds with the alternatives for which it reserves resources. If it cannot support any of the alternatives, it responds with a reply to the MGC that contains empty local and/or remote descriptors.

If the value of a Reserve property is False, the MG must choose one of the alternatives specified in the local descriptor (if present) and one of the alternatives specified in the remote descriptor (if present). If the MG has not yet reserved resources to support the selected alternative, it reserves the resources. If, on the other hand, it already reserved resources for the Termination addressed (because of a prior exchange with ReserveValue and/or ReserveGroup equal to True), it releases any excess resources it reserved previously.

Local and Remote Descriptors.   Local refers to the media received by the MG and Remote refers to the media sent by the MG. The MGC uses Local and Remote descriptors to reserve and commit MG resources for media decoding and encoding for the given Stream(s) and Termination to which they apply. The MG includes these descriptors in its response to indicate what it is actually prepared to support.

If the MG has insufficient resources to support all alternatives requested by the MGC and the MGC requested resources in both Local and Remote, the MG should reserve resources to support at least one alternative each within Local and Remote.

If the MG has insufficient resources to support at least one alternative within a Local (Remote) descriptor received from the MGC, it shall return an empty Local (Remote) in response.

In its response to the MGC, when the MGC included Local and Remote descriptors, the MG must include Local and Remote descriptors for all groups of properties and property values for which it reserved resources. If the MG is incapable of supporting at least one of the alternatives within the Local (Remote) descriptor received from the MGC, it returns an empty Local (Remote) descriptor.

If the Mode property of the LocalControl descriptor is RecvOnly or SendRecv, the MG must be prepared to receive media encoded according to any of the alternatives included in its response to the MGC. If ReserveGroup is False and ReserveValue is false, then the MG should apply the following rules to resolve Local and Remote to a single alternative each:

1. The MG chooses the first alternative in Local for which it is able to support at least one alternative in Remote.
2. If the MG is unable to support at least one Local and one Remote alternative, it returns Error code 510 (Insufficient Resources).

Events Descriptor.   The MGC directs the MG to detect and report on certain events. This information is conveyed to the MG with the Events Descriptor. This parameter contains a RequestIdentifier and a list of events. The RequestIdentifier correlates the request with the notifications. Each event in this descriptor contains an event name, and optional StreamID, and optional KeepActive flag, and optional parameters.

The Event name consists of a Package Name (where the event is defined) and EventID. The ALL wildcard may be used for the EventID, indicating that all events from the specified package have to be detected. The default streamID is 0, indicating that the event to be detected is not related to a particular media stream. Events can have parameters. This allows a single event description to have some variation in meaning without creating large numbers of individual events. Further event parameters are defined in the package.

The default action of the MG, when it detects an event in the Events Descriptor, is to send a Notify command to the MG.

EventBuffer Descriptor. The EventBuffer Descriptor contains a list of events, with their parameters if any, that the MG is requested to detect and buffer. Another parameter, called the LockStep, is used in conjunction with this descriptor to stipulate how buffering occurs. Section 7.1.9 of [BELL00] contains the rules for the buffer operations if you wish more details.

Signals Descriptor. The Signals Descriptor is a parameter that contains the set of signals that the Media Gateway applies to a Termination. Signals are defined in packages, and are named with a Package name (in which the signal is defined) This descriptor also provides for a parameter to define the duration of the signal.

Three types of signals are defined: (a) on/off: the signal lasts until it is turned off, (b) timeout: the signal stays on until it is either turned off by an external intervention, or by the expiration of a timer, (c) brief: a brief signal that is so short it stops on its own, and no time out value is needed.

Megaco provides for a sequential signal list. It is a list containing a sequence of signals that are to be played out sequentially, and is a useful feature for automatic dialing applications.

Some key rules for the use of this descriptor are described next. As always, keep in mind that we are looking at the general functions of Megaco, and the detailed rules for its implementation are in the Internet specifications.

First, the production of a signal on a Termination is stopped by application of a new SignalsDescriptor, or detection of an event on the Termination.

Second, a new SignalsDescriptor replaces any existing SignalsDe-scriptor. Any signals applied to the Termination not in the replacement descriptor are stopped, and new signals are applied, except as follows. Signals present in the replacement descriptor and containing the Keep-Active flag must be continued if they are currently playing and have not already completed. If a replacement signal descriptor contains a signal that is not currently playing and contains the KeepActive flag, that signal must be ignored.

If the replacement descriptor contains a sequential signal list with the identifier as the existing descriptor, then the signal type and se-quence of signals in the sequential signal list in the replacement descrip-tor shall be ignored, and the playing of the signals in the sequential signal list in the existing descriptor shall not be interrupted.

Audit Descriptor. The MGC may wish the MG to check on opera-tions and events occurring at the MG. The Audit Descriptor is used for this purpose, and explains to the MG what information is to be audited. It specifies a list of descriptors that the MG is to return to the MGC. The information that is audited and returned is implementation-specific, and can include any information that is defined in the Megaco implementa-tion, including Descriptors such as Events, Media, Signals, Modem, and so on.

ServiceChange Descriptor. As its name implies, the Service-Change Descriptor contains information about a change is the service of a Termination, and the reason for the change. It contains the address of the changed resource, the method by which it was changed (timeout, ex-ternal intervention, etc.), the time it was changed, and (of course) what was changed.

DigitMap Descriptor. A DigitMap is a dialing plan placed in the MG used for detecting and reporting digit events (the calling party dial-ing a number) received on a Termination. The DigitMap Descriptor con-tains a DigitMap name and the DigitMap to be assigned to the Termina-tion. The map will vary, depending on the requirements for dialing a number from a telephone. For example, a digit map for dialing from a hotel room might be a map to capture 9, 1, area code, exchange code, line code. A digit map for a residence would not contain the 9.

Here are some rules for the use of this descriptor. A digit map may be preloaded into the MG by external means and referenced by name in an EventsDescriptor. It may be defined dynamically and subsequently referenced by name, or the actual digit map itself may be specified in the EventsDescriptor.

The collection of digits according to a DigitMap may be protected by three timers: a start timer (T), short timer (S), and long timer (L).

1. The start timer (T) is used prior to any digits having been dialed.
2. If the Media Gateway can determine that at least one more digit is needed for a digit string to match any of the allowed patterns in the digit map, then the interdigit timer value should be set to a long (L) duration.
3. If the digit string has matched one of the patterns in a digit map, but it is possible that more digits could be received which would cause a match with a different pattern, then instead of reporting the match immediately, the MG must apply the short timer (S) and wait for more digits.

Statistics Descriptor. This descriptor provides information describing the status and usage of a Termination during its existence within a specific Context. A standard of statistics is kept for each termination where appropriate. The particular statistical properties that are reported for a given Termination are determined by the Packages for the Termination.

Packages Descriptor. This descriptor is used only with the Audit-Value command, and returns a list of packages that are pertinent to a specific Termination.

ObservedEvents Descriptor. This descriptor is supplied with the Notify command to inform the MGC of which event(s) were detected. Used with the AuditValue command, the ObservedEventsDescriptor returns events in the event buffer which have not been Notified. This descriptor contains the RequestIdentifier of the EventsDescriptor that triggered the notification, the event(s) detected and the detection time(s).

Topology Descriptor. This descriptor is used to show the directions of traffic flow between the Terminations in a Context. It applies to a Context, and not a Termination. The default topology of a Context is for each Termination's transmissions to be received by all other Terminations. So, this descriptor modifies the default operation.

MEGACO NAMES

Megaco names are hierarchical, and a slash is used to delimit the components of a name. For example, the name sys5/28/24 identifies "sys5" as a T3 (DS3); "28" identifies the 28th DS1 on the DS3 trunk, and "24" identifies the 24th DS0 PCM channel on the DS1 frame.

THE APPLICATION PROGRAMMING INTERFACE (API)

An effective way to gain an understanding of Megaco is to examine how the information (the Descriptors) are conveyed in the Commands. Figure 10–6 shows the format for an Add command, set up for an application programming interface (API).

The input parameters are shown in parentheses after the command name and the return values are placed in front of the Command. All parameters enclosed by square brackets ([. . .]) are optional. For the reader that needs the details for this operation, here is a summary of them.

The TerminationID specifies the termination to be added to the Context. The Termination is either created, or taken from the null Context. For an existing Termination, the TerminationID would be specific. The optional MediaDescriptor describes all media streams.

The optional ModemDescriptor and MuxDescriptor specify a modem and multiplexer if applicable. The EventsDescriptor parameter is op-

```
TerminationID
[,MediaDescriptor]
[,ModemDescriptor]
[,MuxDescriptor]
[,EventsDescriptor]
[,SignalsDescriptor]
[,DigitMapDescriptor]
[,ObservedEventsDescriptor]
[,EventBufferDescriptor]
[,StatisticsDescriptor]
[,PackagesDescriptor]
    Add( TerminationID
        [, MediaDescriptor]
        [, ModemDescriptor]
        [, MuxDescriptor]
        [, EventsDescriptor]
        [, SignalsDescriptor]
        [, DigitMapDescriptor]
        [, AuditDescriptor]
    )
```

Figure 10–6   An Example API: For the Add Command

tional. If present, it provides the list of events that should be detected on the Termination. The SignalsDescriptor parameter is optional. If present, it provides the list of signals that should be applied to the Termination. The DigitMapDescriptor parameter is optional. If present, it defines a DigitMap definition that may be used in an EventsDescriptor. The AuditDescriptor is optional. If present, the command will return descriptors as specified in the AuditDescriptor.

All descriptors that can be modified could be returned by MG if a parameter was underspecified or overspecified. ObservedEvents, Statistics, and Packages, and the EventBuffer Descriptors are returned only if requested in the AuditDescriptor.

EXAMPLES OF MEGACO PROTOCOL EXCHANGES

All the IP Call Processing Protocols define the message exchanges (the protocol flows) between the Gateway Controller and their Gateways. This part of the chapter provides examples of Megaco protocol exchanges between Gateway and Media Gateway Controllers.

The First Example

The first example, depicted in Figure 10–7, is a general illustration, based on [CUER99].[1] and amplified by the author. In this example, the RMGL means "residential Media Gateway, local," and the RMGR means "residential Media Gateway, remote," and "MGC" of course means Media Gateway Controller. The term "local" is used to place the calling party at the local Gateway. The "remote" Gateway supports the called party. In this example, on MGC controls both Gateways.

To keep this example relatively simple, the full contents of the messages are not shown. The intent is to show how the three nodes set up a Context and a Termination. A notation in parentheses represents my tutorial explanation of the protocol exchange. For example, "(ACK)" indicates that the MG or the MGC has responded with an acknowledgment of a previous command. It comes in the form of the same message that precipitated it; for example, a Notify command precipitates a Notify ACK. This ACK often contains additional information, such the result of setting up a new RTP port, naming a null context, etc.

---

[1][CUER99] Cuervo, Fernando, et al, Megaco Protocol, draft-ietf-megaco-protocol-01.txt

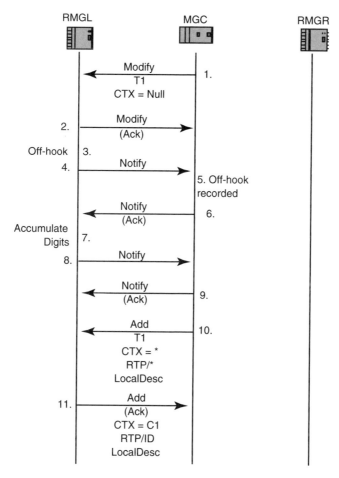

Figure 10–7   (a) Megaco Protocol Flow

Event 1: The MGC issues a Modify command to the RMGL to request that Termination 1 (T1) detect for off-hook. When off-hook is detected, the RMGL is to collect digits. The context is null for the time being, since it is not associated with a connection.

Event 2: The command is acknowledged.

Event 3: The RMGL detects an off-hook condition.

Event 4: It notifies the MGC.

Event 5: The MGC records this event.

Event 6: The MGC acknowledges the Notify message.

Event 7: The RMGL accumulates the digits dialed from the user in accordance with the digit plan that was downloaded from the MGC earlier, usually in a Modify command.

Event 8: The collected digits are sent to the MGC in a Notify command.

Event 9: The MGC acknowledges the receipt of this information.

Event 10: The MGC determines that the digit string is correct, and sufficient to make a call. It sends an Add command to the RMGL to create a context that includes T1. It also specifies an unnamed ephemeral packet termination of RTP/*. The LocalTerminationDescriptor (LocalDesc) may specify a choice of codecs for the call.

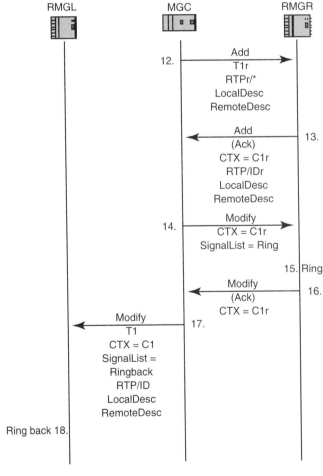

Figure 10–7   (b) Megaco Protocol Flow

Event 11: The RMGL responds to the MGC with an ACK, and a Context named C1. It also sends back a name RTP Termination (RTP/ID). Its LocalTerminationDescriptor (LocalDesc) specifies the supported codecs on the receiving RTP port.

Event 12: Based on the information received from the local gateway RMGL, the MGC now can inform the remote gateway RMGR to add the termination (T1r) that corresponds to the dialed digit string it had received from the local gateway. It also sends an ephermal RTP port. The information in T1's LocalDesc is passed to the remote gateway in the RemoteDesc field, which specifies the codecs for T1r.

Event 13: The RMGR responds to the add command with a named Context of C1r, a named RTP Termination of RTP/IDr, and its LocalDesc specifying the supported codecs on its receiving RTP port.

Event 14: The MGC now uses a Modify command to request that ringing be applied on T1r. The message also requests the gateway to look for off-hook.

Event 15: The RMGR applies ringing to the called party line.

Event 16: It so indicates to the MGC with a response.

Event 17: The MGC then sends a Modify command to the calling RMGL. The command requests that ring-back be applied to T1, and identifies the remote receiving RTP port in the RemoteDesc.

Event 18: Ring back is applied.

Event 19: A reply acknowledges that ring back is being applied and that the RTP settings have been updated.

Event 20: The called party answers the call by going off-hook.

Event 21: The RMGR sends a Notify to convey this information to the MGC, and of course, ringing is cancelled.

Event 22: The MGC acknowledges the Notify.

Event 23: The MGC issues a Modify command to cancel ring back on T1, and to set the two-way talk path (Sendrcv). The information in SignalList is used to cancel ring backEvent 2.

Event 24: The RMGL acknowledges the modify, removes ring back, and the call set up is now completed.

Several observations can be made about this example. First, the MGC initially set up the Termination in the Null Context, which we learned earlier contains all Terminations that are not associated with any Context. In this (typical) example, idle lines are associated with the Null Context. Second, all three nodes use IP addresses to identify who

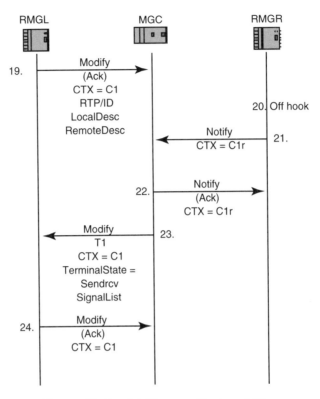

Figure 10–7   (c) Megaco Protocol Flow

sent the MGC message. This sending IP address is placed in the message (of course, it is also in the IP header). Third, the messages contain a variety of parameters, not shown in this general example, such as termination IDs, event descriptors, the send-receive mode and in some messages, SDP coding to describe the profile for the session. The next example shows and explains these parameters.

The Second Example

The second example is a more detailed explanation of a Megaco session, based on [CUER00].[2] The approach in this example is to explain the Megaco messages in considerable detail. Figures 10–8(a) and 10–8(b) are used for this example.

---

[2][CUER00]. Cuervo, Fernando, et al. Megaco Protocol, draft-ietf-megaco-protocol-07.txt, February 21, 2000.

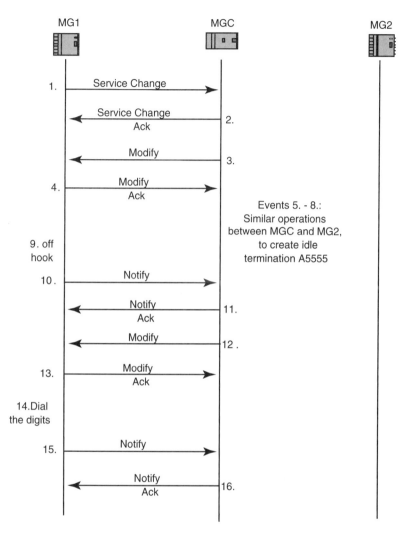

MG1   MGC   MG2

1.   Service Change ────────▶

2.   ◀──── Service Change
                     Ack

3.   ◀──── Modify

4.   Modify ────────▶
                 Ack

                                    Events 5. - 8.:
                                    Similar operations
                                    between MGC and MG2,
9. off   to create idle
hook   termination A5555

10.   Notify ────────▶

11.   ◀──── Notify
                 Ack

12.   ◀──── Modify

13.   Modify ────────▶
                 Ack

14.Dial
the digits

15.   Notify ────────▶

16.   ◀──── Notify
                 Ack

Figure 10–8(a)   Call Setup

We assume both Gateways in this example (MG1 and MG2) are controlled by the same Media Gateway Controller (MGC). The Megaco port for all nodes is 55555. MG1 has the IP address of 124.124.124.222; MG2 is configured for 125.125.125.111; the MGC is configured for 123.123.123.4.

Helpful Hints.   During this analysis, notice that the transaction identifiers in the API, and the resulting messages (Commands) are used to correlate a transaction pair; for example, a Notify and a Notify ACK.

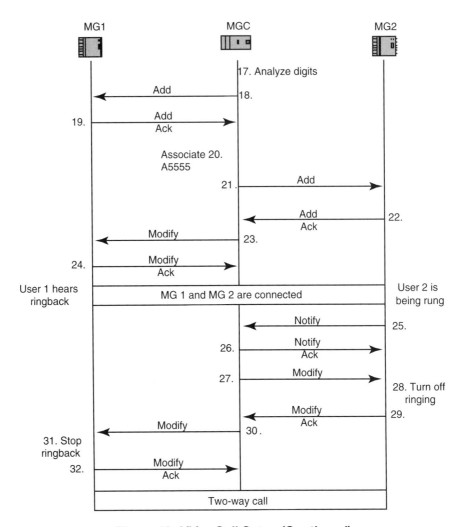

Figure 10–8(b)   Call Setup (Continued)

Each transaction pair must use the same number (that is, the Command and its ACK) in order to keep the Commands and replies correlated.

Also notice that events are also identified with unique values, shown in these examples as "Events" and "ObservedEvents."

The notations for a Context are NULL, and – (also meaning NULL). The "$" is used to note that a parameter is blank, and is (usually) coded in the reply message (filled-in) by the recipient of the message in which this field notation resides.

Finally, you should have read Chapter 5, since these examples use the Session Description Protocol (SDP).

Event 1: The ServiceChange API invocation at MG1 results in the Service Change message being sent to the MGC. This operation serves as a registration of MG1 to the MGC. Using Cuervo's example, the message contains the transaction ID of 9998, and MG1's IP address of 124.124.124.222. It also contains the port number of 55555, and the name of the gateway, ResGW1. The ROOT termination is placed in this API call and the resulting message directs the Gateway that the message pertains to the entire Gateway, and not a Termination in the Gateway. The API invocation for this event is coded as follows:

```
MG1 to MGC:
    MEGACO/1 [124.124.124.222]
    Transaction = 9998 {
        Context = - {
            ServiceChange = ROOT {Services {
                Method=Restart,
                ServiceChangeAddress=55555, Profile=ResGW/1}
            }
        }
    }
```

Event 2: The MGC responds with a Service Change message, which serves to acknowledge event 1. The reply must contain the MGC's IP address of 123.123.123.4, the transaction ID of 9998. It also contains a Context of ROOT Termination, and the port number of 55555. Notice the transaction identifiers in events 1 and 2 are the same, 9998. Remember that each transaction pair must use the same number (that is, the Command and its ACK) in order to keep the Commands and replies correlated. The API invocation for this event is coded as follows:

```
MGC to MG1:
    MEGACO/1 [123.123.123.4]:55555
    Reply = 9998 {
        Context = - {ServiceChange = ROOT {
            Services {ServiceChangeAddress=55555, Profile=ResGW/1}
}
```

Event 3: At the MGC, the API call results in the sending of a Modify message to MG1. The API invocation for this event is coded as follows (and includes the session description):

```
MGC to MG1:
     MEGACO/1 [123.123.123.4]:55555
     Transaction = 9999 {
         Context = - {
             Modify = A4444 {
                 Media { Stream = 1 {
                         LocalControl {
                             Mode = SendReceive,
                             ds0/gain=2,   ; in dB,
                             ds0/ec=G165
                         },
                         Local {
v=0
c=IN IP4 $
m=audio $ RTP/AVP 0
a=fmtp:PCMU VAD=X-NNVAD ; special voice activity
                         ; detection algorithm
                         }
                     }
                 },
                 Events = 2222 {al/of}
             }
         }
     }
```

Event 4: MG1 acknowledges the Modify in event 3. The API invocation for this event is coded as follows:

```
MG1 to MGC:
     MEGACO/1 [124.124.124.222]:55555
     Reply = 9999 {
        Context = - {Modify = A4444}
     }
```

Events 5–8: Similar operations occur between the MGC and MG2. For this side of the connection, termination A5555 is used. Termination A5555 is idle. Since the operations are the same for these events (with different Ids) as described in events 1–4, the coding is not shown in this example.

Event 9: MG1 has been instructed by the MGC to monitor for off-hook on termination A4444. It is doing just that and detects the off-hook condition when its user (User 1) goes off-hook to make a call to User 2, who is connected to MG2.

Event 10: MG1 detects the off-hook event from its user, and sends a Notify Command to the MGC. The API invocation for this event is coded as follows:

```
MG1 to MGC:
    MEGACO/1 [124.124.124.222]:55555
    Transaction = 10000 {
        Context = - {
            Notify = A4444 {ObservedEvents =2222 {
                19990729T22000000:al/of}}
        }
    }
```

Event 11: The MGC acknowledges the Notify Command:

```
MGC to MG1:
    MEGACO/1 [123.123.123.4]:55555
    Reply = 10000 {
        Context = - {Notify = A4444}
    }
```

Event 12: The Termination is modified to look for digits according to Dialplan0 ("DigitMap = DialPlan0"), to play dial tone ("dd/ce"), and to monitor for an on-hook event (al/on). Notice that the digit map for this dial plan is included:

```
MGC to MG1:
    MEGACO/1 [123.123.123.4]:55555
    Transaction = 10001 {
        Context = - {
            Modify = A4444 {
                Events = 2223 {
                    al/on, dd/ce {DigitMap=Dialplan0}
                },
                Signals {cg/dt},
                DigitMap= Dialplan0{
    (0| 00|[1-7]xxx|8xxxxxxx|Fxxxxxxx|Exx|91xxxxxxxxxx|9011x.)}
            }
        }
    }
```

Event 13: The Modify Command that was issued in event 12 is acknowledged:

```
MG1 to MGC:
    MEGACO/1 [124.124.124.222]:55555
    Reply = 10001 {
        Context = - {Modify = A4444}
    }
```

Event 14: User 1 dials the digits of the called party, user 2. These digits are collected by MG1 in accordance with Dialplan0. Dial tone is stopped upon detection of the first dialed digit.

Event 15: After the digits are collected (or an appropriate number of them), MG1 issues a Notify Command:

```
MG1 to MGC:
    MEGACO/1 [124.124.124.222]:55555
    Transaction = 10002 {
        Context = - {
            Notify = A4444 {ObservedEvents =2223 {
                19990729T22010001:dd/ce{ds="916135551212",Meth=
FM}}}
        }
    }
```

Event 16: The Notify Command issues in event 15 is acknowledged:

```
MGC to MG1:
    MEGACO/1 [123.123.123.4]:55555
    Reply = 10002 {
        Context = - {Notify = A4444}
    }
```

Event 17: The MGC analyzes the digits sent in event 15.

Event 18: Based on this analysis, the MGC recognizes that a connection should be made between MG1 and MG2. With this event, Termination A4444 and an RTP Termination is added to a new context in MG1. The remote descriptors for MG2's user have not been ascertained, so the Mode is set to ReceiveOnly. The Media Stream 1 also has defined in this event a network package (nt), and a jitter property for the package (jit). The "jit=40" defines a maximum jitter buffer of 40 ms. The SDP code of ptime gives length of time (in ms) of the media packet. The RTP/AVP 4 profile describes the MGC's preferred codec(s). Notice the "$" notations; they are to be filled in by the Media Gateway's reply. Also note that the SDP code shows two RTP audio ports. In subsequent events, these will be set and filled in for the local port for MG1 and the remote port for MG2:

```
MGC to MG1:
    MEGACO/1 [123.123.123.4]:55555
    Transaction = 10003 {
        Context = $ {
            Add = A4444,
            Add = $ {
                Media {
                  Stream = 1 {
                      LocalControl {
                          Mode = ReceiveOnly,

                          nt/jit=40, ; in ms
                      },
                      Local {
    v=0
    c=IN IP4 $
    m=audio $ RTP/AVP 4
    a=ptime:30
    v=0
    c=IN IP4 $
    m=audio $ RTP/AVP 0
                      }
                  }
              }
          }
      }
    }
```

Event 19: MG1 returns an ACK, and fills in the Context Name ("2000"), the Temination ID ("A4445"), the local IP address ("124.124.124.222"), and the port number ("2222"). The RTP/AVP 4 profile suggested by the MGC is acceptable:

```
MG1 to MGC
    MEGACO/1 [124.124.124.222]:55555
    Reply = 10003 {
      Context = 2000 {
        Add = A4444,
        Add=A4445{
            Media {
                Stream = 1 {
                    Local {
```

```
        v=0
        c=IN IP4 124.124.124.222
        m=audio 2222 RTP/AVP 4
        a=ptime:30
        a=recvonly
                        } ; RTP profile for G.723 is 4
                 }
              }
           }
        }
     }
```

Event 20: The MGC now associates A5555 with a new Context on
MG2.

Event 21: The MGC establishes an RTP stream for A5555. The
Command also directs MG2 to set ring on A5555 ("al/ri"). The RTP
information of MG1 is passed to MG2 in this event. The MG2 RTP
parameters will be filled in by MG2 in the next event and passed
back to the MGC and later, MG1:

```
MGC to MG2:
    MEGACO/1 [123.123.123.4]:55555
    Transaction = 50003 {
        Context = $ {
           Add = A5555  { Media {
                Stream = 1 {
                     LocalControl {Mode = SendReceive} }},
             Events=1234{al/of}
                     Signals {al/ri}
                     },
             Add  = $ {Media {
                     Stream = 1 {
                         LocalControl {
                             Mode = SendReceive,
                             nt/jit=40 ; in ms
                             },
                         Local {
        v=0
        c=IN IP4 $
        m=audio $ RTP/AVP 4
        a=ptime:30
                             },
                         Remote {
        v=0
        c=IN IP4 124.124.124.222
        m=audio 2222 RTP/AVP 4
```

```
                    a=ptime:30
                               } ; RTP profile for G.723 is 4
                        }
                    }
                }
            }
        }
```

Event 22: The Add Command is ACKed, with MG2 filling in the required parameters. Its port number is 1111, which is different from the control port number of 55555:

```
MG2 to MGC:
    MEGACO/1 [124.124.124.222]:55555
    Reply = 50003 {
       Context = 5000 {
          Add = A5555{},
          Add = A5556{
             Media {
                Stream = 1 {
                   Local {
v=0
c=IN IP4 125.125.125.111
m=audio 1111 RTP/AVP 4
}
                   } ; RTP profile for G723 is 4
                }
             }
          }
       }
```

Events 23 and 24: The MG2 information is passed to MG1 and acknowledged:
Event 23:

```
MGC to MG1:
    MEGACO/1 [123.123.123.4]:55555
    Transaction = 10005 {
      Context = 2000 {
        Modify = A4444 {
          Signals {cg/rt}
        },
        Modify = A4445 {
           Media {
                Stream = 1 {
                   Remote {
```

```
      v=0
      c=IN IP4 125.125.125.111
      m=audio 1111 RTP/AVP 4
                      }
                  } ; RTP profile for G723 is 4
              }
          }
        }
      }
      MG1 to MGC:
      MEGACO/1 [124.124.124.222]:55555
      Reply = 10005 {
         Context = 2000 {Modify = A4444, Modify = A4445}
      }
```

Event 24:

```
MG1 to MGC:
    MEGACO/1 [124.124.124.222]:55555
    Reply = 10005 {
       Context = 2000 {Modify = A4444, Modify = A4445}
    }
```

Events 25–29: The two Gateways now have a connection between them. User 2 is being alerted (the user phone has ring applied), and User 1 hears ringback. Events 25 and 26 notify the MGC that user 2 has answered the telephone. Events 27–29 turn off the ringing to user 2.

Event 25:

```
From MG2 to MGC:
    MEGACO/1 [125.125.125.111]:55555
    Transaction = 50005 {
       Context = 5000 {
           Notify = A5555 {ObservedEvents =1234 {
              19990729T22020002:al/of}}
       }
    }
```

Event 26:

```
From MGC to MG2:
    MEGACO/1 [123.123.123.4]:55555
    Reply = 50005 {
        Context = - {Notify = A5555}
    }
```

Event 27:

```
From MGC to MG2:
    MEGACO/1 [123.123.123.4]:55555
    Transaction = 50006 {
      Context = 5000 {
        Modify = A5555 {
           Events = 1235 {al/on},
           Signals { } ; to turn off ringing
        }
      }
    }
```

Event 28: Ringing is turned off.
Event 29:

```
From MG2 to MGC:
    MEGACO/1 [125.125.125.111]:55555
    Reply = 50006 {
     Context = 5000 {Modify = A4445}
    }
```

Events 30–32: To complete the call, the MGC sets the Termination at MG1 to SendReceive, and instructs the Gateway to stop the ringback.
Event 30:

```
MGC to MG1:
    MEGACO/1 [123.123.123.4]:55555
    Transaction = 10006 {
      Context = 2000 {
        Modify = A4445 {
           Media {
              Stream = 1 {
                 LocalControl {
                    Mode=SendReceive
                 }
              }
           }
        },
        Modify = A4444 {
           Signals { }
        }
      }
    }
```

Event 31: Ringback is stopped.
Event 32:

```
MG1 to MGC:
    MEGACO/1 [124.124.124.222]:55555
    Reply = 10006 {
        Context = 2000 {Modify = A4445, Modify = A4444}}
```

MEGACO IP PHONE MEDIA GATEWAY

[BELL00][3] specifies an implementation of the Megaco/H.248 Protocol for control of Internet telephones. It is called the Megaco IP Phone Media Gateway, and this section provides a summary of this working draft.

The telephone is a Media Gateway (MG), controlled by the Megaco/H.248 Protocol, with application control intelligence located in the Media Gateway Controller (MGC). The approach makes use of existing protocol features and user interface related packages, and is thus a straight-forward application of the Megaco/H.248 Protocol. The following require-ments in [BELL00] drive the Megaco IP Phone design:

• The Megaco IP Phone must meet the immediate, basic needs of the business user.
• Provide a path for rapid expansion to support sophisticated busi-ness telephony features.
• Allow a wide range of telephones and similar devices to be defined.
• The approach must encompass a simple, minimal design.
• Allow device cost to be appropriate to capabilities provided.
• Packages and termination types must have characteristics that enable reliability.
• The IP Phone MG must meet the appropriate Megaco/H.248 Proto-col, and be a straight-forward application of the Megaco/H.248 Protocol.

As depicted in Figure 10–9, the Megaco IP Phone is organized as a Media Gateway (MG) that consists of a user interface termination and a set of Audio Transducer terminations. Each Audio Transducer termina-

---

[3][BELL00]. Bell, Robert, et al. Megaco IP Phone Media Gateway Application Pro-file, draft-ietf-megaco-ipphone-02.txt, February, 2000.

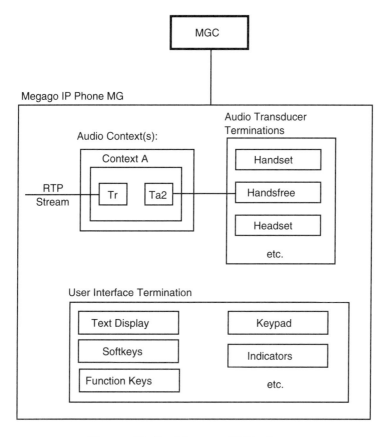

Figure 10–9   Megaco IP Package

tion represents an individually controllable audio input/output element of the telephone device, such as handset, handsfree, headset, etc.

It is also possible to simplify representation of the device by hiding all available audio input/outputs behind a single Audio Transducer termination. For example, the handset, and implement control of multiple real input/outputs locally inside the device.

All non-audio user interface elements are associated with the user interface termination. This special termination includes packages to implement all user interaction with the telephone user interface, including function keys, indicators, the dial pad, etc., as appropriate for the specific device capabilities. This grouping of user interface elements behind a well-known termination simplifies audits to determine actual device configuration, and reduces the number of terminations involved in representing a user interface.

Many Megaco IP Phone MGs may be controlled by a single MGC. This is distinguished from the organization between traditional analog or PBX telephones behind an IP network, where the MGC would control an MG which in turn controls the collection of telephone devices in question. In the case of a Megaco IP Phone MG, the MG directly implements the media terminations like handset, handsfree, and headset, and the user interface. In this case, the Megaco IP Phone itself is the MG.

To provide control of audio paths, audio transducer terminations are manipulated using contexts in the normal way, by sending Add, Move, Subtract and Modify commands addressed to the specific terminations being manipulated. For example, in this figure, creating a context (Context A) containing an RTP termination (Tr) and a handset audio transducer termination (Ta1) creates a voice connection to/from the handset. Moving a handsfree audio transducer termination (Ta2) into the context, and removing the handset, sets up a handsfree conversation.

User input elements, such as keypad or function keys, generate events through Notify commands sent from the user interface termination of the Megaco IP Phone MG to the controlling MGC for handling. These events are defined according to the set of packages supported by the user interface termination of the device.

User output elements such as the text display or Indicators are controlled by signals sent by the MGC, addressed to the user interface termination of the Megaco IP Phone MG, generally as part of a Modify command, using syntax defined in the corresponding package. Since the user interface termination cannot be part of any context, Add, Move, and Subtract commands are not valid.

THE MEGACO MIB

The IETF has a published Management Information Base (MIB). It is available in [AKRA99].[4] Most of the MIB entries are variables in tables, and a few entries are individual scalar variables. The Simple Network Management Protocol (SNMP) is used to support the flow of network management traffic between the MGC and MGs. Conventional SNMP operations are supported such as GETs, SETs, and TRAPs, as shown in Figure 10–10.

---

[4][AKRA99]. Akramovich, Ilya, et al. "Megaco MIB," draft-ietf-megaco-mib-00.txt, October 1999.

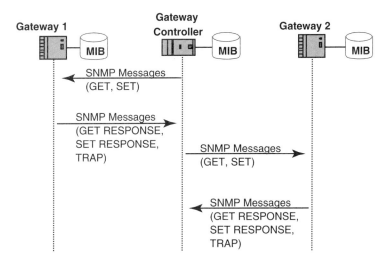

Figure 10–10 SNMP Operations Between Controllers and Gateways

MIB Entries

Figures 10–11(a) and 10–11(b) show the organization of the principal Megaco MIB entries. This section provides a description of each entry in these figures.

Variables

- MediaGatewayNumLinks: Number of Media Gateway links available in this system.
- MediaGatewayMasterMGCaddress: Address of MGC.
- MediaGatewayMaxTerminations: Maximum number of Termination in a Context.
- MediaGatewayActiveContext: Number of active Contexts.

MediaGatewayContextTable. Contains Context information for instances of a Megaco protocol.

- MediaGatewayId: Unique ID (address) of gateway.
- MediaGatewayContextId: The Context ID.
- MediaGatewayNumberofTerminations: Number of Terminations in a Context.

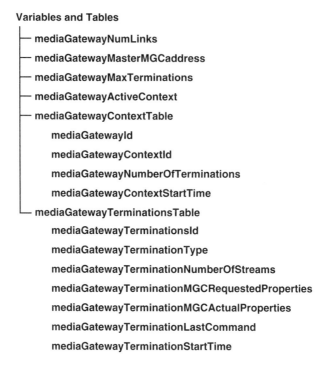

Figure 10–11(a)   Principal Megaco MIB Entries

- MediaGatewayNumberContextStartTime: Date and Time when Context was created.

MediaGatewayTerminationsTable. Contains information about Terminations in a Media Gateway. The list of terminations in this table equals the total number of Terminations for all Contexts in a gateway.

- MediaGatewayTerminationId: ID of the Termination, assigned by the gateway.
- MediaGatewayTerminationType: The Termination type, not defined in the Megaco specification (author has been notified).
- MediaGatewayTerminationNumberOfStreams: The number of streams pertaining to the termination.
- MediaGatewayTerminationMGCRequestedProperties: The list of properties requested by the MGC in the form of Descriptors.
- MediaGatewayTerminationMGCActualProperties: The list of actual Properties for this Termination.

Variables and Tables (continued)

├─ mediaGatewayTable

    mediaGatewayLinkName

    mediaGatewayProtocol

    mediaGatewayAdminStatus

    mediaGatewayOperStatus

    mediaGatewayLastStatusChange

    mediaGatewayNumInMessages

    mediaGatewayNumInOctets

    mediaGatewayNumOutMessages

    mediaGatewayNumOutOctets

    mediaGatewayNumErrors

    mediaGatewayNumTimerRecovery

    mediaGatewayTransportNumLoses

    mediaGatewayTransportNumSwtichover

    mediaGatewayTransportTotalNumAlarms

    mediaGatewayTransportLastEvent

    mediaGatewayTransportLastEventTime

    mediaGatewayResetStatistics

    mediaGatewayLastStatisticsReset

└─ mediaGatewayControllerTable

    mediaGatewayControllerLinkName

    mediaGatewayControllerIndex

    mediaGatewayControllerIPAddress

    mediaGatewayControllerPort

    mediaGatewayControllerOperStatus

Figure 10–11(b)   Principal Megaco MIB Entries (Continued)

- MediaGatewayTerminationLastCommand: The last command that was sent to this Termination.
- MediaGatewayTerminationStartTime: Time and date of this Termination creation.

MediaGatewayTable.   Contains a list of objects about a group of MGCs that share a common signaling link.

- MediaGatewayLinkName: Name of this Media Gateway control group.

- MediaGatewayProtocol: Type of control protocol in use, such as Q.931, Megaco, etc.

- MediaGatewayAdminStatus: Status of group (up or down).

- MediaGatewayOperStatus: Operational status of signaling link (up, down, or unknown).

- MediaGatewayLastStatusChange: Time the link entered it current operational status.

- MediaGatewayNumInMessages: Total number of messages received on the link.

- MediaGatewayNumInOctets: Total number of octets received on the link.

- MediaGatewayNumOutMessages: Total number of messages sent on the link.

- MediaGatewayNumOutOctets: Total number of octets sent on the link.

- MediaGatewayNumErrors: Total number of signal-level errors encountered.

- MediaGatewayNumTimerRecovery: Number of timer recovery events since last reset.

- MediaGatewayTransportNumLosses: Number of times a transport link was lost.

- MediaGatewayTransportNumSwitchover: Number of times signaling was switched to another link.

- MediaGatewayTransportTotalNumAlarms: Total number of alarms issued by for the transport layer.

These variables are a continuation of the description of the **MediaGatewayTable.**

- MediaGatewayTransportLastEvent: Last event reported by transport layer.

- MediaGatewayTransportLastEventTime: The time for the previous event.

- MediaGatewayTransportResetStatistics: Used to reset all statistics for this Media Gateway.

- MediaGatewayLastStatisticsReset: Date and time of the statistics reset.

MediaGatewayControllerTable.   Contains a list of objects an individual MGC.

- MediaGatewayContollerLinkName: The same as MediaGatewayLinkName.
- MediaGatewayContollerIndex: Index number for the MGC entry. Its value is from 1 to the maximum number of controllers per group.
- MediaGatewayContollerIPAddress: IP address of the MGC.
- MediaGatewayContollerPort: TCP port number of the MGC.
- MediaGatewayContollerOperStatus: Status of the transport link to this MGC.

SECURITY SERVICES

The Megaco draft contains some guidelines the use of security services. The idea (identical to MGCP) is that if unauthorized entities could use Megaco, they would be able to set up unauthorized calls, or to interfere with authorized calls. Megaco is supported by security services defined in the IP security architecture in RFC 2401, using either the IP Authentication Header (AH), defined in RFC 2402, or the IP Encapsulating Security Payload (ESP), defined in RFC 2406. However, Megaco defines some additional procedures for the security services. You should check Section 10 of the working draft if you are going to implement IPSec to support Megaco.

SUMMARY

Megaco represents another IP Call Processing Protocol and is now part of the H.xxx specifications, published as H.248. Megaco bears many resemblances to MGCP, but the concepts of Contexts and Terminations are unique to Megaco.

11

The Session Initiation Protocol (SIP)

INTRODUCTION

This chapter describes the Session Initiation Protocol (SIP). The major attributes of SIP are explained, including the roles of servers, clients, and registrars. SIP is published in RFC 2543 [HAND99].[1] In addition to this work, numerous associated and supporting specifications are also being developed, and they will be cited as appropriate.

To understand many of the SIP operations, you should be familiar with the Session Description Protocol (SDP), explained in Chapter 5, and SIP's use of Augmented Backus Naur Form (BNR) explained in Appendix 11A, at the back of this chapter.

SIP FEATURES

SIP is a call processing protocol. Its job is to set up, modify, and tear down sessions between session users. The session may be a multimedia conference, or a point-to-point telephone call. SIP is not dependent upon

---

[1][HAND99] The SIP authors are Mark Handley, Henning Schulzrinne, Eve Schooler, and Jonathan Rosenberg. Their addresses and company associations are available in the final standard (RFC 2543).

any particular conference control protocol, such as H.323, and it does not define any method of transporting the session traffic.

SIP has capabilities other than just signaling operations. It can support sessions via multicast or single unicast, a mesh of unicast sessions, or a combination of these choices. SIP does not act as a Media Gateway, in that it does not transport any media streams.

One of its more distinctive features is its ability to support mobile users. If a user registers his/her location with a SIP server, the system will direct SIP messages to the user, or invoke a proxying operation to another server to a user's current location. The mobile capability is keyed to the individual user, and not the user's terminal (telephone, computer, etc.). This aspect of SIP makes it different from other call control protocols.

More than one server may be able to contact the user. To handle this situation, "forked" messages are sent to multiple servers. The responses are returned to the requesting party in such a manner that the requester can make decisions about the best path for the call.

SIP is an attractive support tool for IP telephony and IP videoconferencing because:

- It can operate as stateless, or stateful. Thus, a stateless implementation provides good scalability, since the servers do not have to maintain information on the call state once the transaction has been processed. Moreover, the stateless approach is very robust, since the server need not remember anything about a call.
- It uses the formats and syntax of HTTP (Hypertext Transfer Protocol), thus providing a convenient way of operating with ongoing browsers.
- The SIP message (the message body) is opaque; it can be of any syntax. Therefore, it can be described in more than one way. As examples, it may be described with the Multipurpose Internet Mail Extension (MIME), or the Extensible Markup Language (XML). It can transport Java, JPEG, etc.
- It identifies a user with a URI (Uniform Resource Identifier), thus providing the user the ability to initiate a call by clicking on a Web link.

THE FIVE MAJOR FEATURES OF SIP

SIP exhibits five major features of establishing and terminating multimedia sessions:

- *User location:* Determination of the end system to be used for communications. In this regard, SIP has capabilities like that of DNS. Actually, it uses DNS to support this feature.

- *User capabilities:* Determination of the media and media parameters to be used. One might think this feature is akin to a media resource reservation protocol, and it is, except SIP merely conveys this information between the interested parties.

- *User availability:* Determination of the willingness of the called party to engage in communications. This feature is similar to conventional signaling protocols such as ISDN's Q.931, SS7's ISUP, and Frame Relay and ATM's switched virtual call services.

- *Call setup:* Establishment of call parameters at both called and calling party. Same as my comments for feature 3.

- *Call handling:* Including transfer and termination of calls. Same as my comments for feature 3.

PROTOCOL PLACEMENT OF SIP

SIP can operate over UDP or TCP. When sent over TCP or UDP, multiple SIP transactions can be carried in a single TCP connection or UDP datagram. UDP datagrams, including all headers, should not be larger than the path maximum transmission unit (MTU) if the MTU is known, or 1500 bytes if the MTU is unknown.

This RFC 2543 rule does not mean that a 1500-byte MTU is the only option. Other MTU sizes are acceptable, depending on the requirements of the underlying protocols, shown in Figure 11–1.

CLARIFICATION OF TERMS

Before proceeding further, it is a good idea to pause and explain some terms and concepts, as defined in RFC 2543.

- *Server:* A server is an application program that accepts requests in order to service requests and sends back responses to those requests. Servers are either proxy, redirect, or user agent servers or registrars.

- *Proxy server:* Acts as both a server and a client for the purpose of making requests on behalf of other clients. Requests are serviced

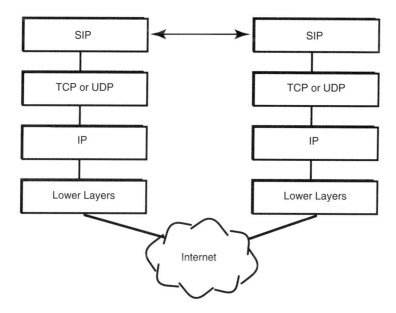

Figure 11–1 **Placement of SIP in the Internet Layered Architecture**

internally or by passing them on to other servers. A proxy interprets and may rewrite a request message before forwarding it.

- *Redirect server:* A server that accepts a SIP request, maps the address new addresses and returns to the client. Unlike a proxy
  server, it does not initiate its own SIP request. Unlike a user agent
  server, it does not accept calls.

- *Registrar:* A registrar is a server that accepts REGISTER requests. A registrar is typically co-located with a proxy or redirect
  server and may offer location services.

- *User agent server (UAS):* A server that contacts the user when a
  SIP request is received and that returns a response on behalf of
  the user.

- *User agent (UA):* An application containing both a user agent
  client and user agent server.

As Figure 11–2 shows, SIP consists of two major components, the
user agent and the network server. The user agent is an end system that
interfaces with the user and acts on behalf of the user. The user agent
consists of two entities, a protocol client, known as the user agent client

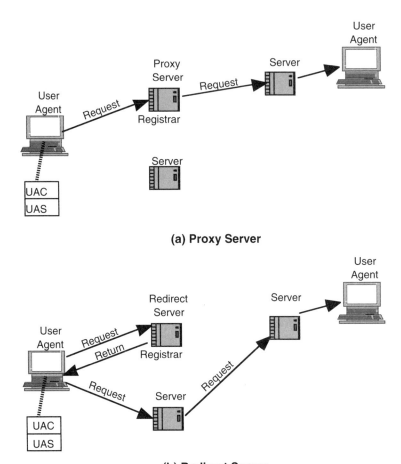

(a) Proxy Server

(b) Redirect Server

Where:
  UAC   User agent client
  UAS   User agent server

Figure 11–2   SIP Clients and Servers

(UAC), and a protocol server, known as the user agent server (UAS). As explained earlier, the UAC initiates the call and the UAS is used to answer the call. Since the user agent contains both a UAC and a UAS, SIP can operate as a peer-to-peer operation while using the client-server model.

The network server in implemented in two types: (a) a proxy server and (b) a redirect server. The SIP proxy server receives a request from a

client and decides which server the request goes to next, if indeed another server is needed. This proxy may send the request to yet another
server, or a redirect server, or a UAS. The response to the request will
travel through the same path as the request, but in reverse order. The
proxy server acts as both a server and a client for making requests on behalf of other clients. A proxy interprets the SIP message, and may
rewrite a request message before forwarding it to another server or a
client.

The redirect server will not forward the request, but will instead direct the client to contact the next server directly; its "redirect" response
contains the address of the next hop server. The SIP message address is
mapped into new addresses and returned to the client. A redirect server
cannot act as a client, in that it does not accept calls.

Another major component of SIP is the registrar. It is usually co-
located with the proxy or redirect server, and may offer location services.
As the name implies, the registrar is used to register SIP parties in a SIP
domain, topics that are discussed later.

SIP may create a forked call introduced earlier, and shown in Figure
11–3. If a server determines that more than one next-hop server may be
able to reach the user, it can fork an incoming request and send it to multiple next-hop servers. The multiple responses are returned to the UAC,
and SIP has rules on merging them.

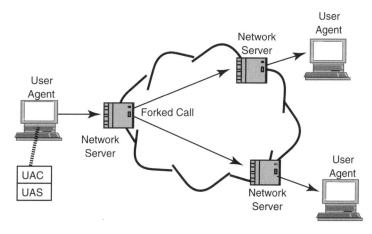

Figure 11–3   Forked Calls

SIP STATUS CODES

Before proceeding further, let us pause and examine the SIP status codes that reside in the SIP messages. Variations of these codes have long been used in Internet protocols, such as Telnet, and FTP. The codes are three digits, and SIP allows the following six values for the first digit:

- 1xx: Informational: Request received, continuing to process the request, and no problems have been encountered.
- 2xx: Success: The action was successfully received, understood, and accepted. This code acts as an ACK.
- 3xx: Redirection: Further action needs to be taken in order to complete the request, which may or may not entail a redirect.
- 4xx: Client Error: The request contains bad syntax or cannot be fulfilled at this server, and the request is rejected.
- 5xx: Server Error: The server failed to fulfill an apparently valid request. All edits on the message passed, but the server failed for internal reasons.
- 6xx: Global Failure: The request cannot be fulfilled at any server.

Table 11–1 shows how SIP establishes rules on the use of these codes by the servers, the registrar, and the user agent server. In effect, the ability or inability to place these codes in the SIP messages defines the properties of the four "servers." The Via header is explained shortly

Table 11–1   SIP Use of the RFC 2543 Status Codes

Property	Redirect Server	Proxy Server	User Agent Server	Registrar
Also acts as an SIP client	no	yes	no	no
Returns 1xxx status	yes	yes	yes	yes
Returns 2xx status	no	yes	yes	yes
Returns 3xx status	yes	yes	yes	yes
Returns 4xx status	yes	yes	yes	yes
Returns 5xx status	yes	yes	yes	yes
Returns 6xx status	no	yes	yes	no
Inserts Via header	no	yes	no	no
Accepts ACK	yes	yes	yes	no

EXAMPLE OF A REQUEST/RESPONSE OPERATION

Figure 11–4 shows an example of a SIP request/response operation. A user at SIP user agent A wants to make a call to another party. Agent A sends out an SIP message to server B (a call invitation) in domain A (event 1). Server A tries to find the called party in domains B and C by forking the request to servers C and D in these domains (events 2 and 3).

In domain C, server D is unable to find the called party, so it returns a error response back through the same route as the original request message (events 4 and 5).

Server C in domain B is able to locate the called party. It sends a handshake message (a request to participate in a session) to the called party's user agent E (event 6). The user agent and server then responds to the invitation (events 7, 8, and 9).

THE SIP METHODS

SIP uses six methods (and message types) for its operations. Methods that are not supported by a proxy or redirect server are treated by that server as if they were an OPTIONS method, and forwarded accordingly. The methods are as follows:

- INVITE: Indicates that a user or server is being invited to participate in a session (a request). The message contains a description of the session, using SDP, and the type of media that is to be used for

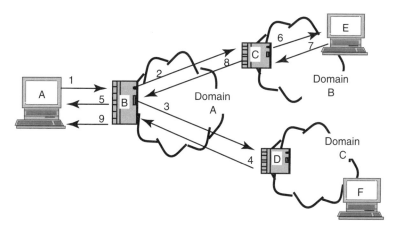

Figure 11–4   A Request/Response Operation

the call, as well as calling and called addresses, user location, caller preferences, and desired features for the response. The user may also indicate a preference for codecs.

- ACK: Used only with INVITE requests, its purpose is to confirm that the client has received a final response to the INVITE request. The ACK may contain information (in the message body) with the final session description to be used by the callee. If there is no such information, the callee uses the session description in the INVITE request.

- OPTIONS: Queries a server about the capabilities of the called party. A called user agent may also send an OPTIONS message reflecting how it would respond to an INVITE if it is busy. A server may respond to this request if believes it can contact the user (for example, the user has recently been active).

- BYE: Issued by user agent to indicate to the server that it wishes to release the call. Either party can issue the BYE. A BYE is forwarded after a party has released the call (hung-up). The party that receives a BYE must cease transmitting streams to the party that issued the BYE request.

- CANCEL: Cancels a pending request, but does not affect or undo a completed request. A user agent client or a proxy client may issue a CANCEL at any time. One obvious use of this request is by a proxy server that has received a response to one of its parallel (forked) searches.

- REGISTER: Used by the client to register an address to a SIP server. SIP permits clients to register from different locations. A user agent may register with a local server on startup by sending an IP multicast to "all SIP servers" (sip.mcast.net, 224.0.1.75). Of course, "all" SIP servers may eventually encompass a lot of machines, so the registration multicast must be restricted to a specific administrative domain.

In addition, a user agent may listen for multicast address 224.0.1.75 in order to glean information about the locations of other users in the domain.

SIP'S USE OF INTERNET RESOURCES

As mentioned earlier, one of the attractive features of SIP is its use of conventional Internet naming and addressing methods. It uses the

Uniform Resource Identifier (URI) to identify the participants in the session.[2] Some people refer to the SIP URI as a SIP address.

As stated earlier, the SIP message syntax also is based on HTTP and SMTP. Thus, SIP integrates well into the client-server world of the Web. This aspect of SIP should not be under emphasized. It allows the pervasive Web to be used as a ready-made platform for the SIP operations.

In addition, since URIs are based on the Domain Name System (DNS), and DNS is used to correlate DNS names to IP addresses, SIP takes advantage of the ongoing Internet naming and addressing architecture.

SIP MESSAGE CODING CONVENTIONS

The SIP message is a request from a client to a server or a response from a server to a client. It takes these forms (and see the appendix at the back of this chapter for a tutorial on how to read SIP messages).

SIP-message = Request | Response

Both messages consist of: (a) start line, (b) one or more header fields (headers), (c) an empty line, (d) carriage-return line-feed (CRLF), indicating the end of the headers, and an optional message-body:

generic-message =   start-line
                    *message-header
                    CRLF
                    [message-body]

start-line =   Request-Line | Status-Line

message-header =   (general-header | request-header | response-header
                    | entity-header)

The start-line is either a Request-Line for a request message, or a Status-Line for a response message, and both are described shortly. The message header varies, depending on the SIP information being con-

---

[2]Tim Berners-Lee, the man behind the invention of the Web, devised the URI, and considers it, in his words, "the most fundamental innovation of the Web." Later, the IETF renamed the URI the URL (L, for Locator). Berners-Lee still prefers the term URI. The IETF considers a URI as a URL. Most people use the two terms synonymously.

veyed. Several headers and several fields for the specific headers are defined, and we will take a look at them later. The message-body is optional.

The request and response message formats are explained in this section. For the request message, it begins with a Request-Line, followed by headers, a CRLF, and an optional message-body. The response message is similar to the request message. It begins with Status-Line, followed by headers, a CRLF, and an optional message-body.

Request =   Request-Line
                    *(general-header | request-header | entity-header)
                    CRLF
                    [message-body]

Response =   Status-Line
                    *(general-header | response-header | entity-header)
                    CRLF
                    [message-body]

The Request-Line begins with a method token, such as INVITE, a single space (SP), the Request-URI (a SIP URI indicating the user or the service to which this request is being addressed; as such, it can be rewritten by proxy servers), an SP (single space), SIP version number, and CRLF. The Response-Line contains the SIP version number, an SP, a status code, an SP, and associated text, and CRLF. Status codes and other information about the SIP request and response messages are covered later.

Request-Line =   Method SP Request-URI SP SIP-Version CRLF
Status-Line =   SIP-version SP Status-Code SP Reason-Phrase
                    CRLF

Figure 11–5 shows an example of how the INVITE message and domain names are used by SIP, and a proxy server. In event 1, the proxy server receives an INVITE message from jgillen@earthlink.net (actually, this message come from a user agent, which is housed at jgillen's host). This server queries a location server to find out more information about the called party, uyless@infoinst.com (event 2).

The location server responds in event 3, and provides a more precise name (and a more precise location, when the name is associated with an IP address). This information is then used by the proxy server to send

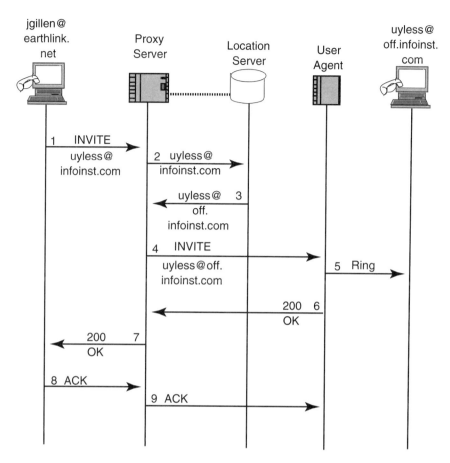

Figure 11–5   Use of INVITE with a Proxy Server

the INVITE (with the more precise name) to the user agent that services the name (uyless@off.infoinst.com). The user agent alerts the called party with a ring in event 5, and sends back a SIP ACK, with a code of 200 (event 6).

The proxy server then sends the ACK to the calling party in event 7. To complete this operation, a SIP ACK message is sent by the calling party (event 8), and relayed to the called party's user agent (event 9).

The main difference between the proxy and the redirect server is shown in Figure 11–6. The redirect server does not forward the message to another server. Rather, it sends back a message to the client, as shown in event 4. The message informs the client that Uyless has moved and can be found at uyless@res.infoinst.com. Thereafter, the operations proceed in a fashion similar to the proxy server scenario.

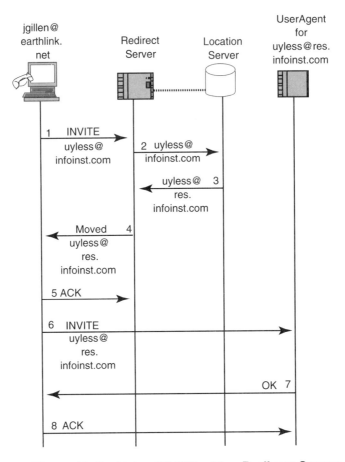

Figure 11–6   Using INVITE with a Redirect Server

THE VIA OPERATION

A party may move between different end systems over time. These locations can be dynamically registered with the SIP server. A location server may also use other protocols such as finger (RFC 1288), rwhois (RFC 2167), LDAP (RFC 1777), etc., to determine the end system where a user might be reachable. A location server can return several locations because the user may be logged in at several hosts simultaneously or because the location server has information not yet received.

As shown in Figure 11–7, if a proxy server forwards a SIP request, it adds itself to the end of the list of forwarders (noted in the Via header described later). This "trace" or "route recording" ensures that replies take

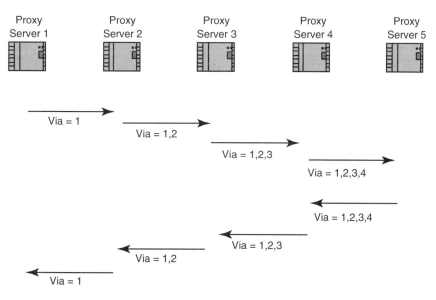

Figure 11-7   Route Tracing with the Via Operation

the same path back to the originator. This operation is important be-cause it ensures correct operation through compliant firewalls and avoids request loops.

On this response path, each host removes its Via identification, so that any internal routing information is hidden from the callee and out-side networks.

SIP HEADERS

Each of the headers in the SIP message contain a number of fields. The contents of these fields are used by the SIP sender to inform the SIP receiver of what the sender is proposing for the session. These fields form the basic architecture and thus warrant our attention. They are listed in Table 11-2 with a general explanation of how they are used in the SIP messages. Subsequent material describes each parameter.

The header fields are similar to HTTP header fields in regard to syntax and semantics. The legend for the table is: o = optional, m = mandatory, – = not applicable, * = header field is needed only if message body is not empty.

The Where column in the table describes the request and response types available for each header field. The legend for this field is: R = used

Table 11–2　SIP Header Fields

Field Name	Where	enc	e-e	ACK	BYE	CAN	INV	OPT	REG
Accept	R		e	—	—	—	o	o	o
Accept	415		e	—	—	—	o	o	o
Accept-Encoding	R		e	—	—	—	o	o	o
Accept-Encoding	415		e	—	—	—	o	o	o
Accept-Language	R		e	—	o	o	o	o	o
Accept-Language	415		e	—	o	o	o	o	o
Allow	200		e	—	—	—	—	m	—
Allow	405		e	o	o	o	o	o	o
Authorization	R		e	o	o	o	o	o	o
Call-ID	gc	n	e	m	m	m	m	m	m
Contact	R		e	—	—	o	o	o	o
Contact	1xx		e	—	—	—	o	o	—
Contact	2xx		e	—	—	—	o	o	o
Contact	3xx		e	—	o	—	o	o	o
Contact	485		e	—	o	—	o	o	o
Content-Encoding	e		e	o	—	—	o	o	o
Content-Length	e		e	o	—	—	o	o	o
Content-Type	e		e	*	—	—	*	*	*
CSeq	gc	n	e	m	m	m	m	m	m
Date	g		e	o	o	o	o	o	o
Encryption	g	n	e	o	o	o	o	o	o
Expires	g		e	—	—	—	o	—	o
From	gc	n	e	m	m	m	m	m	m
Hide	R	n	h	o	o	o	o	o	o
Max-Forwards	R	n	e	o	o	o	o	o	o
Organization	g	c	h	—	—	—	o	o	o
Proxy-Authenticate	407	n	h	o	o	o	o	o	o
Proxy-Authorization	R	n	h	o	o	o	o	o	o
Proxy-Require	R	n	h	o	o	o	o	o	o
Priority	R	c	e	—	—	—	o	—	—
Require	R		e	o	o	o	o	o	o
Retry-After	R	c	e	—	—	—	—	—	o
Retry-After	404, 480, 486, 503, 600, 603	c	e	o	o	o	o	o	o

(continued)

Table 11–2   SIP Header Fields (*continued*)

Field Name	Where	enc	e-e	ACK	BYE	CAN	INV	OPT	REG
Response-Key	R	c	e	—	o	o	o	o	o
Record-Route	R		h	o	o	o	o	o	o
Record-Route	2xx		h	o	o	o	o	o	o
Route	R		h	—	o	o	o	o	o
Server	r	c	e	o	o	o	o	o	o
Subject	R	c	e	—	—	—	o	—	—
Time-stamp	g		e	o	o	o	o	o	o
To	gc(1)	n	e	m	m	m	m	m	m
Unsupported	420		e	o	o	o	o	o	o
User-Agent	g	c	e	o	o	o	o	o	o
Via	gc(2)	n	e	m	m	m	m	m	m
Warning	r		e	o	o	o	o	o	o
WWW-Authenticate	401	c	e	o	o	o	o	o	o

in requests, r = used in responses, numeric value = status codes, g = general header, e = entity header, c = field is copied from the request to the response.

The enc column describes whether this message header field can be encrypted end-to-end. The legend for this field is: n = must not be encrypted, c = should be encrypted. The e-e column is: e = end-to-end, h = hop-by-hop.

This section provides an over view of the functions of these fields.

- *Accept:* Indicates what media types are acceptable in a SIP response, such as html, private, etc. Used only with INVITE, OPTIONS, and REGISTER request methods.
- *Accept-Encoding:* Restricts the content-codings that are in the SIP response. Refer to the content-encoding header field.
- *Accept-Language:* Used to allow the client to indicate to the server in which language it would prefer to receive information.
- *Allow:* Lists the set of methods supported by the resource identified by the Request-URI. It is used by the recipient to restrict methods associated with the resource. Status code 405 (method not allowed) must contain this header field.
- *Authorization:* Used by user agent to authenticate itself with a server. Usually occurs after receiving a 401 response from the

server. The field contains the necessary credentials and authentication information to satisfy the authorization challenge.

- *Call-ID:* Uniquely identifies a particular SIP invitation or all registrations for a specific client. A multimedia conference results in several calls with different call-IDs. The REGISTER and OPTIONS methods use this parameter to match requests and responses.

- *Contact:* This parameter provides a URI where the user can be reached for further communications. SIP defines several rules for using the contact parameter; they are beyond this general tutorial, and I refer you to Section 6.13 of the SIP specification.

- *Content-Encoding:* This field is used as a modifier to the "media-type." It indicates what additional content codings have been applied to the entity-body, and therefore what decoding mechanisms must be applied to obtain the media-type referenced by the content-type field.

- *Content-Length:* This field indicates the length of the message-body, in decimal number of octets.

- *Content-Type:* This field indicates the media type of the message-body, such as SDP, HTML, etc.

- *Cseq:* This field, the command sequence, contains the request method (for example, INVITE), and a sequence number (unique within the call-ID).

- *Date:* This field indicates the time when the SIP request or response message was first sent. Any retransmissions must have the same field in the message.

- *Encryption:* Encryption is optional in SIP. If used, this field specifies that the SIP traffic has been encrypted.

- *Expires:* This field is used to make sure a SIP message does not stay in the system indefinitely. It contains date and time values. Upon examination at a node, when these values are matched or exceeded in relation to a network wall clock, the message content expires.

- *From:* This field indicates the initiator of the SIP request message. It is copied from the request to the response by the server.

- *Hide:* This field indicates that the client wants the path information in the Via header field to be hidden from subsequent proxy servers and user agents.

- *Max-Forwards:* It is possible to limit the number of proxies or gateways that forward requests to subsequent severs. This field supports this service; it is similar to a hop count limit in IP operations.

- *Organization:* This field identifies the organization of the entity issuing the request or response. It can be used by the user, the user agent, or a proxy server.

- *Proxy-Authenticate:* This field is used to support a proxy authentication operation. Its value is a challenge that identifies the authentication scheme, and the parameters that are applicable to the proxy for the operation.

- *Proxy-Authorization:* This field is used by the client to identify itself to a proxy which requires authentication of the user. Its contents are the credentials containing the authentication information of the user agent for the proxy.

- *Proxy-Require:* This field sets the requirements at the proxy server for SIP features desired by the client. If the server cannot support a feature, it must return a negative acknowledgment to the client.

- *Priority:* As its name implies, this field indicates the priority of the request, from the standpoint of the SIP user. It can indicate four levels of priority: (a) emergency, (b) urgent, (c) normal, and (d) nonurgent.

- *Require:* The client uses this field to inform the user agent server of the SIP options that the client expects the server to support. The server must respond with a negative acknowledgment is the option is not supported (a status code of 420: bad extension).

- *Retry-After:* In the event that a service is configured, but unavailable (for example, a called party declines the call due to being in a meeting), this field is used to inform the requesting client when the service will be available again.

- *Response-Key:* The client uses this field to request the key that the called user agent should use to encrypt the response message.

- *Record-Route:* The field is used to ensure SIP traffic follows a specific path through the network. It is created as each proxy server receives and relays the message; the server adds its Request-URI to a list in the message. The responding server must copy this field unchanged into the response message.

- *Route:* This field determines the route taken by a SIP request message. It is similar to the IP source routing option in that each node that receives the message removes the first entry in a list, and then sends (proxies) the request to this "name-addr."

- *Server:* This field contains information about the software used by the server to process the message.

- *Subject:* This field indicates the nature of the call; that is, its subject.

- *Time-stamp:* The field indicates when the client sent the SIP request message to the server. The server must echo this information back to the client, and it may also indicate how much time has elapsed since it received the request. This feature is useful for computing round-trip time and making appropriate adjustments to the retransmission timers.

- *To:* This field identifies the recipient of the request message (name-addr or addr-spec).

- *Unsupported:* The server uses this field to indicate features that it does not support.

- *User-Agent:* This field contains information about the client's user agent originating the response.

- *Via:* This field indicates the path that the request has traversed so far, and used to make certain the response takes the same path as the request. The client originating the request inserts into the request a Via field containing its host name or network address and the port number at which it wishes to receive responses. Each subsequent proxy server that forwards the request adds its own additional Via field before any existing Via fields.

- *Warning:* This field supplements the SIP codes, and is used to convey additional information about the status of a response.

- *WWW-Authenticate:* This field is used to support authentication, and contains a least one challenge indicating the authentication scheme, and applicable parameters.

STRUCTURE FOR SIP MESSAGE

Figure 11–8 shows the general structure for the SIP message. The fields in this example are coded to give you an idea of the general syntax of the message; they do not adhere to the specific rules for coding SIP messages. These rules are covered later in this chapter and in the appendix at the back of this chapter.

The message begins with the first line, followed by headers, and then a message body. I have placed some of the parameters in this exam-

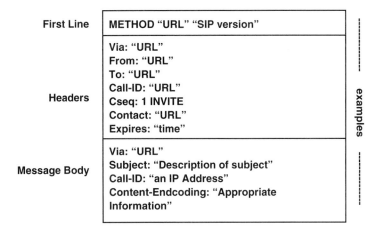

Figure 11–8   General Structure of the SIP Message

ple that were discussed in the previous section. The "METHOD" field is INVITE, REGISTER, BYE; that is, one of the SIP methods. If the message is a request, the first line of the message is a request line. It contains (in this order):

Method SP Request-URI SP SIP-version, CRLF

If the message is a response (not shown in this figure), the first line of the message is called a status line, and it contains (in this order):

SIP version, SP Status-Code SP Reason-Phase CRLF

The fields in the first line of the request and response lines are discussed next.

The first line of the SIP REGISTER message and the common headers are shown in Figure 11–9. The following header fields and parameters are the most important.

The From header field contains the address-of-record of the person responsible for the registration. For first-party registration, it is identical to the To header field value.

The Request-URI names the destination of the registration request, i.e., the domain of the registrar. The user name must be empty. The domains in the Request-URI and the To header field usually have the same value. The REGISTER request is no longer forwarded once it has

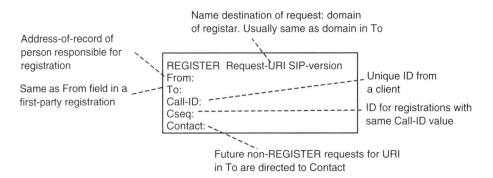

Figure 11-9   Key Message Contents for the REGISTER Method

reached the server whose authoritative domain is the one listed in the Request-URI.

All registrations from a client use the same Call-ID header value, at least within the same reboot cycle. Registrations with the same Call-ID MUST have increasing Cseq header values. However, the server does not reject out-of-order requests. The request MAY contain a Contact header field; future non-REGISTER requests for the URI given in the To header field is directed to the address(es) given in the Contact header.

EXAMPLES OF SIP MESSAGE EXCHANGES

This part of the chapter provides some examples of message exchanges between SIP clients and servers. These examples are sourced from section 16 of RFC 2543, and section 16 of this RFC provides more examples.

An Initial Registration

In Figure 11-10, a user at host saturn.bell-tel.com registers on startup, via multicast, with the local SIP server named bell-tel.com. The user agent on saturn expects to receive SIP requests on UDP port 3890. The registration expires after two hours. Any future invitations for watson@bell-tel.com arriving at sip.bell-tel.com will now be redirected to watson@saturn.bell-tel.com, UDP port 3890.

Figure 11–10   The Registration Operation

Updating a Registration

If the user Watson wants to be reached elsewhere, say, an on-line service he uses while traveling, he must update his reservation after first canceling any existing locations. The message exchanges for this operation are shown in Figure 11–11. Hereafter, the server will forward any request for Watson to the server at example.com, using the Request-URI tawatson@example.com. For the server at example.com to reach Watson, he will need to send a REGISTER there, or inform the server of his current location through some other means.

Third-Party Registration

It is possible to use third-party registration. In Figure 11–12, the secretary jon.diligent registers his boss, T. Watson. The request could be sent to either the registrar at bell-tel.com or the server at example.com. In the latter case, the server at example.com would proxy the request to the address indicated in the Request-URI. Then, the Max-Forwards header could be used to restrict the registration to that server.

An Invitation to a Multicast Conference

The next example in Figure 11–13 shows the operations for an invitation to a multicast conference. The first example invites schooler@cal-tech.edu to a multicast session. All examples use the Session Description Protocol (SDP) (RFC 2327) as the session description format.

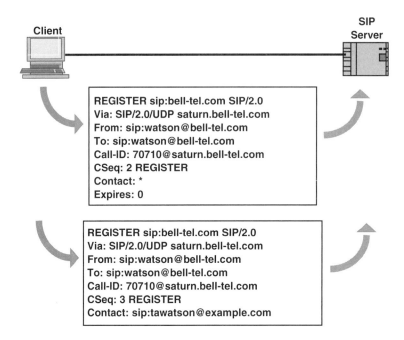

REGISTER sip:bell-tel.com SIP/2.0
Via: SIP/2.0/UDP saturn.bell-tel.com
From: sip:watson@bell-tel.com
To: sip:watson@bell-tel.com
Call-ID: 70710@saturn.bell-tel.com
CSeq: 2 REGISTER
Contact: *
Expires: 0

REGISTER sip:bell-tel.com SIP/2.0
Via: SIP/2.0/UDP saturn.bell-tel.com
From: sip:watson@bell-tel.com
To: sip:watson@bell-tel.com
Call-ID: 70710@saturn.bell-tel.com
CSeq: 3 REGISTER
Contact: sip:tawatson@example.com

Figure 11–11   Protocol Exchange to be Reached "Else-where"

The From/To request headers state that the request was initiated by mjh@isi.edu and addressed to schooler@caltech.edu. The Via fields list the hosts along the path from invitation initiator (the last element of the list) towards the callee. In the example above, the message was last multicast to the administratively scoped group 239.128.16.254 with a time to

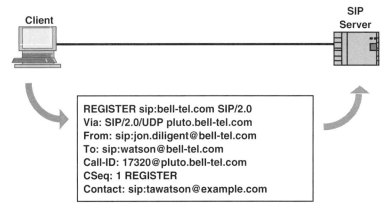

REGISTER sip:bell-tel.com SIP/2.0
Via: SIP/2.0/UDP pluto.bell-tel.com
From: sip:jon.diligent@bell-tel.com
To: sip:watson@bell-tel.com
Call-ID: 17320@pluto.bell-tel.com
CSeq: 1 REGISTER
Contact: sip:tawatson@example.com

Figure 11–12   A Third Party Registration

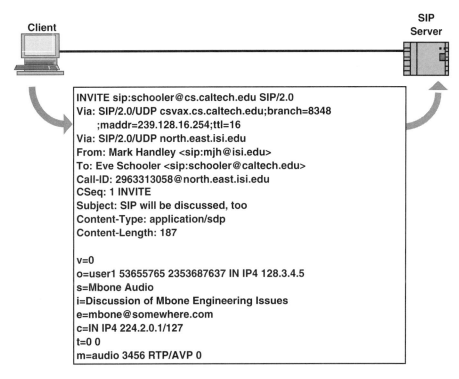

```
INVITE sip:schooler@cs.caltech.edu SIP/2.0
Via: SIP/2.0/UDP csvax.cs.caltech.edu;branch=8348
    ;maddr=239.128.16.254;ttl=16
Via: SIP/2.0/UDP north.east.isi.edu
From: Mark Handley <sip:mjh@isi.edu>
To: Eve Schooler <sip:schooler@caltech.edu>
Call-ID: 2963313058@north.east.isi.edu
CSeq: 1 INVITE
Subject: SIP will be discussed, too
Content-Type: application/sdp
Content-Length: 187

v=0
o=user1 53655765 2353687637 IN IP4 128.3.4.5
s=Mbone Audio
i=Discussion of Mbone Engineering Issues
e=mbone@somewhere.com
c=IN IP4 224.2.0.1/127
t=0 0
m=audio 3456 RTP/AVP 0
```

Figure 11–13   Invitation to a Multicast Conference

live of 16 from the host csvax.cs.caltech.edu. The second Via header field indicates that it was originally sent from the host north.east.isi.edu. The Request-URI indicates that the request is currently being addressed to schooler@cs.caltech.edu, the local address that csvax looked up for the callee. In this case, the session description is using the Session Description Protocol (SDP), as stated in the Content-Type header.

The header is terminated by an empty line and is followed by a body containing the session description.

The Alerting/Ringing Operation

In Figure 11–14, the called user agent, directly or indirectly through proxy servers, indicates that it is alerting ("ringing") the called party.

Responding to an Invitation

A response to the invitation is shown in Figure 11–15. The first line may be added by the invited user's agent if required. The Call-ID is

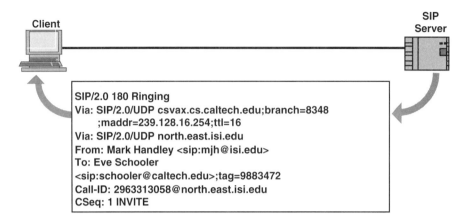

Figure 11–14   Indication that Called Party is Alerted

taken directly from the original request, along with the remaining fields of the request message. The original sense of From field is preserved (i.e., it is the session initiator). In addition, the Contact header gives details of the host where the user was located, or alternatively the relevant proxy contact point which should be reachable from the caller's host.

Confirming the Invitation

In Figure 11–16, the caller confirms the invitation by sending an ACK request to the location named in the Contact header.

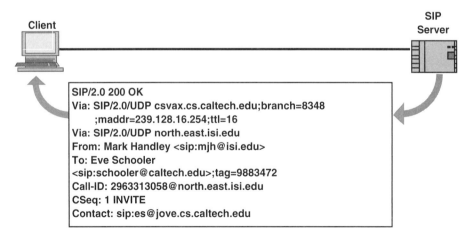

Figure 11–15   Response to the Invitation (for Invited User's Agent)

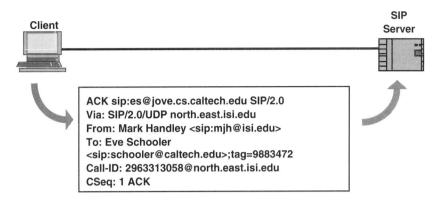

Figure 11–16   Caller confirms the invitation.

SIP Connection Through Two Proxy Servers

Figure 11–17 shows the message exchanges for a successful connection between two users (clients) through two proxy servers. The figure is drawn differently from previous examples. It is not practical to show the SIP messages in one figure since there are 23 of them. For these next examples, the messages are included as part of the text. In addition, these message flows are sourced from [JOHN00],[3] which contains a wealth of SIP message flow examples. The events for this operation are numbered in the figure.

Also please note that this example has a discrepancy in the "Content-Length" field. Sometimes the authors code this field as 147 and other times as 132. This writer counted 133 characters in the Content. I have contacted the authors about this discrepancy.

Client A wishes to set up a connection to client B, and sends an INVITE message to proxy server 1. For this example, we assume A did not furnish authorization information needed by the proxy, so the proxy sends back to client A a 407 (Proxy-Authenticate) message. The user responds correctly (event 4) with the challenge information. In the INVITE message, proxy 1 inserts a Record-Route header to ensure this informa-

[3][JOHN00]. Johnston, Alan et al. "SIP Telephony Call Flow Examples," draft-ietf-sip-call-flows-00.txt, March 2000. This working draft contains many examples beyond what I have shown here. For example, several scenarios are provided to show how SIP can be used to support call features, such as call waiting. I also include more examples from this draft in Chapter 12.

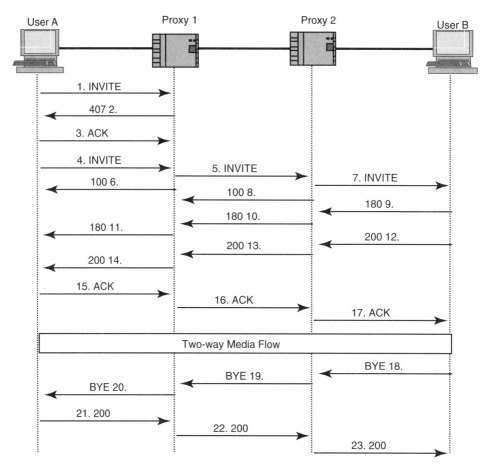

**Figure 11–17   SIP Connection Through Two Proxy Servers
[JOHN00]**

tion is present in all message exchanges. In turn, proxy 2 inserts its record into this header (in event 7). The ACKs and BYEs in this example contain this header. In event 9, a tag is inserted by B since the INVITE message contained more than one Via header, and may be part of a forked operation. The tag provides an unambiguous identification of the entity that returned the reply.

The SIP Messages.   This section contains the SIP messages that are exchanged in the example in Figure 11–17. Port number 5060 is used for this flow at all nodes. The following identifications are used with these examples.

- User A: BigGuy<sip:UserA@here.com>
- User B: LittleGuy<UserB@there.com>
- Proxy 1: ss1.wcom.com
- Proxy 2: ss2.wcom.com

Event 1: The SIP message for this event is coded as shown below. Several observations can be made about this message. First, the URI in the first line identifies Proxy server 1: UserB@ss.1.wcom.com. In accordance with SIP conventions, the host part of the Request-URI typically agrees with one of the host names of the receiving server.

The To field in the request contains the address of the callee: LittleGuy<sip:UserB@there.com. The From field contains the address of the caller: BigGuy<sip.UserA@here.com. The Contact header contains the address where the caller would like to be contacted for transactions from the callee back to the caller. In this example, it is the same address as the From field.

The SDP fields (v, o, s, c, t, m, and a) describe the nature of the session, as viewed by its owner, User A. Again, you may wish to refer to the SDP material in Chapter 5 during the discussion of this example.

```
INVITE sip:UserB@ss1.wcom.com SIP/2.0
Via: SIP/2.0/UDP here.com:5060
From: BigGuy <sip:UserA@here.com>
To: LittleGuy <sip:UserB@there.com>
Call-ID: 12345600@here.com
CSeq: 1 INVITE
Contact: BigGuy <sip:UserA@here.com>
Content-Type: application/sdp
Content-Length: 147


v=0
o=UserA 2890844526 2890844526 IN IP4 here.com
s=Session SDP
c=IN IP4 100.101.102.103
t=0 0
m=audio 49170 RTP/AVP 0
a=rtpmap:0 PCMU/8000
```

Event 2: The server responds by denying the invitation. It wishes User A to authenticate itself before it processes the INVITE. Thus, is sends back a client error code, 407 stating that authorization is required. The field value contains the information needed to effect the challenge and response. The nonce is the value the user must use in conjunction with the MD5 algorithm (and the user's private key) to compute a digital signature.

Many of the fields in the response are the same values as those in the request. The responder must copy the To, From, Call-ID, CSeq and Via fields from the request.

```
SIP/2.0 407 Proxy Authorization Required
Via: SIP/2.0/UDP here.com:5060
From: BigGuy <sip:UserA@here.com>
To: LittleGuy <sip:UserB@there.com>
Call-ID: 12345600@here.com
CSeq: 1 INVITE
Proxy-Authenticate: Digest realm="MCI WorldCom SIP",
domain="wcom.com", nonce="wf84f1ceczx41ae6cbe5aea9c8e88d359",
opaque="", stale="FALSE", algorithm="MD5"
Content-Length: 0
```

Event 3: User A acknowledges the challenge.

```
ACK sip:UserB@ss1.wcom.com SIP/2.0
Via: SIP/2.0/UDP here.com:5060
From: BigGuy <sip:UserA@here.com>
To: LittleGuy <sip:UserB@there.com>
Call-ID: 12345600@here.com
CSeq: 1 INVITE
Content-Length: 0
```

Event 4: The user responds to the server's challenge by resending the INVITE containing the requested authentication information. The response of "42ce3cef44b22f50c6a6071bc8" is User A's computation of MD5 and the user's private key. The server now uses User A's public key and MD5 to determine if the response is valid.

This INVITE uses a different CALL-ID value, and this value will be used hereafter (events 4–23). Also note that the value of CSeq is the same for all the messages (events 1–24). SIP's rules on the CSeq require that a CSeq header field in a request contains the request method and a sequence number chosen by the requesting client, unique within a single value of Call-ID.

The SDP code for this event is the same as for the INVITE in event 1.

```
INVITE sip:UserB@ss1.wcom.com SIP/2.0
Via: SIP/2.0/UDP here.com:5060
```

```
From: BigGuy <sip:UserA@here.com>
To: LittleGuy <sip:UserB@there.com>
Call-ID: 12345601@here.com
CSeq: 1 INVITE
Contact: BigGuy <sip:UserA@here.com>
Authorization:Digest username="UserA", realm="MCI WorldCom SIP",
nonce="wf84f1ceczx41ae6cbe5aea9c8e88d359", opaque="",
uri="sip:ss1.wcom.com", response="42ce3cef44b22f50c6a6071bc8"
Content-Type: application/sdp
Content-Length: 147


v=0
o=UserA 2890844526 2890844526 IN IP4 here.com
s=Session SDP
c=IN IP4 100.101.102.103
t=0 0
m=audio 49170 RTP/AVP 0
a=rtpmap:0 PCMU/8000
```

Event 5: In this event, Proxy 1 accepts the credentials from User A and sends the INVITE message on to Proxy 2. This example does not show authentication occurring between the two Proxies. It assumed this authentication has occurred earlier. The two Via lines trace the route of the INVITE from User A to Proxy 1. Also, notice that the Request-URI now identifies the recipient of the INVITE message, Proxy 2 (ss2.wcom.com).

A new field is added to this message, the Record-Route. It is added to a request by any proxy (Proxy 1, in this example) that insists on being in the path of subsequent requests for the same call leg. SIP requires that the calling user agent client copy the Record-Route header into a Route header field of subsequent requests within the same call leg, reversing the order of requests, so that the first entry is closest to the user agent client. We will not see this rule executed in this example, since the calling UAC makes no further requests.

```
INVITE sip:UserB@ss2.wcom.com SIP/2.0
Via: SIP/2.0/UDP ss1.wcom.com:5060
Via: SIP/2.0/UDP here.com:5060
Record-Route: <sip:UserB@ss1.wcom.com>
From: BigGuy <sip:UserA@here.com>
To: LittleGuy <sip:UserB@there.com>
Call-ID: 12345601@here.com
CSeq: 1 INVITE
Contact: BigGuy <sip:UserA@here.com>
Content-Type: application/sdp
Content-Length: 132
```

```
v=0
o=UserA 2890844526 2890844526 IN IP4 here.com
s=Session SDP
c=IN IP4 100.101.102.103
t=0 0
m=audio 49170 RTP/AVP 0
a=rtpmap:0 PCMU/8000
```

Event 6: Proxy 1 responds to INVITE in event 4 by sending a Trying (100) message to User A. This message simply states that an unspecified action is being taken by the proxy for this call. In this example, Proxy 1 is likely consulting a DNS server to find an IP address for User B.

```
SIP/2.0 100 Trying
Via: SIP/2.0/UDP here.com:5060
From: BigGuy <sip:UserA@here.com>
To: LittleGuy <sip:UserB@there.com>
Call-ID: 12345601@here.com
CSeq: 1 INVITE
Content-Length: 0
```

Event 7: Upon locating the address, Proxy 1 will use IP to forward the INVITE to Proxy 2, the best-known server for User B. Another Via record has been added. In addition, the Record-Route field has ss1.wcom.com added as well.

```
INVITE sip:UserB@there.com SIP/2.0
Via: SIP/2.0/UDP ss2.wcom.com:5060
Via: SIP/2.0/UDP ss1.wcom.com:5060
Via: SIP/2.0/UDP here.com:5060
Record-Route: <sip:UserB@ss2.wcom.com>,<sip:UserB@ss1.wcom.com>
From: BigGuy <sip:UserA@here.com>
To: LittleGuy <sip:UserB@there.com>
Call-ID: 12345601@here.com
CSeq: 1 INVITE
Contact: BigGuy <sip:UserA@here.com>
Content-Type: application/sdp
Content-Length: 132


v=0
o=UserA 2890844526 2890844526 IN IP4 here.com
s=Session SDP
c=IN IP4 100.101.102.103
t=0 0
m=audio 49170 RTP/AVP 0
a=rtpmap:0 PCMU/8000
```

Event 8: Proxy 2 must respond to event 7. It returns a Trying (100) message to Proxy 1.

```
SIP/2.0 100 Trying
Via: SIP/2.0/UDP ss1.wcom.com:5060
Via: SIP/2.0/UDP here.com:5060
From: BigGuy <sip:UserA@here.com>
To: LittleGuy <sip:UserB@there.com>
Call-ID: 12345601@here.com
CSeq: 1 INVITE
Content-Length: 0
```

Event 9: The UAC for User B informs Proxy 2 that its INVITE in event 8 was resulted in alerting User B with a ring. Therefore it sends a Ringing (180) message back in this event. The callee can accept, redirect, or reject the call. In all of these cases, it formulates a response, a Ringing in this example. The response message contains the To, From, Call-ID, CSeq and Via fields from the request message.

The only significant aspect of this message that we have not examined thus far is the tag in the To line. SIP establishes these rules for the tag (and several others, that are beyond this general description):

The responding UAS adds the tag parameter to the To field in the response if the request contains more than one Via header field. Since a request from a UAC may fork and arrive at multiple hosts, the tag parameter serves to distinguish, at the UAC, multiple responses from different UASs. The tag value remains in all subsequent messages for this call leg (events 9–23).

Although not shown in this example, the UAS may also add a Contact header field in the response. It contains an address where the callee would like to be contacted for subsequent transactions, including the ACK for the current INVITE. The UAS stores the values of the To and From field, including any tags. These become the local and remote addresses of the call leg, respectively.

```
SIP/2.0 180 Ringing
Via: SIP/2.0/UDP ss2.wcom.com:5060
Via: SIP/2.0/UDP ss1.wcom.com:5060
Via: SIP/2.0/UDP here.com:5060
From: BigGuy <sip:UserA@here.com>
To: LittleGuy <sip:UserB@there.com>;tag=314159
Call-ID: 12345601@here.com
CSeq: 1 INVITE
Content-Length: 0
```

Event 10: The Ringing message is conveyed to Proxy 1.

```
SIP/2.0 180 Ringing
Via: SIP/2.0/UDP ss1.wcom.com:5060
Via: SIP/2.0/UDP here.com:5060
From: BigGuy <sip:UserA@here.com>
To: LittleGuy <sip:UserB@there.com>;tag=314159
Call-ID: 12345601@here.com
CSeq: 1 INVITE
Content-Length: 0
```

Event 11: The Ringing message is conveyed to User A.

```
SIP/2.0 180 Ringing
Via: SIP/2.0/UDP here.com:5060
From: BigGuy <sip:UserA@here.com>
To: LittleGuy <sip:UserB@there.com>;tag=314159
Call-ID: 12345601@here.com
CSeq: 1 INVITE
Content-Length: 0
```

Event 12: The callee UAS returns a 200 OK message. The notable aspects to this message are found in the SDP coding. The field and attribute names represent User B's profile for the session, including its address (110.111.112.113), and the port number for the session (3456). The audio profile is the same as that of User A.

```
SIP/2.0 200 OK
Via: SIP/2.0/UDP ss2.wcom.com:5060
Via: SIP/2.0/UDP ss1.wcom.com:5060
Via: SIP/2.0/UDP here.com:5060
Record-Route: <sip:UserB@ss2.wcom.com>,<sip:UserB@ss1.wcom.com>
From: BigGuy <sip:UserA@here.com>
To: LittleGuy <sip:UserB@there.com>;tag=314159
Call-ID: 12345601@here.com
CSeq: 1 INVITE
Contact: LittleGuy <sip:UserB@there.com>
Content-Type: application/sdp
Content-Length: 134

v=0
o=UserB 2890844527 2890844527 IN IP4 there.com
s=Session SDP
c=IN IP4 110.111.112.113
t=0 0
m=audio 3456 RTP/AVP 0
```

```
a=rtpmap:0 PCMU/8000
```

Event 13: The information from event 12 is relayed to Proxy 1.

```
SIP/2.0 200 OK
Via: SIP/2.0/UDP ss1.wcom.com:5060
Via: SIP/2.0/UDP here.com:5060
Record-Route: <sip:UserB@ss2.wcom.com>,<sip:UserB@ss1.wcom.com>
From: BigGuy <sip:UserA@here.com>
To: LittleGuy <sip:UserB@there.com>;tag=314159
Call-ID: 12345601@here.com
CSeq: 1 INVITE
Contact: LittleGuy <sip:UserB@there.com>
Content-Type: application/sdp
Content-Length: 134


v=0
o=UserB 2890844527 2890844527 IN IP4 there.com
s=Session SDP
c=IN IP4 110.111.112.113
t=0 0
m=audio 3456 RTP/AVP 0
a=rtpmap:0 PCMU/8000
```

Event 14: The information from events 12 and 13 is relayed to the UAC at User A. The following operations now take place, depending upon the individual circumstances of the call.

Although not shown in the example, multiple responses may arrive at the calling UAC for a single INVITE request, due to a forking proxy. Once again, the tag parameter becomes important. Each response is distinguished by the tag parameter in the To header field, and each represents a distinct call leg.

The caller may choose to acknowledge or terminate the call with each responding UAS. To acknowledge, it sends an ACK request, and to terminate it sends a BYE request. The To header field in the ACK or BYE MUST be the same as the To field in the 200 response, including any tag. The From header field must be the same as the From header field in the 200 (OK) response, including any tag. The Request-URI of the ACK or BYE request may be set to whatever address was found in the Contact header field in the 200 (OK) response, if present.

These are only part of the rules for how the tag is handled at the caller. There are more rules, beyond our scope, and you can read Section 11.3 of RFC 2543 if you need more detailed information.

```
SIP/2.0 200 OK
Via: SIP/2.0/UDP here.com:5060
Record-Route: <sip:UserB@ss2.wcom.com>,<sip:UserB@ss1.wcom.com>
From: BigGuy <sip:UserA@here.com>
To: LittleGuy <sip:UserB@there.com>;tag=314159
Call-ID: 12345601@here.com
CSeq: 1 INVITE
Contact: LittleGuy <sip:UserB@there.com>
Content-Type: application/sdp
Content-Length: 134


v=0
o=UserB 2890844527 2890844527 IN IP4 there.com
s=Session SDP
c=IN IP4 110.111.112.113
t=0 0
m=audio 3456 RTP/AVP 0
a=rtpmap:0 PCMU/8000
```

In events 15, 16, and 17, User A and the proxies acknowledge the
events in 12, 13, and 14. The messages for these exchanges are shown
below.

Event 15:

```
ACK sip:UserB@ss1.wcom.com SIP/2.0
Via: SIP/2.0/UDP here.com:5060
Route: <sip:UserB@ss2.wcom.com>,<sip:UserB@there.com>
From: BigGuy <sip:UserA@here.com>
To: LittleGuy <sip:UserB@there.com>;tag=314159
Call-ID: 12345601@here.com
CSeq: 1 ACK
Content-Length: 0
```

Event 16:

```
ACK sip:UserB@ss2.wcom.com SIP/2.0
Via: SIP/2.0/UDP ss1.wcom.com:5060
Via: SIP/2.0/UDP here.com:5060
Route: <sip:UserB@there.com>
From: BigGuy <sip:UserA@here.com>
To: LittleGuy <sip:UserB@there.com>;tag=314159
Call-ID: 12345601@here.com
CSeq: 1 ACK
```

Event 17:

```
ACK sip: UserB@there.com SIP/2.0
Via: SIP/2.0/UDP ss2.wcom.com:5060
Via: SIP/2.0/UDP ss1.wcom.com:5060
Via: SIP/2.0/UDP here.com:5060
From: BigGuy <sip:UserA@here.com>
To: LittleGuy <sip:UserB@there.com>;tag=314159
Call-ID: 12345601@here.com
CSeq: 1 ACK
```

The two users now have two-way connection between them. The are exchanging audio calls over packet networks. There is no intervening telephone network involved.

For events 18–23 User B goes off hook, which precipitates the exchange of the BYE message and the 200 messages. The coding for these messages are shown below.

Event 18:

```
BYE sip: UserA@ss2.wcom.com SIP/2.0
Via: SIP/2.0/UDP there.com:5060
Route: <sip:UserA@ss1.wcom.com>,<sip:UserA@here.com>
From: LittleGuy <sip:UserB@there.com>;tag=314159
To: BigGuy <sip:UserA@here.com>
Call-ID: 12345601@here.com
CSeq: 1 BYE
Content-Length: 0
```

Event 19:

```
BYE sip: UserA@ss1.wcom.com SIP/2.0
Via: SIP/2.0/UDP ss2.wcom.com:5060
Via: SIP/2.0/UDP there.com:5060
Route: <sip:UserA@here.com>
From: LittleGuy <sip:UserB@there.com>;tag=314159
To: BigGuy <sip:UserA@here.com>
Call-ID: 12345601@here.com
CSeq: 1 BYE
```

Event 20:

```
BYE sip: UserA@here.com SIP/2.0
Via: SIP/2.0/UDP ss1.wcom.com:5060
```

```
Via: SIP/2.0/UDP ss2.wcom.com:5060
Via: SIP/2.0/UDP there.com:5060
From: LittleGuy <sip:UserB@there.com>;tag=314159
To: BigGuy <sip:UserA@here.com>
Call-ID: 12345601@here.com
CSeq: 1 BYE
Content-Length: 0
```

Event 21:

```
SIP/2.0 200 OK
Via: SIP/2.0/UDP ss1.wcom.com:5060
Via: SIP/2.0/UDP ss2.wcom.com:5060
Via: SIP/2.0/UDP there.com:5060
From: LittleGuy <sip:UserB@there.com>;tag=314159
To: BigGuy <sip:UserA@here.com>
Call-ID: 12345601@here.com
CSeq: 1 BYE
Content-Length: 0
```

Event 22:

```
SIP/2.0 200 OK
Via: SIP/2.0/UDP ss2.wcom.com:5060
Via: SIP/2.0/UDP there.com:5060
From: LittleGuy <sip:UserB@there.com>;tag=314159
To: BigGuy <sip:UserA@here.com>
Call-ID: 12345601@here.com
CSeq: 1 BYE
Content-Length: 0
```

Event 23:

```
SIP/2.0 200 OK
Via: SIP/2.0/UDP there.com:5060
From: LittleGuy <sip:UserB@there.com>;tag=314159
To: BigGuy <sip:UserA@here.com>
Call-ID: 12345601@here.com
CSeq: 1 BYE
Content-Length: 0
```

POTENTIAL PROBLEMS WITH SIP

Take a look at the SIP message in event 12. It has an SDP "c" field of "IN IP4 110.111.112. 113. This address is obviously carried in the user message, and not in the L_3 IP datagram header. Port numbers are also carried in the SDP message, such as the SDP "m" field of "audio 3456 RTP/AVP O." If this address is a private address, there may be problems in transporting the resulting media session messages across a firewall or a Network Address Translation (NAT) server. Upon learning of the session partner's address from the SDP fields, the partner will use this address to send IP datagrams containing the media stream to its peer, and this address may not be acceptable to a firewall. If it passes a firewall (which is unlikely), it will not be acceptable to the Internet, because it is not globally-routable.

This problem is a subject of discussion in the Internet's various conferences, and Birds of a Feather (BoF) sessions.

SUMMARY

SIP is an IP Call Processing Protocol and a location server protocol. Clients and servers interact to support unicast or conference calls. SIP registers and "invites" call participants across multiple networks and name domains. SIP integrates easily into the Web-based architecture, because of its use of Web-based syntaxes. It has similar functions to other IP-based telephony call processing systems, but also provides features that are unique, such as tracking locations of users.

APPENDIX 11A   SIP USE OF THE AUGMENTED BACKUS-NAUR FORM NOTATIONS

All SIP mechanisms are described with an Augmented Backus-Naur Form (BNR) notation, similar to that stipulated in RFC 822. Anyone who wishes to know more than just the general concepts of SIP must be familiar with SIP augmented BNR. This section explains these concepts, and Appendix D contains RFC 822.

The basic notation is the name of a rule followed by its definition (and the definition may contain elements, separated by the "=" character):

name = definition

White space is significant only for a rule that spans multiple lines, and is used to signify an indentation. Certain basic rules are coded in uppercase, such as DIGIT, HT, CRLF, etc. Angle brackets are used within

Table 11–A1   SIP URL Syntax

SIP-URL =	"sip:" [userinfo "@"] hostport url-parameters [headers]
userinfo =	user [":" password]
user =	*(unreserved | escaped | "&" | "=" | "+" | "$" | ",")
password =	*(unreserved | escaped | "&" | "=" | "+" | "$" | ",")
hostport =	host [":" port]
host =	hostname | IPv4address
hostname =	*(domainlabel ".") toplabel ["."]
domainlabel =	alphanum | alphanum *(alphanum | "-") alphanum
toplabel =	alpha | alpha *(alphanum | "-") alphanum
IPv4address =	1*digit "." 1*digit "." 1*digit "." 1*digit
port =	*digit
url-parameters =	*(";" url-parameter)
url-parameter =	transport-param | user-param | method-param | ttl-param | maddr-param | other-param
transport-param =	"transport=" ("udp" | "tcp")
ttl-param =	"ttl=" ttl
ttl =	*3DIGIT ; 0 to 255
maddr-param =	"maddr=" host
user-param =	"user=" ("phone" | "ip")
method-param =	"method=" Method
tag-param =	"tag=" UUID
UUID =	1*(hex | "-")
other-param =	(token | (token "=" (token | quoted-string)))
headers =	"?" header *("&" header)
header =	hname "=" hvalue
hname =	1*uric
hvalue =	*uric
uric =	reserved | unreserved | escaped
reserved =	";" | "/" | "?" | ":" | "@" | "&" | "=" | "+" | "$" | ","
digits =	1*DIGIT

the definitions if their presence facilitates discerning the use of the rule names. Literal text is surrounded by quotation marks.

Elements in the definition separated by a bar "|" are alternatives. This example means rule1 or rule 2:

rule1 | rule2

Elements can be enclosed in parentheses, and they are treated as a single element. Square brackets enclose optional elements. The definitions can form a sequence of tokens. In the next example, the definition allows the token sequences of "elem1 foo elem2" or "elem1 bar elem2":

elem1 (foo | bar) elem2

The character "*" preceding an element indicates repetition. Several notations are used for this operation:

Notation	*Meaning*
<n>*<m>element	at least <n> and at most <m> occurrences of element
*element	allows any number
1*element	requires at least one
1*2element	allows one or two

The ISP URLs are used in SIP messages to indicate: (a) originator of message (from), (b) final recipient (to), (c) current destination (request URI), and (d) a redirection address (contact). The URL can be embedded into web pages and other hyper links to indicate that a user or service can be called Via SIP. When used as a hyperlink, the SIP URL indicates the use of the INVITE method.

The URL syntax uses RFC 2396, and is based on Augmented Backus-Naur Form (RFC 822). The basic rules for SIP Augmented BNR are provided in Table 11–A1.

12

Interworking Internets and Telephone Networks

INTRODUCTION

This chapter describes the internetworking operations between IP-based internets and telephony-based ISDNs, SS7 networks, and Intelligent Networks (INs).[1] The internetworking unit used to provide this function is a Signaling Gateway, introduced in Chapter 4. Some literature refers to this unit as an IP/SS7 Gateway.

Whatever your background may be, make sure you understand SS7 and ISDN operations; otherwise, you will not be able to follow the explanations and examples in this chapter. Appendix B provides tutorials on SS7 and ISDN.

INTERNETWORKING SS7 AND THE INTERNET

One of the common criticisms of Internet telephony that is voiced by some people is the absence of the many service features that are common to telephony systems, such as call forwarding, call screening, caller ID,

---

[1]The term Intelligent Network is the preferred term in most parts of the world, and coined in Europe. In North America (and especially in the U.S.) the term to describe a similar network is the Advanced Intelligent Network (we Yankees are not to be out-done by those people across the pond).

and so forth. These features are quite important to many telephone users, and a vital part of the services that produce revenue for telephony service providers.

The initial Internet telephony products are not designed to offer these services, and any VOIP system that is going to succeed in the corporate environment must do so. Certainly, there will be niche applications that run a sparse set of service features, and certain customers will be content with these services. But for VOIP to become a real force in telephony, it must provide these telephony-type services. To be able to provide these services, it must be able to avail itself of the SS7 technology, the lynchpin for telephony service features, and the foundation for the Advanced Intelligent Network (AIN) services.

Reinvent or Use the Telco Platform

If the telco platform is not used, the services that are part of SS7 must be "reinvented" by the Internet task forces—considered by many in the telephony industry to be a ridiculous alternative. Maybe so, but maybe not: Recall from Chapter 1 that a common complaint is the expense and inflexibility of the legacy telephone network architect. In addition, several of the IP Call Processing Protocols (such as SIP and Megaco) have begun to define service features, such as call waiting.

At any rate, the large SS7 vendors, such as Lucent, Nortel Networks, etc., are developing IP/SS7 gateways, and products are now rolling-out. The general topology for this architecture is shown in Figure 12–1.

Much work remains to be done on the development of standards for IP/SS7 gateways. However, it is evident that the configurations explained in this section will be part of the final standards mix. For example, in Figure 12–1 an SS7 network is adjacent to a network that runs IP. The exchanges are SS7, so the traffic being transferred between them is ISUP, SCCP, TCAP, etc. The SS7 nodes may be fully functioning Signaling Transfer Points (STPs), or endpoints, and the full features of MTP3 are available, such as SS7 point code routing, and recovery from failed nodes and links.

The internets are acting as transport services for the SS7 systems. In this support role, the internets must be capable of translating SS7 Global Titles/Point Codes to IP address(es), sufficient to move the traffic through the "internets cloud."

A Scaled-Down Topology

Another approach is shown in Figure 12–2, in which MTP3 is not used. The requirement here is for a simple point-to-point topology.

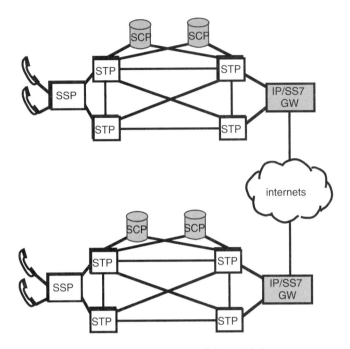

Figure 12–1   Interworking SS7 with Internets

Therefore, MTP3's routing, route recovery, and point code operations are not needed. Addressing is provided with IP addresses or an adaptation layer can map the MTP3 routing label and/or the Global Title to an IP Address. The adaptation layer can also be responsible for backup operations in case of a failure of a link between the nodes. MTP2 at the link layer can be used, but it is not required. An attractive alternative is PPP operating over LAPB.

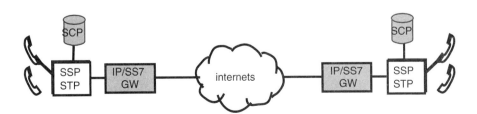

Figure 12–2   A Scaled-down Point-to-Point Configuration

SS7 AND IP COMPONENTS

A variety of SS7-IP components are being proposed in the Internet standards and are under development by the VOIP vendors. Figure 12–3 reflects one example, based on several Internet working drafts, which is called the Architectural Framework (hereafter called the Framework). Most of these entities should look familiar by now:

- *Signaling gateway (SG):* The SG receives and sends public-switched telephone system (PSTS) signals, and it may also receive and send SS7 messages.
- *Media Gateway Controller (MGC):* The MGC acts as the registration and resource management entity. It is similar to the H.323 Gatekeeper, the Megaco MGC, and the MGCP Call Agent, but it also may contain capabilities that establish usage of resources based on policies.
- *Media Gateway (MG):* The Media Gateway acts as the physical interface for PSTN lines and trunks. It also is the interface for VOIP links.
- *Routing tables (RT):* The IP routing tables that are accessed with destination IP addresses in order to route the IP traffic through an internet.
- *Domain Name System (DNS):* Database for domain names, URLs, and associated IP addresses and SS7 point codes.

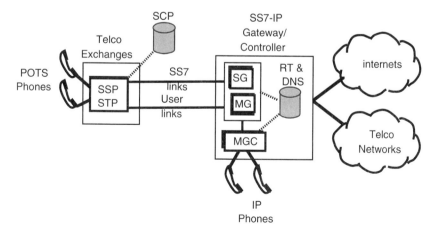

Figure 12–3   Architectural Framework

THE INTEGRATION OF THE TELEPHONE AND INTERNET SERVICE PROVIDERS

In the United States, where deregulation legislation is taking effect, there is a lot of activity in the service providers' acquisitions and mergers. In addition, as voice over data becomes more pervasive, the traditional data-only ISPs are increasing their interfaces into the traditional telephony architecture, such as the LEC equipment and SS7. Figure 12–4 shows the emerging architecture.

The customer still uses an LEC to connect to the ISP. The data traffic is exchanged through the ISP, the ISP's internet, and to the other user. The ISP's network access server supports a modem pool, and acts as a VOIP gateway.

In this example, the ISP is acting as an IXC by transporting the IP traffic over the ISP's network. The "ISP Network" in this figure also connotes the ISP's connection with the Internet.

Figure 12–4 also shows the interworking of the ISP with SS7, and the Intelligent Network (IN) components (shown at the top of the figure). The modem server, VOIP Gateway connects to the IN components through an SS7 network, or through a Feature Server, which in turn connects to the Service Control Point (SCP). The SCP to Feature Server connection can be authenticated with RADIUS. The job of the SCP is to allow the ISP to exploit the IN capabilities (billing, call screening, etc.), plus IP-specific features, such as routing, and billing by volume.

The IN service node and intelligent peripheral are also shown in this figure as part of the ISP architecture. This specific configuration will eventually be commonplace, but it is unusual at this stage of the evolution toward integrating voice and data networks. Moreover, the SN/IP operations may be part of the Feature Server node. The end offices are using the traditional circuit switches. Eventually, they will be replaced with packet switches.

THE IP/SS7 INTERNETWORKING MODEL (RFC 2719)

RFC 2719 defines the functions of the IP/SS7 internetworking nodes and other entities. Most of the definitions have been covered in earlier chapters, but a brief review should be helpful to make certain all definitions are understood. Refer to Figure 12–5 during this discussion.

- *Switched Circuit Network (SCN):* A network that carries traffic within channelized bearers of predefined sizes, such as 64 kbit/s .000125 sec slots.

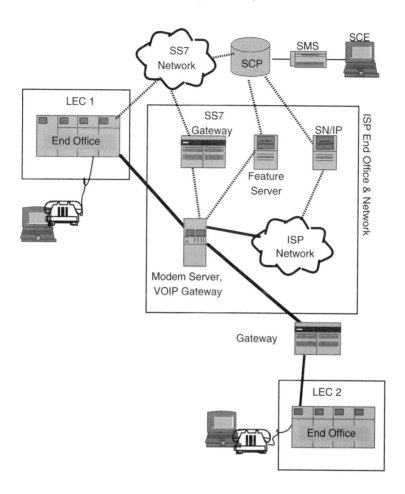

Where:
- IP   Internet Protocol
- ISP   Internet service provider
- LEC   Local exchange carrier
- SCE   Service creation environment
- SMS   Serviced management system
- SN   Service node
- VOIP Voice over IP

Figure 12–4   Integration of the Telephone and Internet Service Providers

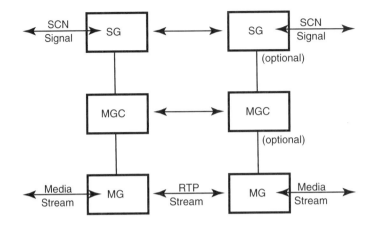

Where:
  MG   Media Gateway
  MGC   Media Gateway controller
  SG   Signaling gateway

Figure 12–5   The Internetworking (SIG) Nodes, as Defined in RFC 2719

- *Signaling Transport (SIG):* A protocol stack for transport of SCN signaling protocols over an IP network.
- *Media Gateway (MG):* Terminates SCN media streams, packetizes the media data (if necessary) and delivers this traffic to the packet network. It performs these functions in reverse order for media streams flowing from the packet network to the SCN.
- *Media Gateway Controller (MGC):* Handles the registration and management of resources at the MG. The MGC may have the ability to authorize resource usage based on local policy. For signaling transport purposes, the MGC serves as a possible termination and origination point for SCN application protocols, such as SS7's ISUP and Q.931.
- *Signaling Gateway (SG):* A signaling agent that receives/sends SCN native signaling at the edge of the IP network. The SG function may relay, translate or terminate SS7 signaling in an SS7-internet gateway. The SG function may also be co-resident with the MG function to process SCN signaling associated with line or trunk terminations controlled by the MG (e.g., signaling back-haul).

The following are terms defined in RFC 2719 for physical entities relating to signaling transport in a distributed gateway model:

- *Media Gateway Unit (MGU):* An MG-Unit is a physical entity that contains the MG function. It may contain other functions, such as an SG function for handling facility-associated signaling.
- *Media Gateway Control Unit (MGCU):* An MGC-Unit is a physical entity containing the MGC function.
- *Signaling Gateway Unit (SGU):* An SG-Unit is a physical entity containing the SG function.
- *Signaling Endpoint (SEP):* This is a node in an SS7 network that originates or terminates signaling messages. One example is a central office switch.

RFC 2719 describes the functions of these nodes by defining the signaling transport. It provides transparent transport of message-based signaling protocols over IP networks, including definition of encapsulation methods, end-to-end protocol mechanisms and use of IP capabilities to support the functional and performance requirements for signaling.

Signaling transport shall be used for transporting SCN signaling between a signaling gateway unit (SGU, a physical entity in the SG), and Media Gateway controller unit (MGCU, a physical unit in the MG). Signaling transport may also be used for transport of message-based signaling between an MGU and Media Gateway controller unit (MGCU, a physical entity in the MGU), between dispersed MGUs, and between two SGUs connecting signaling endpoints or signal transfer points in the SCN.

Signaling transport is defined to support encapsulation and carriage of a variety of SCN protocols. It is defined in such a way as to be independent of any SCN protocol translation functions taking place at the endpoints of the signaling, since its function is limited to the transport of the SCN protocol.

Implementations of the IP/SS7 Functions

Figure 12–6 shows examples (not all-inclusive) of three implementations of the IP/SS7 functions in physical entities as used for interworking of SS7 and IP networks for VOIP, voice over ATM, network access servers, etc. The use of signaling transport is independent of the implementation, and recall that signaling transport is used to carry SCN signaling.

For interworking with SS7-controlled SCN networks, the SG terminates the SS7 link and transfers the signaling information to the MGC

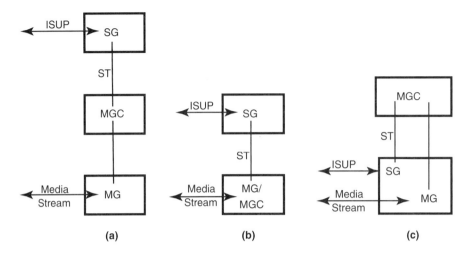

Where:
   MG   Media Gateway
   MGC   Media Gateway controller
   SG   Signaling gateway
   ST   Signaling transport

Figure 12–6   Implementations of the IP/SS7 Functions

using signaling transport. The MG terminates the interswitch trunk and controls the trunk based on the control signaling it receives from the MGC.

As shown in case (a), the SG, MGC, and MG may be implemented in separate physical units, or as in case (b), the MG/MGC may be implemented in a single physical unit. In case (c), a facility-associated SS7 link is terminated by the same device (i.e., the MGU) that terminates the interswitch trunk. In this case, the SG function is co-located with the MG function, and signaling transport is used to "backhaul" control signaling to the MGCU.

SS7 links may also be terminated directly on the MGCU by cross-connecting at the physical level before or at the MGU.

LAYERED PROTOCOLS FOR SS7 AND IP SIGNALING

Based on RFC 2719, just discussed, a number of Internet Drafts have been published to define in more detail the frame architecture set out in this RFC. These specifications are shown in Figure 12–7. At the top of the figure, the SG sits between as SS7 SEP or STP and an IP-

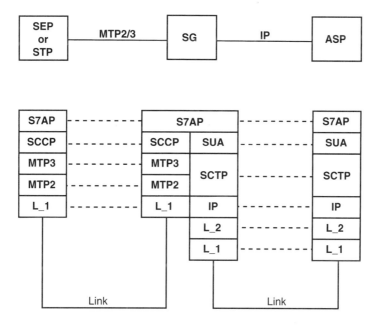

Figure 12–7 The Framework Architecture for Signaling Transport

based application server process (ASP). The ASP is an entity such as a Media Gateway Controller. At the bottom of the figure the layered protocol structure is shown. The protocol stack on the left is the conventional SS7 OAM stack. The protocol stack in the middle (residing in the SG) is a combination of SS7 and SS7/IP interworking protocols, and the protocol stack on the right is a combination of SS7, the new interworking protocols, and IP. The dashed lines in the figure indicate the logical protocol flow between the layers in the three nodes.

Let's turn our attention to the new protocols in this stack: (a) the SS7 SCCP-User Adaptation Layer (SUA) [LOUG00],[2] and (b) the Stream Control Transmission Protocol (SCTP) [STEW00].[3]

SCTP operates over IP. It offers several services similar to TCP, but it provides more flexibility than TCP in managing connections. SUA sup-

---

[2] [LOUG00]. Loughney, J., et al, SS7 SCCP-User Adaptation Layer (SUA), draft-ietf-sigtran-sua-02.txt, July 2, 2000.

[3] [STEW00]. Stewart, R.R., et al. Stream Control Transmission Protocol, draft-ietf-sigtran-sctp-13.txt, July 11, 2000.

ports the transfer of SS7 protocols (such as TCAP) over IP (using SCTP). It also supports the transfer of SCCP-user messages between two end-points within an IP network.

SCTP

SCTP provides the following services:

- Acknowledged error-free non-duplicated transfer of user data.
- Data fragmentation to conform to discovered path MTU size.
- Sequenced delivery of user messages within multiple streams, with an option for order-of-arrival delivery of individual user messages.
- Optional bundling of multiple user messages into a single SCTP packet.
- Network-level fault tolerance through supporting of multi-homing at either or both ends of an association.
- Resistance to flooding and masquerade attacks.

Why not TCP?   A number of vendors and enterprises have built their proprietary applications to replace TCP (usually running on top of UDP). [STEW00] and the author summarize the problems with TCP:

- TCP provides both reliable data transfer and strict order-of-transmission delivery of data. Some applications need reliable transfer without sequence maintenance, while others are satisfied with partial ordering of the data. In both of these cases the head-of-line blocking offered by TCP causes unnecessary delay.
- The stream-oriented nature of TCP is often an inconvenience. Applications must add their own record marking to delineate their messages, and must make explicit use of the push facility to ensure that a complete message is transferred in time.
- The TCP NAK (negative acknowledgment) is not efficient.
- The limited scope of TCP sockets complicates the task of providing highly-available data transfer capability using multi-homed hosts.
- TCP is relatively vulnerable to denial of service attacks, such as SYN attacks, wherein a hacker can inundate a node with a flood of SYNs, causing the node to consume its resources to handle these phony connection requests.

- TCP does not support more than one transport address (IP address and a port).

Major Functions of SCTP

Regarding the last statement, SCTP supports multiple transport addresses by which to reach an endpoint. The endpoint can also originate SCTP packets from these multiple transport addresses. In addition, SCTP consists of a number of other functions. They are as follows:

- *Association startup and takedown:* This function is concerned with setting up a session (called an association) between two SCTP users (the application resting on top of SCTP in the layered model). The function establishes mechanisms to combat against security attacks during this handshake. Like TCP, SCTP provides for a graceful close, wherein the closing handshake takes measures to ensure that all traffic has been accounted for. Unlike TCP, SCTP does not support a half-open state.
- *Sequenced delivery within streams:* The term "stream" in SCTP does not mean a sequence of bytes, as it does in TCP. Rather, it refers to a sequence of user messages. A user can inform SCTP of the number of streams that are to be supported by the association, and they are negotiated with the other user. Thereafter, stream numbers identify each stream, and sequence numbers are used for each stream. If a user does not wish SCTP to deliver the messages in sequential order, SCTP will present them to the user as they are received.
- *User data fragmentation:* SCTP is used to make sure the user messages are not too big for the L_2 protocol's maximum transmission unit size (MTU). For example, if an egress interface is configured for an MTU of 512 bytes, and the user message is passed to SCTP in larger units, then SCTP will fragment the message to meet the egress interface MTU requirements.
- *Acknowledgment and congestion avoidance:* Like TCP, SCTP acknowledges the receipt of traffic. It also has congestion avoidance operations that are similar to TCP.
- *Chunk building:* The SCTP user has the option of requesting more than one user message to be "chunked" into one SCTP packet. If this operation is performed, the receiving SCTP will make certain

the messages are "unchunked" properly at the receiving end. During periods of congestion, SCTP may do chunk building on its own.

- *Packet validation:* The SCTP header contains a validation tag field and a 32-bit checksum field. They are used to guard against a blind masquerade attack as well as a replay attack.
- *Path Management:* Path management is responsible for monitoring the remote transport addresses for reachability. It also selects the correct destination transport address for each outgoing packet, based on the user's instructions, and its perception of the reachability of the transport address.

This brief summary of SCTP can be followed up by studying [STEW00].

Major Functions of SUA

SUA supports the interworking of the SS7 OAM messages over IP between two signaling points. It is designed to support the following operations:

- Transfer of SCCP-User Part messages
- Support for SCCP connectionless service
- Support for SCCP connection-oriented service
- Support for seamless operation of SCCP-user protocol peers
- Support for distributed IP-based signaling nodes
- Support for asynchronous reporting of status changes to management

In providing these support functions, one of the key SUA operations is address translation. For example, if an SS7 application protocol is invoked at an SG, SUA will translate an SS7 Global Title to an appropriate SCTP association (IP address and port number).

This brief summary of SUA can be followed-up by studying [LONG00].

H.323 AND SS7

We have learned that H.323 (and the supporting protocols, H.225 and H.245) are used to support Internet Call Processing operations in local and wide area networks. In addition, the H.323 Gatekeeper acts as

Call Agent with a telephony network, and must therefore be able to correlate H.323 and ISUP message flows. [MA98] has developed the basic scheme for the interworking of H.323 and an SS7 Gateway. In this section, we examine the major features and the protocol flow of the H.323/SS7 Gateway operations, and use some examples from [MA98]. The interworking of H.323 and ISUP is fairly straight forward because the operations of the H Recommendations are similar to ISUP. For example, all of these signaling protocols use the bearer capability concept, so mapping the H.224 SETUP message to the ISUP IAM message is a relatively simple procedure.

Figure 12–8 shows the operations for the setting up of a call. Here is a description of each event.

Event 1: The H.323 Gatekeeper issues a SETUP message to the Signaling Gateway.

Event 2: The Signaling Gateway uses the information in the SETUP message to form the ISUP IAM message. It sends this message to the next transit (and maybe final) telephony exchange (the SS7 exchange in the figure).

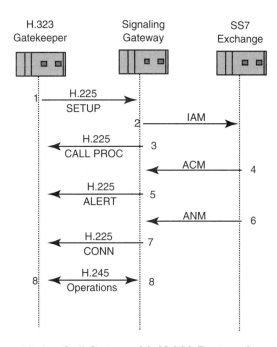

Figure 12–8   Call Setup with H.323 Protocols and ISUP

Event 3: The Signaling Gateway sends the CALL PROCEEDING message to the Gatekeeper.

Event 4: The ISUP ACM message is sent by the transit exchange.

Event 5: The receipt of the ACM message in event 5 precipitates the sending of the ALERT message by the Signaling Gateway to the Gatekeeper.

Event 6: The transit exchange informs the Signaling Gateway that the called party has answered the call by sending the ANM message.

Event 7: In turn, the Signaling Gateway sends the CONNECT message to the Gatekeeper.

Event 8: Thereafter, the H.323 Gatekeeper and the Signaling Gateway enter into the H.245 operations to perform capability exchanges and logical channel setup.

H.245 Operations During the Handshake

As shown in Figure 12–9, it is possible for the Signaling Gateway to begin the H.245 operations immediately after receiving the H.225 SETUP message, since the message contains the TSAP address. So, it

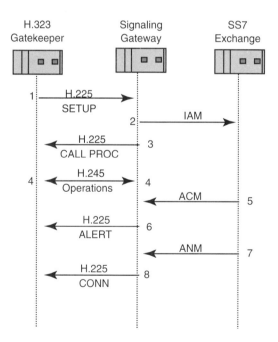

Figure 12–9   Initiating H.245 Operations After Receiving the SETUP Message

need not wait for the called party to respond. This approach will reduce the delay between the Gatekeeper and the Signaling Gateway after the ANM is received.

The call setup obviously can be made in the opposite direction, in which case the IAM from the SS7 exchange starts the set up operations between the Gatekeeper and the Signaling Gateway. And both sides of this operation may initiate call termination operations, refuse calls, and so on. I trust you have an idea of the interworking relationships between H.323 and SS7, but if you wish more details, I refer you to [MA99].

Call Initiated from SS7 Side

For the call initiated from the ISDN or PSTN side to the H.323 terminal, the call setup procedure flow is similar to the earlier examples, but in a reverse order of the message exchanges. Figure 12–10 shows the message flow for this scenario.

The H.245 logical channel setup procedure can be performed based on the bearer capability information in the ISUP IAM without waiting for the H.225 CONNECT message. This figure shows a successful call setup from an ISDN calling party, through the SS7 network, to a called H.323 terminal.

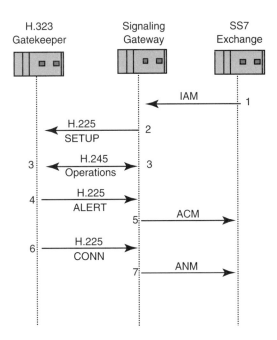

Figure 12–10   Call Initiated from the SS7 Side

An Unsuccessful Connection

Figure 12–11 shows the unsuccessful call setup initiated by the called exchange. In an ISDN or PSTN, many factors can lead to an unsuccessful call setup, such as called party busy, resource unavailable, bearer service not implemented, and others. After the destination exchange receives the IAM and determines that the call is not able to be completed, it sends back an ISUP REL message with the reason. At the originating exchange (the Signaling Gateway), the ISUP REL message is mapped into the H.225 END SESSION message and sent to the calling party to end the call.

Releasing the Session

To complete this discussion of the H.232/SS7 Gateway, Figure 12–12 shows the message flow for the release of the session, both from the local and remote sides. Figure 12–12(a) shows the release emanating from the local side, and Figure 12–12(b) shows the release emanating from the remote side.

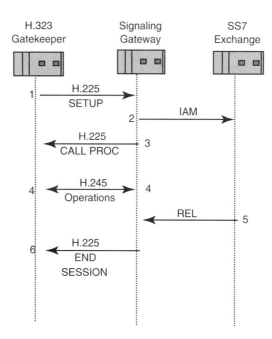

Figure 12–11   Unsuccessful Call, Signaled from Called Side

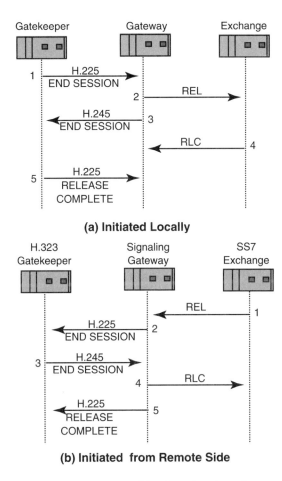

(a) Initiated Locally

(b) Initiated from Remote Side

Figure 12–12   Closing the Session

SIP AND SS7

We now return to SIP, explained in Chapter 11. This part of the chapter shows several examples of how SIP internetworks with the PTSN's SS7, ISDN, and conventional analog operations. These examples are only a few from [JOHN00],[4] whose working draft contains implementation guidelines for building a SIP/PTSN Gateway. It is important that you read Chapter 11 before studying these examples.

---

[4][JOHN00]. Johnston, Alan et al. "SIP Telephony Call Flow Examples", draft-ietf-sip-call-flows-00.txt, March 2000.

In the following examples, User A is placing calls from the PSTN to User B in a SIP network. User A's telephone switch signals to a Network Gateway (NGW 1) using ISUP.

Since the called SIP User Agent does not send in-band signaling information, no early media path needs to be established on the IP side. As a result, the SIP 183 Session Progress response diagnostic is not used. However, NGW 1 will establish a one way speech path prior to call completion, and generate ringing for the PSTN caller. Any tones or recordings are generated by NGW 1 and played in this speech path. When the call completes successfully, NGW 1 bridges the PSTN speech path with the IP media path. Alternatively, the NGW1 could redirect the call to an Announcement Server which would complete the call and play announcements or tones as directed by the Gateway.

Successful PTSN to SIP Call

In Figure 12–13, User A from the PSTN calls User B through a Network Gateway NGW1 and Proxy Server Proxy 1. When User B answers the call the media path is setup end-to-end. The call terminates when User A hangs up the call, with User A's telephone switch sending an ISUP RELEASE (REL) message which is mapped to a BYE by NGW 1. Please note that the "users" in these examples are not the subscribers, but the agents that represent the subscribers, such as SIP UACs, UASs, proxy servers, and IP/SS7 Gateways.

The SIP Messages.   The SIP messages used during this exchange are similar to those we examined in Chapter 11. Of course, the fields in the messages differ. Notwithstanding, our approach here is to concentrate on the functions of the message flows.

Event 1: The calling party sends an ISUP IAM to its gateway, NGW1. The SS7 dialing plans accompany the calling party and called party numbers. In addition, the ISUP message contains parameters that provide information about the nature of the call (speech, data, fax, etc.).

Events 2 and 3: NGW 1 maps the IAM information into a SIP INVITE. It passes this message to Proxy 1. Both NGW1 and Proxy 1 must correlate the called part y address (such as a telephone number) to an IP address. During these events NGW1 and Proxy 1 are setting up resources to receive traffic (port numbers for example).

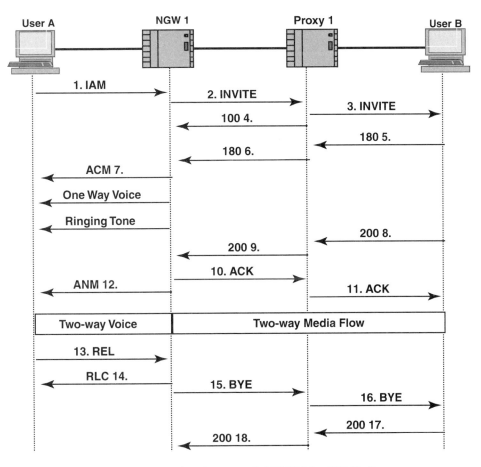

Figure 12–13   Successful PTSN to SIP Call

Events 4, 5, and 6: In event 4, Proxy 1 informs NGW1 that it is trying to reach the called party. In events 5 and 6, the SIP ringing (180) message is sent back to the calling party.

Event 7: Upon receiving the ringing message in event 6, the NGW1 sends the ISUP IAM to user A. The connection at the calling end is one-way (until all parameters have been negotiated, and the called party goes off hook. Also, ringing is given to the calling party.

Events 8–12: The called party answers the call; the required ACKs are sent to acknowledge the 200 OK messages. The message in event 9 causes the NGW1 to send the ISUP ANM to the calling party. Thereafter, the calling and called parties can engage in a two-way media flow (voice, video, or data).

Events 13–18: User A hangs up, an action that precipitates the message flow in these events.

Call from a PBX

In this example in Figure 12–14, User A dials from PBX A to User B through GW 1 and Proxy 1, and several of the SIP messages are shown in this scenario. This is an example of a call that appears destined for the PSTN but instead is routed to a SIP Client. Signaling between PBX A and GW 1 is Feature Group B (FGB) circuit signaling, in-band Multi-Frequency (MF) outpulsing (explained in Chapter 2).

After receiving the 180 Ringing from User B, GW 1 generates ringing tone for User A. User B answers the call by sending a 200 OK. The call terminates when User A hangs up, causing GW1 to send a BYE.

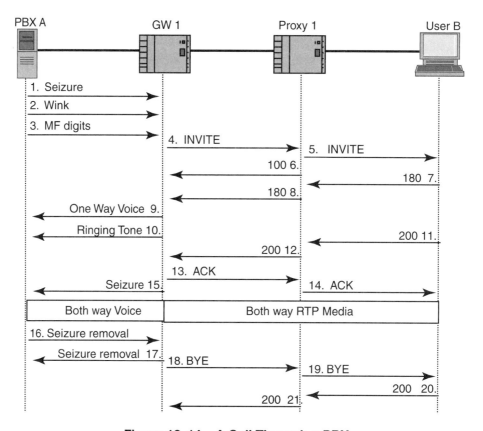

Figure 12–14   A Call Through a PBX

The Enterprise Gateway can only identify the trunk group that the call came in on, it cannot identify the individual line on PBX A that is placing the call. The SIP URL used to identify the caller is shown in these flows as sip:IdentifierString@gw1.wcom.com. A unique Identifier-String is provisioned on the Gateway against each incoming trunk group.

For this example, the control port for all nodes is 5060. The calling PBX is URL sip:IdentifierString@gw1.wcom.com. The called URL is sip:+1-972-555-2222@ss1.wcom.com. GW 1 is gw1.wcom.com, and Proxy 1 is ss1.wcom.com. The other parameters in the SIP messages in this example have been explained in the SDP and SIP chapters.

Events 1–4: PBX A does a hand shake with BW1 and in event 3, sends over the dialed digits; this stream is KP 1 792 555 2222 ST, in accordance with the rules explained in Chapter 2. In event 3, GW1 sends a SIP INVITE message to Proxy 1.

```
INVITE sip:+1-972-555-2222@ss1.wcom.com;user=phone SIP/2.0
Via: SIP/2.0/UDP gw1.wcom.com:5060
From: PBX_A <sip:IdentifierString@gw1.wcom.com>;user=phone
To: sip:+1-972-555-2222@ss1.wcom.com;user=phone
Call-ID: 12345602@gw1.wcom.com
CSeq: 1 INVITE
Contact: PBX_A <sip:IdentifierString@gw1.wcom.com>;user=phone
Content-Type: application/sdp
Content-Length: 150

v=0
o=GATEWAY1 2890844527 2890844527 IN IP4 gatewayone.wcom.com
s=Session SDP
c=IN IP4 gatewayone.wcom.com
t=0 0
m=audio 3456 RTP/AVP 0
a=rtpmap:0 PCMU/8000
```

Event 5: Proxy 1 uses a location manager to determine where the phone number +1-972-555-2222 is located. Based upon location analysis the call is forwarded to SIP User B.

```
INVITE sip:UserB@there.com SIP/2.0
Via: SIP/2.0/UDP ss1.wcom.com:5060
Via: SIP/2.0/UDP gw1.wcom.com:5060
Record-Route: <sip:+1-972-555-2222@ss1.wcom.com>
From: PBX_A <sip:IdentifierString@gw1.wcom.com>;user=phone
To: sip:+1-972-555-2222@ss1.wcom.com;user=phone
```

```
Call-ID: 12345602@gw1.wcom.com
CSeq: 1 INVITE
Contact: PBX_A <sip:IdentifierString@gw1.wcom.com>;user=phone
Content-Type: application/sdp
Content-Length: 150


v=0
o=GATEWAY1 2890844527 2890844527 IN IP4 gatewayone.wcom.com
s=Session SDP
c=IN IP4 gatewayone.wcom.com
t=0 0
m=audio 3456 RTP/AVP 0
a=rtpmap:0 PCMU/8000
```

Events 6–21: The remaining events take place as shown in Figure 12–14. There is nothing more to add to this example that has not already been explained in Chapter 11.

H.323 AND SIP

H.323 is the most widely-used Call Processing protocol in the industry, and SIP is slated to become one of the major players, information we learned in Chapter 1. Some think that SIP will supplant or eclipse H.323 in the future. For now, it is evident that some of the user systems will be using H.323 and others will be using SIP. Consequently, it is essential that a gateway be defined that allows these two systems to interwork with each other. Fortunately, considerable work has been expended on these efforts, and is available in "Interworking Between SIP/SDP and H.323" [SING00].[5] This part of the chapter provides a tutorial and summary of this Internet draft, which addresses the interworking of H.323v2 and SIPv2.

The H.323 and SIP Configuration

Figure 12–15 shows the configuration for the interworking of H.323 and SIP systems. An H.323 Gatekeeper and a SIP server can be part of the Gateway. The SIP server can be a proxy, and also provides the SIP Registrar functions. As explained in the remainder of this section, this Gateway provides mapping and translation services for the H.323 and SIP networks.

---

[5][SIGN00]. Singh, Kundan and Schulzrinne, Henning. Interworking Between SIP/SDP and H.323," draft-singh-sip-h323.txt, January 10, 2000.

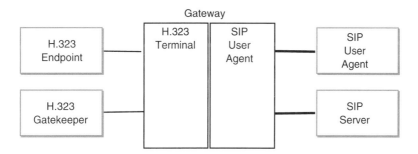

Figure 12–15   The H.323/SIP Gateway [SING00]

Gateway Initialization

When receiving a SIP REGISTER request (see Figure 12–16), the GW generates an H.323 RAS RRQ request to its local Gatekeepers. The callSignalAddress of the RAS message contains the network address of the Gateway; the terminalType is set to "gateway" and the terminalAlias is derived from the SIP To SIP-Address. Any address resolution request coming from the H.323 cloud to a SIP address can be resolved by H.323 Gatekeeper(s) using H.323 RAS requests. Any request coming from the

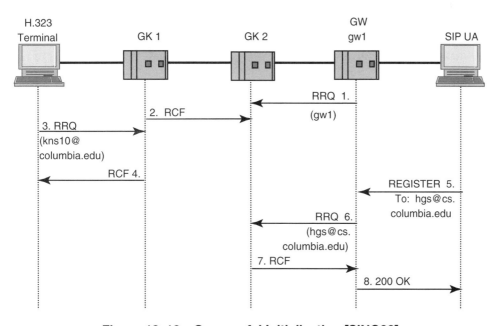

Figure 12–16   Successful Initialization [SING00]

SIP network to H.323 is forwarded to the H.323 Gatekeeper(s) by the Gateway. H.323 Gatekeeper(s) resolve this address using RAS/H.323.

The conventional H.323 operations take place between the H.323 Gateways and Gatekeepers, with the exchanges of RRQ and RCF messages. Upon receiving the REGISTER message from the SIP User Agent, the Gateway (gw1) sends an RRQ message to the H.323 Gatekeeper (GK2 in the figure).

SIP AND IN

Some telephony engineers have begun to examine how SIP could interwork (and co-exist) with the pervasive IN.[6] This chapter concludes by showing the relationships of the IN call states and the SIP "call states." SIP does not actually implement call states. Nonetheless, Figures 12–17 and 12–18 show that SIP's activities can be correlated with IN call states.

Figure 12–17 represents the states in the originating call model for an AIN in relation to the SIP operations. The SIP INVITE is associated with the first six states, and the next four SIP operations are associated with the final four call model states. Here is a brief description of the originating states:

Null	Line or trunk interface is idle (no call exists), and switch provides supervision.
Authorizing origination attempt	Switch verifies authority of the user to place a call with the given properties (e.g., line restrictions). Any glare situation detected is resolved.
Collecting information	Switch collects initial information (e.g., service codes, address information) from user according to a specified dialing plan.
Analyzing information	Switch interprets and translates the collected information according to the specified numbering plan, determining the called party ID, type of call, carrier, and route index.
Select route	Switch interprets the analysis results to select the outgoing route (e.g., point to a local dialed number).

---

[6]Don't forget, IN and AIN are used synonymously in this book.

SIP Call States   **IN Call States**

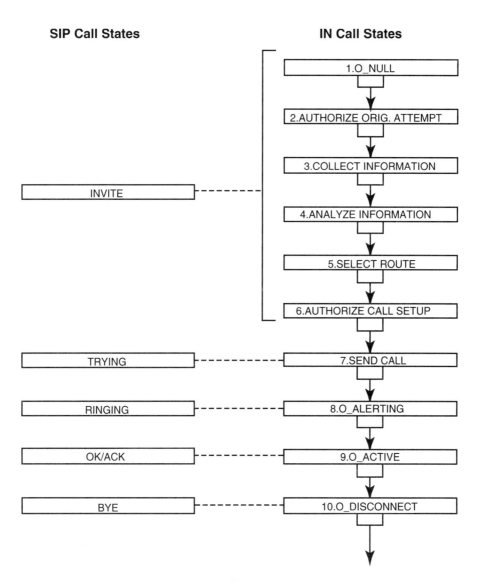

**Figure 12–17   Interworking SIP with the Intelligent Network
(IN): Origination**

Authorizing call setup   Switch verifies that the calling party is
                              authorized to place the call (e.g., checks
                              toll restrictions).

Call send   Switch sends an indication of desire to
                              set up a call to the specified called party
                              ID to the terminating call portion.

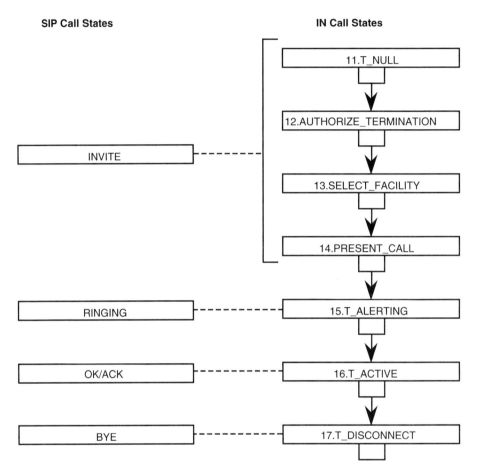

Figure 12–18   Interworking SIP with the Intelligent Network (IN): Termination

Figure 12–18 represents the states in the terminating call model for an (advanced) intelligent network in relation to the SIP operations. The SIP INVITE is associated with the first four states, and the next three SIP operations are associated with the final three call model states. Here is a brief description of the terminating states:

Null	A disconnect and call clearing occurs.
Authorize termination attempt	Indication of incoming call received from originating half BCSM.
Select facility	Authority to route call to specified termination resource group verified.

Present call	Available terminating resource identified.
Alerting	Terminating Party alerted of incoming call.
Active	An indication is sent to the originating part of call model that the terminating party has accepted and answered the call (e.g., terminating party goes off-hook).
Disconnect	A disconnect indication is received from the terminating party.

SUMMARY

For VOIP to become a major force in telephony, it must provide telephony-type services. To be able to provide these services, it must be able to avail itself of the SS7 technology, the lynchpin for telephony service features, and the foundation for the Advanced Intelligent Network (AIN) services. Alternately, the IETF must define native-mode service features using the Web architecture. For the near future, both scenarios will be implemented in vendors' products.

Appendix A
IP Call Processing and QOS

IP CALL PROCESSING AND QOS

In the past few years, it has become evident that network service providers need to differentiate between different types of traffic and treat these traffic types differently. Increasingly, the customer is asking for services from the provider that reflect the needs of the customer's organization. The current arrangement of giving a customer a channel of a fixed capacity and restricting the customer to this raw bit rate is insufficient to handle the customer's diverse requirements.

Moreover, customers are now asking network providers to establish different levels of service, and to charge back to the customer the actual level of service provided. In other words, you get what you pay for.

One of the functions of IP Call Processing could be to support QOS negotiations between the users and the network. However, at this point in the evolution of IP Call Processing, these support features are limited.

For the near future, it is likely that QOS will not be a big part of IP Call Processing. The reason for this statement it the fact that efforts are underway to define separate protocols for QOS. These efforts focus on DiffServ and RSVP and will be explained in this appendix.

ROLE OF IP CALL PROCESSING IN THE QOS OPERATIONS

I see great potential in using, say, Megaco or SIP to set up and negotiate QOS in a multimedia internet. From the standpoint of the messaging tasks, one only has to extend SDP. The QOS tasks, such jitter control, bandwidth management, admission policys, policing traffic, etc. are external to any type of protocol flow. That means RSVP, Megaco, SIP, etc. could be used to negotiate the QOS. We will see what happens in the next year of so. It is likely that the IP Call Processing Protocols will be extended to support the negotiation of QOS. For now, let's find out what QOS is all about.

QOS COMPONENTS

The term quality-of-service (QOS) was first used in the Open Systems Interconnection (OSI) Model about 20 years ago, and its meaning refers to the ability of a service provider to support a user's application requirements with regard to at least four service categories: (a) bandwidth, (b) latency (delay), (c) jitter, and (d) traffic loss.

The provision of bandwidth for an application means the network has sufficient capacity to support the application's throughput requirements, measured say, in packets per second.

The second service category is latency, which describes the time it takes to send a packet from a sending node to a receiving node. Latency is also measured in round-trip-time (RTT), which is the time it takes to send a packet to a destination node and receive a reply from that node. RTT includes the transmission time in both directions and the processing time at the destination node. Applications, such as voice and video, have stringent latency requirements, and if the packet arrives too late, it is not useful, and is ignored, resulting in wasted bandwidth and a reduction in the quality of the service to the application.

The third service category, jitter, is the variation of the delay between packets, and usually occurs on an output link where packets are competing for the shared link. Variable delay is onerous to speech. It complicates the receiver's job of playing-out the speech image to the listener.

The last service category is traffic (packet loss). Packet loss is quite important in voice and video applications, since the loss may affect the outcome of the decoding process at the receiver, and may also be detected by the end-user's ears or eyes.

There is another aspect of traffic loss; it deals with the complete loss of service in a network. This "hard down" situation of course is much more serious than a partial traffic loss, but it is not the subject of this discussion, and is best left to another text. The assumption for this discussion this that the network is up and running. The question is how the network will meet the customer's QOS requirements.

These four categories have a common theme: congestion management. They are all influenced by the contention for resources of a service system that has limited resources. Therefore, traffic may become congested while waiting for a resource to be freed up to service the traffic.

Congestion and the resultant drop in throughput and increased delays are such an ingrained part of the Internet that most of us take it for granted. Indeed, best effort is the only method of handling users' traffic. Best effort does not support any of the QOS categories previously described.

But this situation will change. The use of QOS features, and giving a customer the option of purchasing QOS service levels will surely create new applications as well as new opportunities and products.

DECISIONS TO SUPPORT QOS

The provisioning and supply of adequate QOS for an application is not a simple process. Because of its complexity, in the past, internets treated all applications' traffic alike, and delivered the traffic on a best effort basis: that is, the traffic was delivered if the network had the resources to support the delivery. However, if the network became congested, the traffic was simply discarded. Some networks have attempted to establish some method of feedback (flow control) to the user in order to "request" the user to reduce the infusion of traffic into the network. But as often as not, this technique is not very effective, because many traffic flows in data networks are very short, maybe just a few packets in a user-to-user session. So, by the time the user application receives the feedback it is finished sending traffic. The feedback packets are worthless, and have done nothing but create yet more traffic.

The best effort concept means traffic is discarded randomly, no attempt is made to do any kind of intelligent filtering. This approach has the effect of discarding more packets from applications that have high bandwidth requirements and are placing more packets into the network than those that have lesser requirements and are not sending as many packets into the network. So, the biggest "customers," those needing more bandwidth, are the very ones that are the most penalized! Assuming the customer who is supposedly given a bigger pipe is paying more for that pipe, then it is reasonable to further assume that this customer should be given a fair return on the customer's investment in the service.

It is charitable to say that the best effort approach is not a very good model. What is needed is a way to manage the QOS based on the customer's requirements and investment.

QOS EFFORTS

The Internet Engineering Task Force has two working groups that are working to develop QOS standards. The first group that was formed deals with Integrated Services (IntServ). The focus is on long-lived unicast and multicast flows, and the Resource Reservation Protocol (RSVP) is used with this approach. This model guarantees each flow's QOS requirements through the complete path, from the sender to the receiver. Each node (router) in the path is aware of each flow's requirements and participates in the QOS support operation.

The second group is working on Differentiated Services (DiffServ). This model does not work with individual flows. Rather it combines flows with the same service requirements into a single aggregated flow. This aggregated flow then receives levels of service relative to other traffic flows.

These two approaches are quite different in how they provide QOS to the user, and we devote much time to them later. For now, it is interesting to note that both IntServ and DiffServ specify QOS at layer 3 in contrast to Frame Relay and ATM, which define QOS at layer 2.[1]

If QOS is to be provided end-to-end—between two end users—the scope of the QOS becomes quite important. This term refers to the topological extent over which the customer is offered the QOS is provided.[2] The scope may be restricted to one provider, or many. But for meaningful

---

[1]The supposedly layer 2 operations of Frame Relay and ATM are actually a combination of layer 2 and layer 3 operations. X.25 provides the model: its virtual circuits are managed at its layer 3 in a separate layer 3 header. For Frame Relay and ATM, virtual circuit management has been "pushed down" to layer 2, and the layer 3 header has been eliminated.

[2][BERN99] Bernet, Y. et al. "A Framework for Differentiated Services," draft-ietf-difserv-framework-02-.txt., February, 1999.

QOS to be obtained, the scope of service should include all providers that are involved in handling the users' traffic.

The concept has become more visible in the past few years as customers have had their traffic transported through more than one service provider. The first major breech of a one service provider concept occurred in the United States with the 1984 break up of the Bell System, leading to the use of local exchange carriers (LECs) and interchange carriers (IXCs). As the Internet matured, it became commonplace to use LECs, IXCs, as well as more than one Internet Service Provider (ISP) to provide end-to-end service to a customer.

SERVICE LEVEL AGREEMENTS (SLAs)

Wide area networks (WANs) that offer QOS features are common today. Throughput and delay are examples of these features. Others are traffic loss guarantees. That is the good news. The bad news is that it may be quite difficult for the customer to know if the network provider is living up to the service level agreement (SLA) contract (the contract between the customer and the service provider).

In a large customer internet, there may be hundreds of connections and services with different network providers. SLA contracts have been signed, and the SLAs are supposedly being supported. Nothing is simple in life, even SLAs. The problem stems from the fact that the SLA for QOS support may be difficult to monitor (commercially speaking, it is not an insurmountable technical problem).

In a public data network (such as a Frame Relay network), a customer enterprise is often billed based on its bandwidth usage on each permanent virtual circuit (PVC). It is important for the customer to be able to know how the service provider has billed for the PVC and the traffic across the PVC. In the past, software was not readily available to monitor these circuits and provide meaningful information to the customer. This situation is changing, and a number of vendors now have products that enables Frame Relay customers to gather information for monitoring their SLAs.

This figure shows the topology for implementing an SLA monitor. The enhanced channel service unit/data service unit (CSU/DSU) collects performance data by monitoring the traffic passing through it. The data are passed to software that generates reports on key QOS operations: (a) availability, (b) delay, (c) throughput by PVC or physical port, (d) traffic discards, (e) port utilization over time, and (f) percentage of bandwidth being used by a protocol (SNA, IP, etc.).

The price for these enhanced CSU/DSUs range from $1000 to $4000. They are available from a number of vendors [TAYL98][3] and [JAND99].[4]

MORE INFORMATION ON QOS

We have only touched on the subject of QOS. If you want more details take a look a companion book to this series, *QOS in Wide Area Networks.*

---

[3][TAYL98] Taylor, Steven, and Wexler, Joanie, "Maturing Frame Relay Make New Demands," *Business Communications Review,* July, 1998.

[4][JAND99] Jander, Mary, "SAL Monitoring Tools," *Data Communications,* February, 1999.

Appendix B

ISDN and SS7

INTRODUCTION

If you have read any of the main body of this book, you have come across considerable material on ISDN and SS7. IP Call Processing must integrate with ISDN and SS7, so it is a good idea to have at least a rudimentary knowledge of these systems. This appendix is devoted to that end. It is a very general view of these protocols, but it is sufficient for us to understand how they interwork with IP Call Processing.

ISDN CONNECTION MANAGEMENT MESSAGES

ITU-T Q.931 messages are used to manage ISDN connections. Table B–1 lists these messages and a short explanation is provided later in this section about the functions of the more significant messages. For this discussion, the call establishment and call disestablishment messages are used, as their names imply, to set up and tear down a connection.

EXAMPLE OF AN ISDN CONNECTION

Figure B–1 provides an example of how a call is setup with the Q.931 messages. The two persons involved in this connection are using conventional telephone handsets that are attached to ISDN terminals,

Table B–1   SDN Layer 3 Messages Used with IP Call Processing*

Call Establishment
  ALERTING
  CALL PROCEEDING
  CONNECT
  CONNECT ACKNOWLEDGE
  PROGRESS
  SETUP
  SETUP ACKNOWLEDGE
Call Disestablishment
  DISCONNNECT (DISC)
  RELEASE (RLS or RLSE)
  RELEASE COMPLETE
  RESTART
  RESTART ACKNOWLEDGE
Miscellaneous
  CANCEL
  CANCEL ACKNOWLEDGE
  CANCEL REJECT
  CONGESTION CONTROL
  FACILITY (FAC)
  FACILITY ACKNOWLEDGE
  FACILITY REJECT
  INFORMATION (INFO)

*Note: use of these messages varies across vendors and national boundaries.

shown in this figure as the calling terminal and the called terminal. The exchange terminations (ET) are located at the central offices.

The calling party goes off-hook and dials the telephone number of the called party. This information is used by the calling terminal to create an ISDN SETUP message, which is sent across the ISDN line to the local ET. This ET acknowledges the message with the SETUP ACK message, and initiates actions to set up a circuit to the next ET, which is shown in the figure with the dashed arrow. The SETUP ACK and INFORMATION messages are optional, and are not used in some of the IP/ISDN interworking operations. The local ET sends a CALL PROCEEDING message to the calling terminal to indicate that the call is being processed.

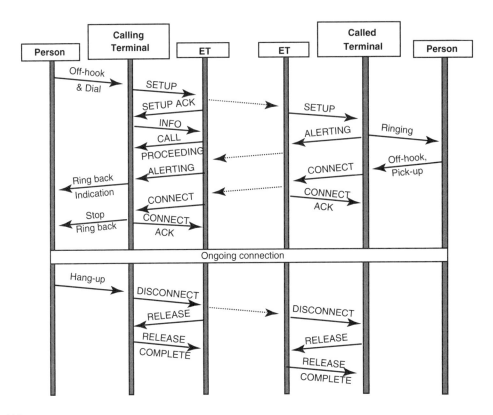

Where:
  BC   Bearer capability
  CDN   Called party number
  CGN   calling party number
  CSE   Cause code

Figure B–1   ISDN Signaling Example

At the called end, the SETUP message is forwarded to the called terminal by the terminating ET. This terminal examines the contents of the message to determine who is being called and what services are being requested. It checks the called party's line to see if it is idle, and if so, places the ringing signal on the line. When the ringing signal is placed on the line, the called terminal transmits an ALERTING message in the backwards direction, which is passed all the way to the calling terminal. This message indicates to the calling terminal that the called party has been signaled, which allows a ring back signal to be placed on the line to the calling party.

When the called party answers the call, the called terminal sends a CONNECT message in the backward direction, which is passed to the calling terminal. Upon receiving this message, ring back is removed from the line, and the connection is cut-through to the calling party. The CONNECT messages are acknowledged with CONNECT ACK messages.

The on-hook action initiates the ISDN connection termination operations. The DISCONNECT messages are used to indicate that the connection is to be terminated. The RELEASE and RELEASE COMPLETE messages follow the DISCONNECT messages.

SS7

Figure B–2 depicts a typical SS7 topology. The subscriber lines are connected to the SS7 network through the Service Switching Points (SSPs). The SSPs receive the signals from the customer premises equipment (CPE) and perform call processing on behalf of the user. SSPs are implemented at end offices or access tandem devices. They serve as the source and destination for SS7 messages. In so doing, SSP initiates SS7 messages either to another SSP or to a signaling transfer point (STP).

The STP is tasked with the translation of the SS7 messages and the routing of those messages between network nodes and databases. The STPs are switches that relay messages between SSPs, STPs, and service control points (SCPs). Their principal functions are similar to the layer 3 operations of the OSI Model.

The SCPs contain software and databases for the management of the call. For example, 800 services and routing are provided by the SCP. They receive traffic (typically requests for information) from SSPs via STPs and return responses (via STPs) based on the query.

Although the figure shows the SS7 components as discrete entities, they are often implemented in an integrated fashion by a vendor's equipment. For example, a central office can be configured with a SSP, a STP, and a SCP or any combination of these elements.

The STP is installed as a national STP, an international STP, or a gateway STP. Even though SS7 is an international standard, countries may vary in how some of the features and options are implemented. The STP provides the conversions of the messages that flow between dissimilar systems. For example, in the United States the STP provides conversions between ANSI SS7 and ITU-T SS7.

STPs also offer screening services, such as security checks on incoming and/or outgoing messages. The STP can also screen messages to make certain they are acceptable (conformant) to the specific network.

Other STP functions include the acquisition and storage of traffic and usage statistics for OAM and billing. If necessary, the STP provides an originating SCP with the address of the destination SCP.

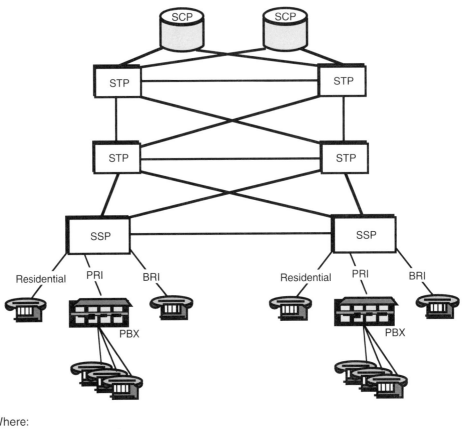

Where:
  BRI   Basic rate interface
  PBX   Private branch exchange
  PRI   Primary rate interface
  SCP   Service control point
  SSP   Service switching point
  STP   Signaling transfer point

Figure B–2   Typical SS7 Topology

RELATIONSHIP OF ISDN AND SS7

This appendix has discussed SS7 and ISDN as separate subjects. Indeed, they are separate, and they perform different operations in a transport and signaling network architecture. However, SS7 and ISDN are "partners" in that ISDN assumes SS7 will set up the connections within a network and SS7 assumes ISDN will set up connections at network boundaries (outside the network). Therefore (see Figure B–3), we can

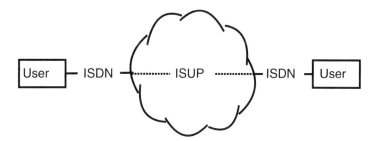

Figure B–3   ISDN and ISUP

view ISDN as a user network interface (UNI) operating between the user device and the network node, and we can view SS7 as a network node interface (NNI) operating between the nodes within the network. Of course, nothing precludes using SS7 as an internetworking interface allowing two networks to communicate with each other.

The ISDN user part (ISUP) is used to coordinate the activities of ISDN and SS7. In effect ISUP "bridges" the two ISDN UNIs across the SS7 network.

Table B–2 shows the names of the major ISUP messages, their abbreviations, and their functions. Most of these messages are used in IP/SS7 Gateways, a subject of Chapter 12.

Table B–2   ISUP Call Processing Messages

Message	Name	Function
ACM	Address Complete Message	Indicates all information necessary to complete a call that has been received
ANM	Answer Message	Indicates called party has answered (used also for billing start in toll calls)
CPG	Call Progress	Indicates an event of significance to the originator has occurred (backwards direction only)
IAM	Initial Address Message	Invitation to establish a call
RLC	Release Complete	Indicates circuit has been placed in an idle state
RLS	Release	Indicates circuit is being released for reasons given (see cause value)

INTERWORKING ISDN AND SS7

In this section, we piece together some of the information explained earlier by providing an example of how the SS7 signaling procedures and call setup occur. This example in Figure B–4 also shows the relationship of ISDN and SS7 connections.

A call setup begins when a telephone or PBX (in this example) sends an ISDN Setup message, which is used to create the SS7 initial address message (IAM). This message is sent to an exchange. The IAM contains all the information required to set up and route the call. All codes and digits required for the call routing through the national (and international) network will be sent in this message. Other signals may also be sent in certain situations. For example, the end of pulsing (ST) signal is sent to indicate the final digit has been sent of the digits in the national or international numbers. Also, since the SS7 network does not pass over the speech path, it must provide facilities to provide a continuity check of the speech circuit to be used. It also makes cross-office checks to ensure the reliability of the connection through the various digital exchanges.

A call is processed by the outgoing exchange analyzing the address signals in the message. Based on these address messages, an appropriate outgoing circuit is seized and an initial address message (IAM) is forwarded to the next exchange.

This exchange analyzes the address message to determine (a) the circuit to be seized; (b) routing through another country, if necessary; (c) the nature of the circuit (terrestrial or satellite); (d) if echo control is needed; (e) the calling parties category; and, (f) the need for continuity checks. The exchanges will disable any echo suppressers (if necessary) at this time.

If all the checks are completed successfully, the network begins the call establishment (when enough address signals are received to determine routing). The address messages are analyzed to determine if all the required signals have been received, at which time the speech path setup is completed. The destination exchange provides a ringing tone back to the originator, and upon the receiving telephone user answering the call, the answer signals are returned by the originating exchange to the user.

At the receiving end, the SS7 IAM is mapped back to the ISDN Setup message and sent to the terminating PBX. Notice the Call Proceeding messages that are sent in response to the Setup messages.

Once the terminating end answers the call, an ISDN Connect message is sent to the network, which maps this message into an SS7 answer message (ANM), which is then mapped into an ISDN Connect message and given to the originating caller.

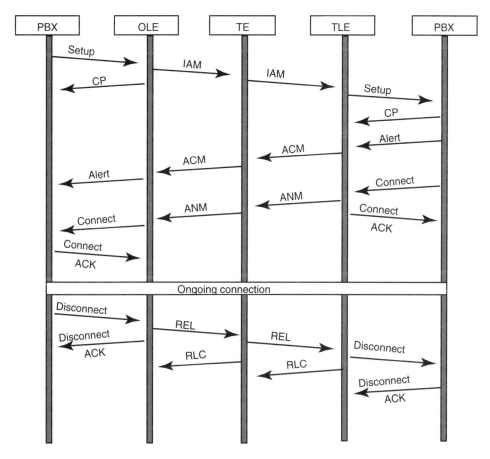

Where:
ACM   Address complete message
ANM   Answer message
CP   Call proceeding
IAM   Initial address message
OLE   Originating local exchange
PBX   Private branch exchange
RLC   Release complete
TE   Transit exchange
TLE   Terminating local exchange

Figure B–4   ISDN and SS7 Operations

Eventually one of the subscribers hangs up, which activates an ISDN Disconnect message, and in turn, the messages shown in the bottom part of this figure. After a certain period of waiting, if no other signals emanate from the end user, additional supervisory signals are exchanged between the two exchanges to make the circuit available for new traffic.

OTHER SS7 PROTOCOLS

This discussion is really just a brief view of the capabilities of SS7. There is a wealth of application features that are covered in other books in this series. Chapter 12 makes references to some of these features. If you wish to pursue this "lead" in more detail, take a look at the ISDN and SS7, and the AIN books in this series. Also, Appendix C in this book should be helpful.

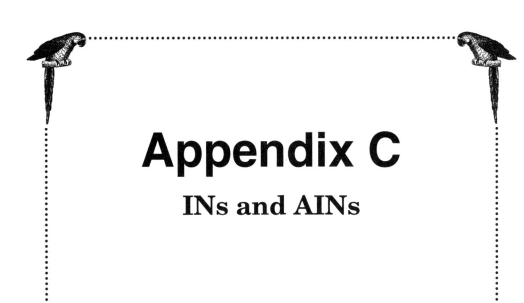

Appendix C

INs and AINs

IN BASICS

The main body of this text has stated that it is important for an IP-based call processing system to have access to the many data bases of the telephone networks, such as 800, 911, and 411 services, as well as service features, such as call screening, caller ID, and so on. A fundamental component of the intelligent network (IN) [or advanced intelligent network (AIN)] is the ability to support the these important information repositories, and the creation of services for the end customer in a rapid manner. The IN uses the technology of Signaling System Number 7 (SS7) and adds its functionality at the application layer to achieve these key goals:

- Provide timely creation of new services for the customer
- Support a wide-range of services (generic and tailored)
- Allows the ease of maintenance of the AIN system (standardized building blocks)
- Require a seamless environment between vendors' systems (minimum conversions between the systems)

IN SERVICES

A frequently asked question is, "What is an IN service?" Another common question is, "What is an example of an IN service?"

The term "IN service" is misleading, because IN is designed to be service independent. In fact, service independence is one of the key components of IN. The value of IN is that it standardizes the procedures and protocols to bring in IN services to a customer in accordance with the four goals cited in the previous paragraph.

The intelligent network is an evolving concept, based on the implementation of a service independent and machine independent architecture from which network service providers can create new services for the customer.

One of the key components to the success of the network and customer satisfaction with the network is the allowance and support of new services in a flexible and expeditious manner. In a nutshell, future architecture is focused on faster provisioning and customized services for the user.

A fundamental component of the AIN is the ability to support the creation of services for the end customer in a rapid manner. While this goal is laudable and on the surface appears to be a simple task, it is in fact difficult and complex to achieve. The difficulty stems from (a) the breadth of some customers requests, and (b) the ability to create the services to support these requests through the modification and/or addition to the network's existing hardware and software architecture.

Consider that a service request may impact scores of hardware components and hundreds of software modules containing thousands of lines of code. Therefore, service creation requires a structured and disciplined approach. It usually entails modeling, building generic blocks for simulation, specifying the service through special languages; in other words, it requires the development of a formal method or model.

EXAMPLE OF AN IN SERVICE

Figure C–1 shows an example of how an IN application can be implemented to provide simple, useful services to an end user. We assume that a customer wishes to order a pizza, and consults his yellow pages to find Pizza a Go-Go, willing and able to provide the service. In event 1, the customer dials the number furnished in the yellow pages (800-1234), which is forwarded to the local central office.

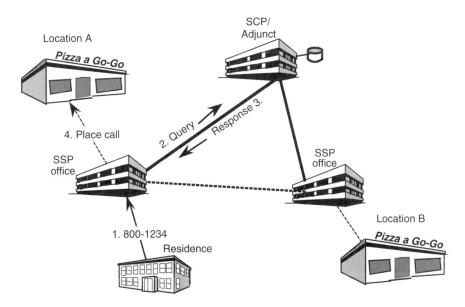

Figure C–1   Example of an AIN Service

This office serves as a SSP office and (under the SSP function) analyzes the number. It discovers that it must route a *query* message to another office that services this telephone number. Therefore in event 2, the SSP office forms an AIN query and sends it to an SSP/adjunct node. As we shall see, the calling and called addresses in this message are the SS7 destination and source point codes and the message itself is coded as a TCAP message.

The SCP/adjunct node uses these addresses to make a query to a database to discover the location of the nearest Pizza a Go-Go outlet. In event 3, it sends this information back to the SSP office. Upon receipt of this message in event 4, the SSP places a call to the pizza parlor, thus connecting the customer to the Pizza a Go-Go.

SS7 SUPPORT FOR THE INTELLIGENT NETWORK

Figure C–2 shows the elements that exist today for the intelligent network. It is evident that they rest on SS7 architecture. The SCP continues to fill the role we described earlier in this material. The switch is now divided into two functions: (a) the service switching point (SSP) and (b) the signaling transfer point (STP).

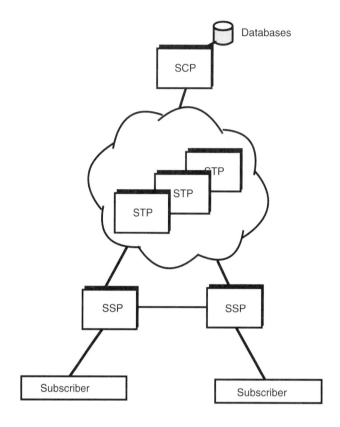

Where:
  SCP   Service control point
  SSP   Service switching point
  STP   Signaling transfer point

Figure C–2   Elements of the Intelligent Network

The SSP is the interface to the called and calling parties labeled in this figure as subscriber. This switch interprets the called party address (the dialed number) and determines what actions are to be taken. If the actions require the services of the SCP, a request message is created at the SSP and forwarded to the SCP through the backbone signaling network (which is supported by switches known as signaling transfer points [STP]).

Therefore, the underlying architecture for the intelligent network consists of three types of machines shown in this figure: the SSP, the STP, and the SCP. These three functions could very well be implemented in one hardware architecture with different software modules. And, indeed, this is the case in many situations.

Likewise, one machine may perform one or two or three of these functions. The actual physical implementation of these entities depends on the operating environment of the network.

During the evolution from a conventional service-specific environment to a service-independent environment, it was recognized that the implementation of other components would enhance and improve the network, mainly by aiding the rapid creation of services, and the efficient maintenance of these services. These components are called the service creation environment (SCE), the service management system (SMS), the intelligent peripheral (IP), the adjunct, and the network access point (NAP). Their position in the AIN topology is illustrated in Figure C–3. Notice that we have included a "cloud" that depicts the SS7 backbone. Inside this cloud are the STPs and their associated links. With a few exceptions (explained shortly), the AIN does not impose additional tasks for the STPs.

The SCE provides design and implementation tools to assist in creating and customizing services in the SCP. The SMS is a powerful data-

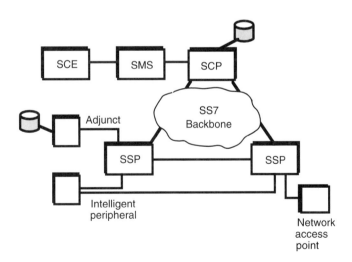

Note: The SCP, adjunct, and intelligent peripheral house the AIN applications programs.

Where:
  SCE   Service creation environment
  SMS   Service management system

Figure C–3   Other Parts of the AIN

base management system. It is used to manage the master database that controls the AIN customer services. This service includes ongoing database maintenance, backup and recovery, log management, and audit trails.

The intelligent peripheral can connect to an AIN call. It provides the following services: (a) tone generation, (b) voice recognition, (c) playback, (d) compression, (e) call control, (f) record, (g) DTMF detection and collection. As this figure illustrates, the IP is connected to one or more SSPs. It is designed to be application-independent, and to support generic services for more than one application.

The adjunct performs the same operations as an SCP, but it is configured for one (or few) services for a single switch. Other switches that wish to use the services of the adjunct must come through the SSP to which the adjunct is directly connected.

The NAP is a switch that has no AIN functions. It is connected off an SSP, and connects to trunks with SS7 or frequency tones. Based on the called and calling number received at the NAP, it may route the call to its attached SSP or AIN services.

The AIN STPs perform two functions beyond their usual operations. They employ pseudo-addressing that enables them to balance the load between SCPs. Second, they can employ alternate routing in the event of a problem in the network.

Figure C–4 shows the ITU-T IN nodes and their functional entities. These functions can be summarized as follows:

The service switching function (SSF) provides the means to recognize calls requiring AIN service processing and to interact with call processing and the service logic on behalf of those calls.

The call control function (CCF) (or call processing) provides the means for establishing and controlling bearer services on behalf of network users.

The call control agent function (CCAF) provides users with access to the services, and represents the users to call processing. The CCAF represents the interface between the user and the network control functions.

The service control function (SCF) contains AIN service logic providing the logical control to be applied to a call involving an AIN service. the SCF handles service related processing activities such as analysis, translation, screening, and routing.

The service data function (SDF) handles service-related and network data. It provides the SCF with a logical view of the data. The SDF contains data that directly relates to the provision or operation of (A)IN services, and may include access to user defined service related data.

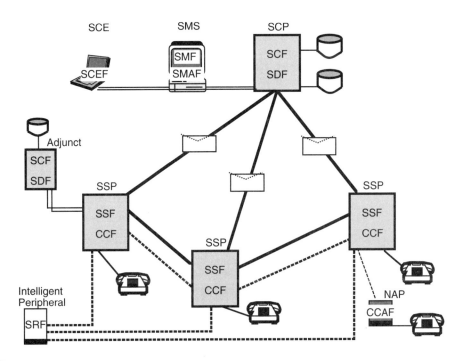

Where:

CCAF	Call control agent function
CCF	Call control function
SCEF	Service creation environment function
SCF	Service control function
SDF	Service data function
SMAF	Service management access function
SMF	Service management function
SRF	Specialized resource function (may reside in Intelligent Peripheral)
SSF	Service switching function

Figure C–4   The ITU-T IN Entities

The specialized resource function (SRF) provides end-user interaction with the AIN through control over resources such as DTMF receivers, voice recognition capabilities, protocol conversion, and announcements.

The service management function (SMF) provides the service provisioning, deployment and management control. The SMF allows access to all AIN functional entities for the transfer of information related to service logic and service data.

The service management access function (SMAF) controls access to service management functions.

Table C–1 Functional Entities and Their Placements

Functional Entity	Description	Placement
Call Control Access Function (CAF)	Allows user to access the CCF; handles call setup, termination, hold-on etc., can also provide user with CLASS (Customer Local Area Signaling Services).	SSP, NAP
Call Control Function (CCF)	Supports establishment of conventional bearer services.	SSP
Service Switching Function (SSF)	Recognizes calls requiring IN service processing. Interacts with call processing and service logic.	SSP
Service Control Function (SCF)	Furnishes control for a call requiring IN service and handles service related processing activities.	SCP, AD, SN
Service Data Function (SDF)	Supports access to network data and provides a logical view of the data to the SCF.	SCP, AD, SN
Specialized Resource Function (SRF)	Supports user interaction with the IN resources through interaction with resources such as DTMF, voice recognition, announcements.	SN, IP
Service Management Function (SMF)	Allows access to IN resources for the transfer of information.	SMS
Service Creation Environment Function (SCEF)	Deals with the creation, validation, and evaluation of new IN services	SCE

Where: IN =   Intelligent Peripheral
      NAP =   Network Access Point
      SCE =   Service Creation Environment
      SCP =   Service Control Point
      SMS =   Service Management System
      SN =   Service node
      SSP =   Service Switching Point

The service creation environment function (SCEF) supports the creation, verification and testing of new AIN services.

Table C–1 summarizes the functional entities and the placement in the IN components. The table is provided from The Conference on Intelligent Networks, May 9, 1996, sponsored by IBC Technical Services Ltd.

Appendix D

RFC 822

RFC 822 is provided in this Appendix. I have eliminated the RFC front matter and the header on each page to conserve space. Also, I have not included the appendices to this RFC, because most of these appendices show examples of coding, and many examples are already provided in the chapters of this text. If you wish to see the appendices and, of course, the complete RFC, go to www.ietf.org.

```
1. INTRODUCTION

1.1. SCOPE

     This standard specifies a syntax for text messages that are
sent among computer users, within the framework of "electronic
mail". The standard supersedes the one specified in ARPANET Re-
quest for Comments #733, "Standard for the Format of ARPA Net-
work Text Messages".
     In this context, messages are viewed as having an envelope
and contents. The envelope contains whatever information is
needed to accomplish transmission and delivery. The contents
compose the object to be delivered to the recipient. This stan-
dard applies only to the format and some of the semantics of
message contents. It contains no specification of the informa-
tion in the envelope.
```

However, some message systems may use information from the
contents to create the envelope. It is intended that this standard facilitate the acquisition of such information by programs.

Some message systems may store messages in formats that differ from the one specified in this standard. This specification
is intended strictly as a definition of what message content
format is to be passed BETWEEN hosts.

Note: This standard is NOT intended to dictate the internal
       formats used by sites, the specific message system fea-
       tures that they are expected to support, or any of the
       characteristics of user interface programs that create or
       read messages.

A distinction should be made between what the specification
REQUIRES and what it ALLOWS. Messages can be made complex and
rich with formally-structured components of information or can
be kept small and simple, with a minimum of such information.
Also, the standard simplifies the interpretation of differing
visual formats in messages; only the visual aspect of a message
is affected and not the interpretation of information within it.
Implementors may choose to retain such visual distinctions.

The formal definition is divided into four levels. The bottom
level describes the meta-notation used in this document. The second level describes basic lexical analyzers that feed tokens to
higher-level parsers. Next is an overall specification for messages; it permits distinguishing individual fields. Finally,
there is definition of the contents of several structured fields.

1.2. COMMUNICATION FRAMEWORK

Messages consist of lines of text. No special provisions are
made for encoding drawings, facsimile, speech, or structured
text. No significant consideration has been given to questions
of data compression or to transmission and storage efficiency,
and the standard tends to be free with the number of bits con-
sumed. For example, field names are specified as free text,
rather than special terse codes.

A general "memo" framework is used. That is, a message consists of some information in a rigid format, followed by the
main part of the message, with a format that is not specified in
this document. The syntax of several fields of the rigidly-for-
mated ("headers") section is defined in this specification; some
of these fields must be included in all messages.

The syntax that distinguishes between header fields is specified separately from the internal syntax for particular fields.
This separation is intended to allow simple parsers to operate
on the general structure of messages, without concern for the

detailed structure of individual header fields. Appendix B is
provided to facilitate construction of these parsers.

In addition to the fields specified in this document, it is
expected that other fields will gain common use. As necessary,
the specifications for these "extension-fields" will be published through the same mechanism used to publish this document.
Users may also wish to extend the set of fields that they use
privately. Such "user-defined fields" are permitted.

The framework severely constrains document tone and appearance and is primarily useful for most intra-organization communications and well-structured inter-organization communication. It
also can be used for some types of inter-process communication,
such as simple file transfer and remote job entry. A more robust
framework might allow for multi-font, multi-color, multidimension
encoding of information. A less robust one, as is present in most
single-machine message systems, would more severely constrain the
ability to add fields and the decision to include specific fields.
In contrast with paper-based communication, it is interesting to
note that the RECEIVER of a message can exercise an extraordinary
amount of control over the message's appearance. The amount of actual control available to message receivers is contingent upon the
capabilities of their individual message systems.

2. NOTATIONAL CONVENTIONS

This specification uses an augmented Backus-Naur Form (BNF)
notation. The differences from standard BNF involve naming rules
and indicating repetition and "local" alternatives.

2.1. RULE NAMING

Angle brackets ("<", ">") are not used, in general. The name
of a rule is simply the name itself, rather than "<name>". Quotation-marks enclose literal text (which may be upper and/or
lower case). Certain basic rules are in uppercase, such as
SPACE, TAB, CRLF, DIGIT, ALPHA, etc. Angle brackets are used in
rule definitions, and in the rest of this document, whenever
their presence will facilitate discerning the use of rule names.

2.2. RULE1 / RULE2: ALTERNATIVES

Elements separated by slash ("/") are alternatives. Therefore "foo / bar" will accept foo or bar.

2.3. (RULE1 RULE2): LOCAL ALTERNATIVES

Elements enclosed in parentheses are treated as a single element. Thus, "(elem (foo / bar) elem)" allows the token sequences "elem foo elem" and "elem bar elem".

2.4. *RULE: REPETITION

The character "*" preceding an element indicates repetition.
The full form is:

<l>*<m>element

indicating at least <l> and at most <m> occurrences of element.
Default values are 0 and infinity so that "*(element)" allows
any number, including zero; "1*element" requires at least one;
and "1*2element" allows one or two.

2.5. [RULE]: OPTIONAL

Square brackets enclose optional elements; "[foo bar]" is
equivalent to "*1(foo bar)".

2.6. NRULE: SPECIFIC REPETITION

"<n>(element)" is equivalent to "<n>*<n>(element)"; that is,
exactly <n> occurrences of (element). Thus 2DIGIT is a 2-digit
number, and 3ALPHA is a string of three alphabetic characters.

2.7. #RULE: LISTS

A construct "#" is defined, similar to "*", as follows:

<l>#<m>element

indicating at least <l> and at most <m> elements, each separated
by one or more commas (","). This makes the usual form of lists
very easy; a rule such as '(element *("," element))' can be
shown as "1#element". Wherever this construct is used, null elements are allowed, but do not contribute to the count of elements present. That is, "(element),,(element)" is permitted, but
counts as only two elements. Therefore, where at least one element is required, at least one non-null element must be present.
Default values are 0 and infinity so that "#(element)" allows
any number, including zero; "1#element" requires at least one;
and "1#2element" allows one or two.

2.8. ; COMMENTS

A semi-colon, set off some distance to the right of rule
text, starts a comment that continues to the end of line. This
is a simple way of including useful notes in parallel with the
specifications.

3. LEXICAL ANALYSIS OF MESSAGES

3.1. GENERAL DESCRIPTION

    A message consists of header fields and, optionally, a body. The body is simply a sequence of lines containing ASCII charac- ters. It is separated from the headers by a null line (i.e., a line with nothing preceding the CRLF).

3.1.1. LONG HEADER FIELDS

Each header field can be viewed as a single, logical line of ASCII characters, comprising a field-name and a field-body. For convenience, the field-body portion of this conceptual entity can be split into a multiple-line representation; this is called "folding". The general rule is that wherever there may be lin- ear-white-space (NOT simply LWSP-chars), a CRLF immediately fol- lowed by AT LEAST one LWSP-char may instead be inserted. Thus, the single line

    To: "Joe & J. Harvey" <ddd @Org>, JJV @ BBN

can be represented as:

    To: "Joe & J. Harvey" <ddd @ Org>,

        JJV@BBN

and

        To: "Joe & J. Harvey"

                <ddd@ Org>, JJV

        @BBN

and

    To: "Joe &
     J. Harvey" <ddd @ Org>, JJV @ BBN

    The process of moving from this folded multiple-line repre- sentation of a header field to its single line representation is called "unfolding". Unfolding is accomplished by regarding CRLF immediately followed by a LWSP-char as equivalent to the LWSP- char.

Note: While the standard permits folding wherever linear-white- space is permitted, it is recommended that structured fields, such as those containing addresses, limit folding to higher-level syntactic breaks. For address fields, it is recommended that such folding occur

3.1.2. STRUCTURE OF HEADER FIELDS

Once a field has been unfolded, it may be viewed as being composed of a field-name followed by a colon (":"), followed by a
field-body, and terminated by a carriage-return/line-feed. The
field-name must be composed of printable ASCII characters (i.e.,
characters that have values between 33. and 126., decimal, except colon). The field-body may be composed of any ASCII characters, except CR or LF. (While CR and/or LF may be present in the
actual text, they are removed by the action of unfolding the
field.)
    Certain field-bodies of headers may be interpreted according
to an internal syntax that some systems may wish to parse. These
fields are called "structured fields". Examples include fields
containing dates and addresses. Other fields, such as "Subject"
and "Comments", are regarded simply as strings of text.

Note: Any field which has a field-body that is defined as other
      than simply <text> is to be treated as a structured
      field.

    Field-names, unstructured field bodies and structured field
bodies each are scanned by their own, independent "lexical" analyzer.

3.1.3. UNSTRUCTURED FIELD BODIES

For some fields, such as "Subject" and "Comments", no structur-
ing is assumed, and they are treated simply as <text>s, as in
the message body. Rules of folding apply to these fields, so
that such field bodies which occupy several lines must therefore
have the second and successive lines indented by at least one
LWSP-char.

3.1.4. STRUCTURED FIELD BODIES

To aid in the creation and reading of structured fields, the
free insertion of linear-white-space (which permits folding by
inclusion of CRLFs) is allowed between lexical tokens. Rather
than obscuring the syntax specifications for these structured
fields with explicit syntax for this linear-white-space, the existence of another "lexical" analyzer is assumed. This analyzer
does not apply for unstructured field bodies that are simply
strings of text, as described above. The analyzer provides an
interpretation of the unfolded text composing the body of the
field as a sequence of lexical symbols.

These symbols are:
    - individual special characters

- quoted-strings
- domain-literals
- comments
- atoms

The first four of these symbols are self-delimiting. Atoms are not; they are delimited by the self-delimiting symbols and by linear-white-space. For the purposes of regenerating sequences of atoms and quoted-strings, exactly one SPACE is assumed to exist, and should be used, between them. (Also, in the "Clarifications" section on "White Space", below, note the rules about treatment of multiple contiguous LWSP-chars.)

So, for example, the folded body of an address field

```
    ":sysmail"@ Some-Group. Some-Org,
      Muhammed.(I am the greatest) Ali @(the)Vegas.WBA
```
is analyzed into the following lexical symbols and types:

:sysmail	quoted string
@	special
Some-Group	atom . special
Some-Org	atom
,	special
Muhammed	atom
.	special
(I am the greatest)	comment
Ali	atom
@	atom
(the)	comment
Vegas	atom
.	special
WBA	atom

The canonical representations for the data in these addresses are the following strings:

```
        ":sysmail"@Some-Group.Some-Org
```

and

```
        Muhammed.Ali@Vegas.WBA
```

Note: For purposes of display, and when passing such structured information to other systems, such as mail protocol services, there must be NO linear-white-space between \<word\>s that are separated by period (".") or at-sign ("@") and exactly one SPACE between all other \<word\>s. Also, headers should be in a folded form.

```
3.2. HEADER FIELD DEFINITIONS
```

These rules show a field meta-syntax, without regard for the
particular type or internal syntax. Their purpose is to permit
detection of fields; also, they present to higher-level parsers
an image of each field as fitting on one line.

```
field = field-name ":" [ field-body ] CRLF

field-name = 1*<any CHAR, excluding CTLs, SPACE, and ":">

field-body = field-body-contents [CRLF LWSP-char field-body]

field-body-contents =
            <the ASCII characters making up the field-body, as
            defined in the following sections, and consisting
            of combinations of atom, quoted-string, and
            specials tokens, or else consisting of texts>
```

```
3.3. LEXICAL TOKENS
```

    The following rules are used to define an underlying lexical
analyzer, which feeds tokens to higher level parsers. See the
ANSI references, in the Bibliography.

```
                                          ; ( Octal, Decimal.)
CHAR       = <any ASCII character>        ; ( 0-177, 0.-127.)
ALPHA      = <any ASCII alphabetic character>
                                          ; (101-132, 65.- 90.)
                                          ; (141-172, 97.-122.)
DIGIT      = <any ASCII decimal digit>    ; ( 60- 71, 48.- 57.)
CTL        = <any ASCII control           ; (  0- 37,  0.- 31.)
             character and DEL>           ; (    177,     127.)
CR         = <ASCII CR, carriage return>  ; (     15,      13.)
LF         = <ASCII LF, linefeed>         ; (     12,      10.)
SPACE      = <ASCII SP, space>            ; (     40,      32.)
HTAB       = <ASCII HT, horizontal-tab>   ; (     11,       9.)
<">        = <ASCII quote mark>           ; (     42,      34.)
CRLF       = CR LF
LWSP-char  = SPACE / HTAB                 ; semantics = SPACE
linear-white-space =  1*([CRLF] LWSP-char) ; semantics = SPACE
                                          ; CRLF => folding
specials   = "(" / ")" / "<" / ">" / "@"  ; Must be in quoted-
             / "," / ";" / ":" / "\" / <"> ; string, to use
             / "." / "[" / "]"            ; within a word.
delimiters = specials / linear-white-space / comment
text       = <any CHAR, including bare    ; => atoms, specials,
             CR & bare LF, but NOT        ; comments and
             including CRLF>              ; quoted-strings are
                                          ; NOT recognized.
```

```
atom         = 1*<any CHAR except specials, SPACE and CTLs>
quoted-string = <"> *(qtext/quoted-pair) <">; Regular qtext or
                                            ; quoted chars.
qtext        = <any CHAR excepting <">,    ; => may be folded
               "\" & CR, and including
               linear-white-space>
domain-literal = "[" *(dtext / quoted-pair) "]"
dtext          = <any CHAR excluding "[",  ; => may be folded
                 "]", "\" & CR, & including
                 linear-white-space>
comment        = "(" *(ctext / quoted-pair / comment) ")"
ctext          = <any CHAR excluding "(",  ; => may be folded
                 ")", "\" & CR, & including
                 linear-white-space>
quoted-pair    = "\" CHAR                   ; may quote any char
phrase         = 1*word                     ; Sequence of words
word           = atom / quoted-string
```

3.4. CLARIFICATIONS

3.4.1. QUOTING

Some characters are reserved for special interpretation, such as delimiting lexical tokens. To permit use of these characters as uninterpreted data, a quoting mechanism is provided. To quote a character, precede it with a backslash ("\").

This mechanism is not fully general. Characters may be quoted only within a subset of the lexical constructs. In particular, quoting is limited to use within:

> - quoted-string
> - domain-literal
> - comment

Within these constructs, quoting is REQUIRED for CR and "\" and for the character(s) that delimit the token (e.g., "(" and ")" for a comment). However, quoting is PERMITTED for any character.

Note: In particular, quoting is NOT permitted within atoms. For example when the local-part of an addr-spec must contain a special character, a quoted string must be used. Therefore, a specification such as:

> Full\ Name@Domain

is not legal and must be specified as:

```
                    "Full Name"@Domain
```

3.4.2. WHITE SPACE

Note: In structured field bodies, multiple linear space ASCII
        characters (namely HTABs and SPACEs) are treated as sin-
        gle spaces and may freely surround any symbol. In all
        header fields, the only place in which at least one LWSP-
        char is REQUIRED is at the beginning of continuation
        lines in a folded field.

When passing text to processes that do not interpret text according to this standard (e.g., mail protocol servers), then NO
linear-white-space characters should occur between a period
(".") or at-sign ("@") and a <word>. Exactly ONE SPACE should be
used in place of arbitrary linear-white-space and comment sequences.

Note: Within systems conforming to this standard, wherever a
        member of the list of delimiters is allowed, LWSP-chars
        may also occur before and/or after it.

Writers of mail-sending (i.e., header-generating) programs
should realize that there is no network-wide definition of the
effect of ASCII HT (horizontal-tab) characters on the appearance
of text at another network host; therefore, the use of tabs in
message headers, though permitted, is discouraged.

3.4.3. COMMENTS

A comment is a set of ASCII characters, which is enclosed in
matching parentheses and which is not within a quoted-string The
comment construct permits message originators to add text which
will be useful for human readers, but which will be ignored by
the formal semantics. Comments should be retained while the message is subject to interpretation according to this standard.
However, comments must NOT be included in other cases, such as
during protocol exchanges with mail servers.
    Comments nest, so that if an unquoted left parenthesis oc-
curs in a comment string, there must also be a matching right
parenthesis. When a comment acts as the delimiter between a sequence of two lexical symbols, such as two atoms, it is lexi-
cally equivalent with a single SPACE, for the purposes of
regenerating the sequence, such as when passing the sequence

onto a mail protocol server. Comments are detected as such only
within field-bodies of structured fields.

   If a comment is to be "folded" onto multiple lines, then the
syntax for folding must be adhered to. (See the "Lexical Analysis of Messages" section on "Folding Long Header Fields" above,
and the section on "Case Independence" below.) Note that the official semantics therefore do not "see" any unquoted CRLFs that
are in comments, although particular parsing programs may wish
to note their presence. For these programs, it would be reasonable to interpret a "CRLF LWSP-char" as being a CRLF that is
part of the comment; i.e., the CRLF is kept and the LWSP-char is
discarded. Quoted CRLFs (i.e., a backslash followed by a CR followed by a LF) still must be followed by at least one LWSP-char.

3.4.4. DELIMITING AND QUOTING CHARACTERS

The quote character (backslash) and characters that delimit syntactic units are not, generally, to be taken as data that are
part of the delimited or quoted unit(s). In particular, the quotation-marks that define a quoted-string, the parentheses that
define a comment and the backslash that quotes a following character are NOT part of the quoted-string, comment or quoted character. A quotation-mark that is to be part of a quoted-string, a
parenthesis that is to be part of a comment and a backslash that
is to be part of either must each be preceded by the quote-char-
acter backslash ("\"). Note that the syntax allows any character
to be quoted within a quoted-string or comment; however only
certain characters MUST be quoted to be included as data. These
characters are the ones that are not part of the alternate text
group (i.e., ctext or qtext).

   The one exception to this rule is that a single SPACE is assumed to exist between contiguous words in a phrase, and this
interpretation is independent of the actual number of LWSP-chars
that the creator places between the words. To include more than
one SPACE, the creator must make the LWSP-chars be part of a
quoted-string.

   Quotation marks that delimit a quoted string and backslashes
that quote the following character should NOT accompany the
quoted-string when the string is passed to processes that do not
interpret data according to this specification (e.g., mail protocol servers).

3.4.5. QUOTED-STRINGS

Where permitted (i.e., in words in structured fields) quoted-
strings are treated as a single symbol. That is, a quoted-string
is equivalent to an atom, syntactically. If a quoted-string is
to be "folded" onto multiple lines, then the syntax for folding

must be adhered to. (See the "Lexical Analysis of Messages" section on "Folding Long Header Fields" above, and the section on
"Case Independence" below.) Therefore, the official semantics do
not "see" any bare CRLFs that are in quoted-strings; however
particular parsing programs may wish to note their presence. For
such programs, it would be reasonable to interpret a "CRLF LWSP-
char" as being a CRLF which is part of the quoted-string; i.e.,
the CRLF is kept and the LWSP-char is discarded. Quoted CRLFs
(i.e., a backslash followed by a CR followed by a LF) are also
subject to rules of folding, but the presence of the quoting
character (backslash) explicitly indicates that the CRLF is data
to the quoted string. Stripping off the first following LWSP-
char is also appropriate when parsing quoted CRLFs.

3.4.6. BRACKETING CHARACTERS

There is one type of bracket which must occur in matched pairs
and may have pairs nested within each other:

    o Parentheses ("(" and ")") are used to indicate com-
       ments.

There are three types of brackets which must occur in matched
pairs, and which may NOT be nested:

    o Colon/semi-colon (":" and ";") are used in address
       specifications to indicate that the included list of
       addresses are to be treated as a group.
    o Angle brackets ("<" and ">") are generally used to in-
       dicate the presence of a one machine-usable reference
       (e.g., delimiting mailboxes), possibly including
       source-routing to the machine.
    o Square brackets ("[" and "]") are used to indicate the
       presence of a domain-literal, which the appropriate
       name-domain is to use directly, bypassing normal name-
       resolution mechanisms.

3.4.7. CASE INDEPENDENCE

Except as noted, alphabetic strings may be represented in any
combination of upper and lower case. The only syntactic units
which requires preservation of case information are:

                    - text
                    - qtext
                    - dtext
                    - ctext
                    - quoted-pair
                    - local-part, except "Postmaster"

When matching any other syntactic unit, case is to be ignored. For example, the field-names "From", "FROM", "from", and even "FroM" are semantically equal and should all be treated identically.

When generating these units, any mix of upper and lower case alphabetic characters may be used. The case shown in this specification is suggested for message-creating processes.

Note: The reserved local-part address unit, "Postmaster", is an exception. When the value "Postmaster" is being interpreted, it must be accepted in any mixture of case, including "POSTMASTER", and "postmaster".

3.4.8. FOLDING LONG HEADER FIELDS

Each header field may be represented on exactly one line consisting of the name of the field and its body, and terminated by a CRLF; this is what the parser sees. For readability, the field-body portion of long header fields may be "folded" onto multiple lines of the actual field. "Long" is commonly interpreted to mean greater than 65 or 72 characters. The former length serves as a limit, when the message is to be viewed on most simple terminals which use simple display software; however, the limit is not imposed by this standard.

Note: Some display software often can selectively fold lines, to suit the display terminal. In such cases, sender-provided folding can interfere with the display software.

3.4.9. BACKSPACE CHARACTERS

ASCII BS characters (Backspace, decimal 8) may be included in texts and quoted-strings to effect overstriking. However, any use of backspaces which effects an overstrike to the left of the beginning of the text or quoted-string is prohibited.

3.4.10. NETWORK-SPECIFIC TRANSFORMATIONS

During transmission through heterogeneous networks, it may be necessary to force data to conform to a network's local conventions. For example, it may be required that a CR be followed either by LF, making a CRLF, or by <null>, if the CR is to stand alone). Such transformations are reversed, when the message exits that network.

When crossing network boundaries, the message should be treated as passing through two modules. It will enter the first module containing whatever network-specific transformations that

were necessary to permit migration through the "current" network. It then passes through the modules:

> o Transformation Reversal
>   The "current" network's idiosyncracies are re-
>   moved and the message is returned to the canoni-
>   cal form specified in this standard.
> o Transformation
>   The "next" network's local idiosyncracies are im-
>   posed on the message.

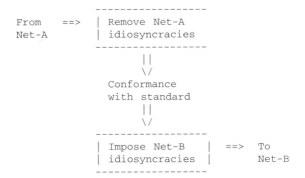

```
                              ------------------
          From     ==>     |  Remove Net-A
          Net-A            |  idiosyncracies
                              ------------------
                                     ||
                                     \/
                              Conformance
                              with standard
                                     ||
                                     \/
                              ------------------
                           |  Impose Net-B   |    ==>   To
                           |  idiosyncracies |          Net-B
                              ------------------
```

4. MESSAGE SPECIFICATION

4.1. SYNTAX

Note: Due to an artifact of the notational conventions, the
       syntax indicates that, when present, some fields, must be
       in a particular order. Header fields are NOT required to
       occur in any particular order, except that the message
       body must occur AFTER the headers. It is recommended
       that, if present, headers be sent in the order "Return-
       Path", "Received", "Date", "From", "Subject", "Sender",
       "To", "cc", etc.

       This specification permits multiple occurrences of most
       fields. Except as noted, their interpretation is not
       specified here, and their use is discouraged.

     The following syntax for the bodies of various fields should
be thought of as describing each field body as a single long
string (or line). The "Lexical Analysis of Message" section on
"Long Header Fields", above, indicates how such long strings can

be represented on more than one line in the actual transmitted
message.

```
Message      = fields *( CRLF *text )      ; Everything after
                                           ; first null line
                                           ; is message body
fields       = dates                       ; Creation time,
                 source                    ; author id & one
                 1*destination             ; address required
                *optional-field            ; others optional
source       = [ trace ]                   ; net traversals
                 originator                ; original mail
                 [ resent ]                ; forwarded
trace        = return                      ; path to sender
                 1*received                ; receipt tags
return       = "Return-path" ":" route-addr ; return address
received     = "Received" ":"              ; one per relay
                 ["from" domain]           ; sending host
                 ["by" domain]             ; receiving host
                 ["via" atom]              ; physical path
                 *("with" atom)            ; link/mail protocol
                 ["id" msg-id]             ; receiver msg id
                 ["for" addr-spec]         ; initial form
                 ";" date-time             ; time received
originator   = authentic                   ; authenticated addr
                 [ "Reply-To" ":" 1#address] )
authentic    = "From"        ":" mailbox   ; Single author
               / ( "Sender"  ":" mailbox   ; Actual submittor
                 "From"      ":" 1#mailbox) ; Multiple authors
                                           ; or not sender
resent       = resent-authentic
                 [ "Resent-Reply-To"  ":" 1#address] )
resent-authentic     =
             = "Resent-From"        ":" mailbox
               / ( "Resent-Sender"  ":" mailbox
                 "Resent-From"      ":" 1#mailbox )
dates        = orig-date                   ; Original
                 [ resent-date ]           ; Forwarded
orig-date    = "Date"        ":" date-time
resent-date  = "Resent-Date" ":" date-time
destination  = "To"          ":" 1#address      ; Primary
               / "Resent-To" ":" 1#address
               / "cc"        ":" 1#address      ; Secondary
               / "Resent-cc" ":" 1#address
               / "bcc"       ":"  #address      ; Blind carbon
               / "Resent-bcc" ":"  #address
optional-field       =
               / "Message-ID"     ":" msg-id
```

```
          / "Resent-Message-ID"  ":" msg-id
          / "In-Reply-To"        ":" *(phrase / msg-id)
          / "References"         ":" *(phrase / msg-id)
          / "Keywords"           ":" #phrase
          / "Subject"            ":" *text
          / "Comments"           ":" *text
          / "Encrypted"          ":" 1#2word
          / extension-field              ; To be defined
          / user-defined-field           ; May be pre-empted
msg-id         = "<" addr-spec ">"       ; Unique message id
extension-field =
          <Any field which is defined in a document published as
          a formal extension to this specification; none will
          have names beginning with the string "X-">
user-defined-field =
          <Any field which has not been defined in this specifi-
          cation or published as an extension to this specifica-
          tion; names for such fields must be unique and may be
          pre-empted by published extensions>
```

4.2. FORWARDING

     Some systems permit mail recipients to forward a message,
retaining the original headers, by adding some new fields. This
standard supports such a service, through the "Resent-" prefix
to field names.
     Whenever the string "Resent-" begins a field name, the field
has the same semantics as a field whose name does not have the
prefix. However, the message is assumed to have been forwarded
by an original recipient who attached the "Resent-" field. This
new field is treated as being more recent than the equivalent,
original field. For example, the "Resent-From", indicates the
person that forwarded the message, whereas the "From" field indicates the original author.
     Use of such precedence information depends upon partici-
pants' communication needs. For example, this standard does not
dictate when a "Resent-From:" address should receive replies, in
lieu of sending them to the "From:" address.

Note: In general, the "Resent-" fields should be treated as
       containing a set of information that is independent of
       the set of original fields. Information for one set
       should not automatically be taken from the other. The in-
       terpretation of multiple "Resent-" fields, of the same
       type, is undefined.

In the remainder of this specification, occurrence of legal "Resent-" fields are treated identically with the occurrence of fields whose names do not contain this prefix.

4.3. TRACE FIELDS

Trace information is used to provide an audit trail of message handling. In addition, it indicates a route back to the sender of the message.

The list of known "via" and "with" values are registered with the Network Information Center, SRI International, Menlo Park, California.

4.3.1. RETURN-PATH

This field is added by the final transport system that delivers the message to its recipient. The field is intended to contain definitive information about the address and route back to the message's originator.

Note: The "Reply-To" field is added by the originator and serves to direct replies, whereas the "Return-Path" field is used to identify a path back to the originator.

While the syntax indicates that a route specification is optional, every attempt should be made to provide that information in this field.

4.3.2. RECEIVED

A copy of this field is added by each transport service that relays the message. The information in the field can be quite useful for tracing transport problems.

The names of the sending and receiving hosts and time-of-receipt may be specified. The "via" parameter may be used, to indicate what physical mechanism the message was sent over, such as Arpanet or Phonenet, and the "with" parameter may be used to indicate the mail-, or connection-, level protocol that was used, such as the SMTP mail protocol, or X.25 transport protocol.

Note: Several "with" parameters may be included, to fully specify the set of protocols that were used.

Some transport services queue mail; the internal message identifier that is assigned to the message may be noted, using the "id" parameter. When the sending host uses a destination address specification that the receiving host reinterprets, by ex-

pansion or transformation, the receiving host may wish to record
the original specification, using the "for" parameter. For example, when a copy of mail is sent to the member of a distribution
list, this parameter may be used to record the original address
that was used to specify the list.

4.4. ORIGINATOR FIELDS

The standard allows only a subset of the combinations possible with the From, Sender, Reply-To, Resent-From, Resent-Sender,
and Resent-Reply-To fields. The limitation is intentional.

4.4.1. FROM / RESENT-FROM

This field contains the identity of the person(s) who wished
this message to be sent. The message-creation process should default this field to be a single, authenticated machine address,
indicating the AGENT (person, system or process) entering the
message. If this is not done, the "Sender" field MUST be present. If the "From" field IS defaulted this way, the "Sender"
field is optional and is redundant with the "From" field. In all
cases, addresses in the "From" field must be machine-usable
(addr-specs) and may not contain named lists (groups).

4.4.2. SENDER / RESENT-SENDER

This field contains the authenticated identity of the AGENT
(person, system or process) that sends the message. It is intended for use when the sender is not the author of the message,
or to indicate who among a group of authors actually sent the
message. If the contents of the "Sender" field would be completely redundant with the "From" field, then the "Sender" field
need not be present and its use is discouraged (though still
legal). In particular, the "Sender" field MUST be present if it
is NOT the same as the "From" Field.
The Sender mailbox specification includes a word sequence
which must correspond to a specific agent (i.e., a human user or a
computer program) rather than a standard address. This indicates
the expectation that the field will identify the single AGENT
(person, system, or process) responsible for sending the mail and
not simply include the name of a mailbox from which the mail was
sent. For example in the case of a shared login name, the name, by
itself, would not be adequate. The local-part address unit, which
refers to this agent, is expected to be a computer system term,
and not (for example) a generalized person reference which can be
used outside the network text message context. Since the critical
function served by the "Sender" field is identification of the
agent responsible for sending mail and since computer programs

cannot be held accountable for their behavior, it is strongly
recommended that when a computer program generates a message, the
HUMAN who is responsible for that program be referenced as part of
the "Sender" field mail-box specification.

4.4.3. REPLY-TO / RESENT-REPLY-TO

This field provides a general mechanism for indicating any
mailbox(es) to which responses are to be sent. Three typical
uses for this feature can be distinguished. In the first case,
the author(s) may not have regular machine-based mail-boxes and
therefore wish(es) to indicate an alternate machine address. In
the second case, an author may wish additional persons to be
made aware of, or responsible for, replies. A somewhat different
use may be of some help to "text message teleconferencing"
groups equipped with automatic distribution services: include
the address of that service in the "Reply-To" field of all messages submitted to the teleconference; then participants can
"reply" to conference submissions to guarantee the correct distribution of any submission of their own.

Note: The "Return-Path" field is added by the mail transport
        service, at the time of final deliver. It is intended to
        identify a path back to the orginator of the message. The
        "Reply-To" field is added by the message originator and
        is intended to direct replies.

4.4.4. AUTOMATIC USE OF FROM / SENDER / REPLY-TO

For systems which automatically generate address lists for
replies to messages, the following recommendations are made:

o The "Sender" field mailbox should be sent notices of
  any problems in transport or delivery of the original
  messages. If there is no "Sender" field, then the
  "From" field mailbox should be used.
o The "Sender" field mailbox should NEVER be used automatically, in a recipient's reply message.
o If the "Reply-To" field exists, then the reply should
  go to the addresses indicated in that field and not
  to the address(es) indicated in the "From" field.
o If there is a "From" field, but no "Reply-To" field,
  the reply should be sent to the address(es) indicated
  in the "From" field.

Sometimes, a recipient may actually wish to communicate with the person that initiated the message transfer. In such cases, it is reasonable to use the "Sender" address.

This recommendation is intended only for automated use of originator-fields and is not intended to suggest that replies may not also be sent to other recipients of messages. It is up to the respective mail-handling programs to decide what additional facilities will be provided.

Examples are provided in Appendix A.

4.5. RECEIVER FIELDS

4.5.1. TO / RESENT-TO

This field contains the identity of the primary recipients of the message.

4.5.2. CC / RESENT-CC

This field contains the identity of the secondary (informational) recipients of the message.

4.5.3. BCC / RESENT-BCC

This field contains the identity of additional recipients of the message. The contents of this field are not included in copies of the message sent to the primary and secondary recipients. Some systems may choose to include the text of the "Bcc" field only in the author(s)'s copy, while others may also include it in the text sent to all those indicated in the "Bcc" list.

4.6. REFERENCE FIELDS

4.6.1. MESSAGE-ID / RESENT-MESSAGE-ID

This field contains a unique identifier (the local-part address unit) which refers to THIS version of THIS message. The uniqueness of the message identifier is guaranteed by the host which generates it. This identifier is intended to be machine readable and not necessarily meaningful to humans. A message identifier pertains to exactly one instantiation of a particular message; subsequent revisions to the message should each receive new message identifiers.

4.6.2. IN-REPLY-TO

The contents of this field identify previous correspondence which this message answers. Note that if message identifiers are used in this field, they must use the msg-id specification format.

4.6.3. REFERENCES

The contents of this field identify other correspondence which this message references. Note that if message identifiers are used, they must use the msg-id specification format.

4.6.4. KEYWORDS

This field contains keywords or phrases, separated by commas.

4.7. OTHER FIELDS

4.7.1. SUBJECT

This is intended to provide a summary, or indicate the nature, of the message.

4.7.2. COMMENTS

Permits adding text comments onto the message without disturbing the contents of the message's body.

4.7.3. ENCRYPTED

Sometimes, data encryption is used to increase the privacy of message contents. If the body of a message has been encrypted, to keep its contents private, the "Encrypted" field can be used to note the fact and to indicate the nature of the encryption. The first <word> parameter indicates the software used to encrypt the body, and the second, optional <word> is intended to aid the recipient in selecting the proper decryption key. This code word may be viewed as an index to a table of keys held by the recipient.

Note: Unfortunately, headers must contain envelope, as well as contents, information. Consequently, it is necessary that they remain unencrypted, so that mail transport services may access them. Since names, addresses, and "Subject" field contents may contain sensitive information, this requirement limits total message privacy.

Names of encryption software are registered with the Network Information Center, SRI International, Menlo Park, California.

4.7.4. EXTENSION-FIELD

A limited number of common fields have been defined in this document. As network mail requirements dictate, additional fields may be standardized. To provide user-defined fields with

a measure of safety, in name selection, such extension-fields
will never have names that begin with the string "X-".
    Names of Extension-fields are registered with the Network
Information Center, SRI International, Menlo Park, California.

4.7.5. USER-DEFINED-FIELD

    Individual users of network mail are free to define and use
additional header fields. Such fields must have names which are
not already used in the current specification or in any definitions of extension-fields, and the overall syntax of these user-
defined-fields must conform to this specification's rules for
delimiting and folding fields. Due to the extension-field publish-
ing process, the name of a userdefined-field may be pre-empted

Note: The prefatory string "X-" will never be used in the names
       of Extension-fields. This provides user-defined fields
       with a protected set of names.

5. DATE AND TIME SPECIFICATION

5.1. SYNTAX

```
date-time     = [ day "," ] date time     ; dd mm yy
                                           ; hh:mm:ss zzz
day           = "Mon" / "Tue" / "Wed" / "Thu"
              / "Fri" / "Sat" / "Sun"
date          = 1*2DIGIT month 2DIGIT     ; day month year

; e.g. 20 Jun 82
month         = "Jan" / "Feb" / "Mar" / "Apr"
              / "May" / "Jun" / "Jul" / "Aug"
              / "Sep" / "Oct" / "Nov" / "Dec"
time          = hour zone                 ; ANSI and Military
hour          = 2DIGIT ":" 2DIGIT [":" 2DIGIT]
                                          ; 00:00:00 - 23:59:59
zone          = "UT" / "GMT"              ; Universal Time
                                          ; North American: UT
              /"EST" / "EDT"              ; Eastern: - 5/ - 4
              / "CST" / "CDT"             ; Central: - 6/ - 5
              / "MST" / "MDT"             ; Mountain: - 7/ - 6
              / "PST" / "PDT"             ; Pacific: - 8/ - 7
              / 1ALPHA                    ; Military: Z = UT;
                                          ; A:-1; (J not used)
                                          ; M:-12; N:+1; Y:+12
              / ( ("+" / "-") 4DIGIT )    ; Local differential
                                          ; hours+min. (HHMM)
```

5.2. SEMANTICS

   If included, day-of-week must be the day implied by the date
specification.
   Time zone may be indicated in several ways. "UT" is Universal Time (formerly called "Greenwich Mean Time"); "GMT" is permitted as a reference to Universal Time. The military standard
uses a single character for each zone. "Z" is Universal Time.
"A" indicates one hour earlier, and "M" indicates 12 hours earlier; "N" is one hour later, and "Y" is 12 hours later. The letter "J" is not used. The other remaining two forms are taken
from ANSI standard X3.51-1975. One allows explicit indication of
the amount of offset from UT; the other uses common 3-character
strings for indicating time zones in North America.

6. ADDRESS SPECIFICATION

6.1. SYNTAX

```
address         = mailbox                    ; one addressee
                / group                      ; named list
group           = phrase ":" [#mailbox] ";"
mailbox         = addr-spec                  ; simple address
                / phrase route-addr          ; name & addr-spec
route-addr      = "<" [route] addr-spec ">"
route           = 1#("@" domain) ":"         ; path-relative
addr-spec       = local-part "@" domain      ; global address
local-part      = word *("." word)           ; uninterpreted
                                             ; case-preserved
domain          = sub-domain *("." sub-domain)
sub-domain      = domain-ref / domain-literal
domain-ref      = atom                       ; symbolic reference
```


6.2. SEMANTICS

   A mailbox receives mail. It is a conceptual entity which
does not necessarily pertain to file storage. For example, some
sites may choose to print mail on their line printer and deliver
the output to the addressee's desk.
   A mailbox specification comprises a person, system or
process name reference, a domain-dependent string, and a name-
domain reference. The name reference is optional and is usually
used to indicate the human name of a recipient. The name-domain
reference specifies a sequence of sub-domains. The domain-dependent string is uninterpreted, except by the final sub-domain;
the rest of the mail service merely transmits it as a literal
string.

6.2.1. DOMAINS

A name-domain is a set of registered (mail) names. A name-domain specification resolves to a subordinate name-domain spec-ification or to a terminal domain-dependent string. Hence, domain specification is extensible, permitting any number of registration levels. Name-domains model a global, logical, hier-archical addressing scheme. The model is logical, in that an ad-dress specification is related to name registration and is not necessarily tied to transmission path. The model's hierarchy is a directed graph, called an in-tree, such that there is a single path from the root of the tree to any node in the hierarchy. If more than one path actually exists, they are considered to be different addresses.

The root node is common to all addresses; consequently, it is not referenced. Its children constitute "top-level" name-do-mains. Usually, a service has access to its own full domain specification and to the names of all top-level name-domains.

The "top" of the domain addressing hierarchy — a child of the root — is indicated by the right-most field, in a domain specification. Its child is specified to the left, its child to the left, and so on.

Some groups provide formal registration services; these con-stitute name-domains that are independent logically of specific machines. In addition, networks and machines implicitly compose name-domains, since their membership usually is registered in name tables.

In the case of formal registration, an organization imple-ments a (distributed) data base which provides an address-to-route mapping service for addresses of the form:

                        person@registry.organization

Note that "organization" is a logical entity, separate from any particular communication network.

A mechanism for accessing "organization" is universally available. That mechanism, in turn, seeks an instantiation of the registry; its location is not indicated in the address spec-ification. It is assumed that the system which operates under the name "organization" knows how to find a subordinate reg-istry. The registry will then use the "person" string to deter-mine where to send the mail specification.

The latter, network-oriented case permits simple, direct, attachment-related address specification, such as:

                        user@host.network

Once the network is accessed, it is expected that a message will go directly to the host and that the host will resolve the user name, placing the message in the user's mailbox.

6.2.2. ABBREVIATED DOMAIN SPECIFICATION

Since any number of levels is possible within the domain hierarchy, specification of a fully qualified address can become inconvenient. This standard permits abbreviated domain specification, in a special case:

>   For the address of the sender, call the left-most sub-domain Level N. In a header address, if all of the sub-domains above (i.e., to the right of) Level N are the same as those of the sender, then they do not have to appear in the specification. Otherwise, the address must be fully qualified.

>   This feature is subject to approval by local subdomains. Individual sub-domains may require their member systems, which originate mail, to provide full domain specification only. When permitted, abbreviations may be present only while the message stays within the sub-domain of the sender.

>   Use of this mechanism requires the sender's sub-domain to reserve the names of all top-level domains, so that full specifications can be distinguished from abbreviated specifications.

For example, if a sender's address is:

    sender@registry-A.registry-1.organization-X

and one recipient's address is:

    recipient@registry-B.registry-1.organization-X

and another's is:

    recipient@registry-C.registry-2.organization-X

then ".registry-1.organization-X" need not be specified in the the message, but "registry-C.registry-2" DOES have to be specified. That is, the first two addresses may be abbreviated, but the third address must be fully specified.

When a message crosses a domain boundary, all addresses must be specified in the full format, ending with the top-level name-domain in the right-most field. It is the responsibility of mail forwarding services to ensure that addresses conform with this requirement. In the case of abbreviated addresses, the relaying service must make the necessary expansions. It should be noted that it often is difficult for such a service to locate all oc-

currences of address abbreviations. For example, it will not be
possible to find such abbreviations within the body of the message. The "Return-Path" field can aid recipients in recovering
from these errors.

Note: When passing any portion of an addr-spec onto a process
       which does not interpret data according to this standard
       (e.g., mail protocol servers). There must be NO LWSP-
       chars preceding or following the at-sign or any delimit-
       ing period ("."), such as shown in the above examples,
       and only ONE SPACE between contiguous <word>s.

6.2.3. DOMAIN TERMS

    A domain-ref must be THE official name of a registry, net-
work, or host. It is a symbolic reference, within a name subdo-
main. At times, it is necessary to bypass standard mechanisms for
resolving such references, using more primitive information, such
as a network host address rather than its associated host name.
    To permit such references, this standard provides the do-
main-literal construct. Its contents must conform with the needs
of the sub-domain in which it is interpreted.
    Domain-literals which refer to domains within the ARPA In-
ternet specify 32-bit Internet addresses, in four 8-bit fields
noted in decimal, as described in Request for Comments #820,
"Assigned Numbers." For example:

                         [10.0.3.19]

Note: THE USE OF DOMAIN-LITERALS IS STRONGLY DISCOURAGED. It is
       permitted only as a means of bypassing temporary system
       limitations, such as name tables which are not complete.

    The names of "top-level" domains, and the names of domains
under in the ARPA Internet, are registered with the Network Information Center, SRI International, Menlo Park, California.

6.2.4. DOMAIN-DEPENDENT LOCAL STRING

    The local-part of an addr-spec in a mailbox specification
(i.e., the host's name for the mailbox) is understood to be
whatever the receiving mail protocol server allows. For example,
some systems do not understand mailbox references of the form
"P. D. Q. Bach", but others do.
    This specification treats periods (".") as lexical separa-
tors. Hence, their presence in local-parts which are not quoted-
strings, is detected. However, such occurrences carry NO
semantics. That is, if a local-part has periods within it, an

address parser will divide the local-part into several tokens,
but the sequence of tokens will be treated as one uninterpreted
unit. The sequence will be re-assembled, when the address is
passed outside of the system such as to a mail protocol service.

For example, the address:

                        First.Last@Registry.Org

is legal and does not require the local-part to be surrounded
with quotation-marks. (However, "First Last" DOES require quoting.) The local-part of the address, when passed outside of the
mail system, within the Registry.Org domain, is "First.Last",
again without quotation marks.

6.2.5. BALANCING LOCAL-PART AND DOMAIN

    In some cases, the boundary between local-part and domain
can be flexible. The local-part may be a simple string, which is
used for the final determination of the recipient's mailbox. All
other levels of reference are, therefore, part of the domain.
    For some systems, in the case of abbreviated reference to
the local and subordinate sub-domains, it may be possible to
specify only one reference within the domain part and place the
other, subordinate name-domain references within the local-part.
This would appear as:

                        mailbox.sub1.sub2@this-domain

    Such a specification would be acceptable to address parsers
which conform to RFC #733, but do not support this newer Internet standard. While contrary to the intent of this standard, the
form is legal.
    Also, some sub-domains have a specification syntax which
does not conform to this standard. For example: uses a different
parsing sequence for local-part than for domain.

Note: As a rule, the domain specification should contain fields
       which are encoded according to the syntax of this stan-
       dard and which contain generally-standardized informa-
       tion. The local-part specification should contain only
       that portion of the address which deviates from the form
       or intention of the domain field.

6.2.6. MULTIPLE MAILBOXES

    An individual may have several mailboxes and wish to receive
mail at whatever mailbox is convenient for the sender to access.

This standard does not provide a means of specifying "any member of" a list of mailboxes.

A set of individuals may wish to receive mail as a single unit (i.e., a distribution list). The <group> construct permits specification of such a list. Recipient mailboxes are specified within the bracketed part (":" - ";"). A copy of the transmitted message is to be sent to each mailbox listed. This standard does not permit recursive specification of groups within groups.

While a list must be named, it is not required that the contents of the list be included. In this case, the <address> serves only as an indication of group distribution and would appear in the form:

name:;

Some mail services may provide a group-list distribution facility, accepting a single mailbox reference, expanding it to the full distribution list, and relaying the mail to the list's members. This standard provides no additional syntax for indicating such a service. Using the <group> address alternative, while listing one mailbox in it, can mean either that the mailbox reference will be expanded to a list or that there is a group with one member.

6.2.7. EXPLICIT PATH SPECIFICATION

At times, a message originator may wish to indicate the transmission path that a message should follow. This is called source routing. The normal addressing scheme, used in an addr-spec, is carefully separated from such information; the <route> portion of a route-addr is provided for such occasions. It specifies the sequence of hosts and/or transmission services that are to be traversed. Both domain-refs and domain-literals may be used.

Note: The use of source routing is discouraged. Unless the sender has special need of path restriction, the choice of transmission route should be left to the mail transport service.

6.3. RESERVED ADDRESS

It often is necessary to send mail to a site, without knowing any of its valid addresses. For example, there may be mail system dysfunctions, or a user may wish to find out a person's correct address, at that site.

This standard specifies a single, reserved mailbox address (local-part) which is to be valid at each site. Mail sent to that address is to be routed to a person responsible for the site's mail system or to a person with responsibility for general site operation. The name of the reserved local-part address is:

Postmaster

so that "Postmaster@domain" is required to be valid.

Note: This reserved local-part must be matched without sensitivity to alphabetic case, so that "POSTMASTER", "postmaster", and even "poStmASteR" is to be accepted.

7. BIBLIOGRAPHY

ANSI. "USA Standard Code for Information Interchange," X3.4. American National Standards Institute: New York (1968). Also in: Feinler, E. and J. Postel, eds., "ARPANET Protocol Handbook", NIC 7104.

ANSI. "Representations of Universal Time, Local Time Differentials, and United States Time Zone References for Information Interchange," X3.51-1975. American National Standards Institute: New York (1975).

Bemer, R.W., "Time and the Computer." In: Interface Age (Feb. 1979).

Bennett, C.J. "JNT Mail Protocol". Joint Network Team, Rutherford and Appleton Laboratory: Didcot, England.

Bhushan, A.K., Pogran, K.T., Tomlinson, R.S., and White, J.E. "Standardizing Network Mail Headers," ARPANET Request for Comments No. 561, Network Information Center No. 18516; SRI International: Menlo Park (September 1973).

Birrell, A.D., Levin, R., Needham, R.M., and Schroeder, M.D. "Grapevine: An Exercise in Distributed Computing," Communications of the ACM 25, 4 (April 1982), 260-274.

Crocker, D.H., Vittal, J.J., Pogran, K.T., Henderson, D.A. "Standard for the Format of ARPA Network Text Message," ARPANET Request for Comments No. 733, Network Information Center No. 41952. SRI International: Menlo Park (November 1977).

Feinler, E.J. and Postel, J.B. ARPANET Protocol Handbook, Network Information Center No. 7104 (NTIS AD A003890). SRI International: Menlo Park (April 1976).

Harary, F. "Graph Theory". Addison-Wesley: Reading, Mass. (1969).

Levin, R. and Schroeder, M. "Transport of Electronic Messages through a Network," TeleInformatics 79, pp. 29-33. North Holland (1979). Also as Xerox Palo Alto Research Center Technical Report CSL-79-4.

Myer, T.H. and Henderson, D.A. "Message Transmission Protocol," ARPANET Request for Comments, No. 680, Network Information Center No. 32116. SRI International: Menlo Park (1975).

NBS. "Specification of Message Format for Computer Based Message Systems, Recommended Federal Information Processing Standard." National Bureau of Standards: Gaithersburg, Maryland (October 1981).

NIC. Internet Protocol Transition Workbook. Network Information Center, SRI-International, Menlo Park, California (March 1982).

Oppen, D.C. and Dalal, Y.K. "The Clearinghouse: A Decentralized Agent for Locating Named Objects in a Distributed Environment," OPD-T8103. Xerox Office Products Division: Palo Alto, CA. (October 1981).

Postel, J.B. "Assigned Numbers," ARPANET Request for Comments, No. 820. SRI International: Menlo Park (August 1982).

Postel, J.B. "Simple Mail Transfer Protocol," ARPANET Request for Comments, No. 821. SRI International: Menlo Park (August 1982).

Shoch, J.F. "Internetwork naming, addressing and routing," in Proc. 17th IEEE Computer Society International Conference, pp. 72-79, Sept. 1978, IEEE Cat. No. 78 CH 1388-8C.

Su, Z. and Postel, J. "The Domain Naming Convention for Internet User Applications," ARPANET Request for Comments, No. 819. SRI International: Menlo Park (August 1982).

Appendix E

RFC 2234

RFC 2234 is provided in this appendix. I have eliminated the RFC front matter and header on each page to conserve space. If you wish to study the references cited in Section 8, go to www.ietf.org. and the ANSI standards (www.ansi.org).

1. INTRODUCTION

Internet technical specifications often need to define a format syntax and are free to employ whatever notation their authors deem useful. Over the years, a modified version of Backus-Naur Form (BNF), called Augmented BNF (ABNF), has been popular among many Internet specifications. It balances compactness and simplicity, with reasonable representational power. In the early days of the Arpanet, each specification contained its own definition of ABNF. This included the email specifications, RFC733 and then RFC822 which have come to be the common citations for defining ABNF. The current document separates out that definition, to permit selective reference. Predictably, it also provides some modifications and enhancements.

The differences between standard BNF and ABNF involve naming rules, repetition, alternatives, order-independence, and value ranges. Appendix A (Core) supplies rule definitions and encoding for a core lexical analyzer of the type common to several Inter-

---

347

net specifications. It is provided as a convenience and is otherwise separate from the meta language defined in the body of
this document, and separate from its formal status.

2. RULE DEFINITION

2.1 Rule Naming

The name of a rule is simply the name itself; that is, a sequence of characters, beginning with an alphabetic character,
and followed by a combination of alphabetics, digits and hyphens
(dashes).

NOTE: Rule names are case-insensitive

The names <rulename>, <Rulename>, <RULENAME> and <rUlENamE> all
refer to the same rule.

Unlike original BNF, angle brackets ("<", ">") are not required.
However, angle brackets may be used around a rule name whenever
their presence will facilitate discerning the use of a rule
name. This is typically restricted to rule name references in
free-form prose, or to distinguish partial rules that combine
into a string not separated by white space, such as shown in the
discussion about repetition, below.

2.2 Rule Form

A rule is defined by the following sequence:

                      name = elements crlf

where <name> is the name of the rule, <elements> is one or more
rule names or terminal specifications and <crlf> is the end-of-
line indicator, carriage return followed by line feed. The equal
sign separates the name from the definition of the rule. The elements form a sequence of one or more rule names and/or value
definitions, combined according to the various operators, defined in this document, such as alternative and repetition.
     For visual ease, rule definitions are left aligned. When a
rule requires multiple lines, the continuation lines are indented. The left alignment and indentation are relative to the
first lines of the ABNF rules and need not match the left margin
of the document.

2.3 Terminal Values

Rules resolve into a string of terminal values, sometimes called
characters. In ABNF a character is merely a non-negative integer. In certain contexts a specific mapping (encoding) of values
into a character set (such as ASCII) will be specified.
   Terminals are specified by one or more numeric characters
with the base interpretation of those characters indicated explicitly. The following bases are currently defined:

```
b           = binary
d           = decimal
x           = hexadecimal
Hence:
CR          = %d13
CR          = %x0D
```

respectively specify the decimal and hexadecimal representation
of [US-ASCII] for carriage return.
A concatenated string of such values is specified compactly,
using a period (".") to indicate separation of characters within
that value. Hence:

```
CRLF        = %d13.10
```

ABNF permits specifying literal text string directly, enclosed
in quotation-marks. Hence:

```
command     = "command string"
```

Literal text strings are interpreted as a concatenated set of
printable characters.

NOTE: ABNF strings are case-insensitive and the character set
       for these strings is us-ascii.

```
Hence:
    rulename    = "abc"
and:
    rulename    = "aBc"
```

will match "abc", "Abc", "aBc", "abC", "ABc", "aBC", "AbC" and
"ABC".

       To specify a rule which IS case SENSITIVE,
          specify the characters individually.

```
For example:
    rulename    = %d97 %d98 %d99
```

or
```
    rulename     = %d97.98.99
```

will match only the string which comprises only lowercased characters, abc.

2.4 External Encodings

External representations of terminal value characters will vary
according to constraints in the storage or transmission environment. Hence, the same ABNF-based grammar may have multiple external encodings, such as one for a 7-bit US-ASCII environment,
another for a binary octet environment and still a different one
when 16-bit Unicode is used. Encoding details are beyond the
scope of ABNF, although Appendix A (Core) provides definitions
for a 7-bit US-ASCII environment as has been common to much of
the Internet.
By separating external encoding from the syntax, it is intended
that alternate encoding environments can be used for the same
syntax.

3. OPERATORS

3.1 Concatenation   Rule1 Rule2

A rule can define a simple, ordered string of values — i.e., a
concatenation of contiguous characters — by listing a sequence
of rule names. For example:

```
    foo          = %x61          ; a
    bar          = %x62          ; b
    mumble       = foo bar foo
```

So that the rule <mumble> matches the lowercase string "aba".

LINEAR WHITE SPACE: Concatenation is at the core of the ABNF
parsing model. A string of contiguous characters (values) is
parsed according to the rules defined in ABNF. For Internet
specifications, there is some history of permitting linear white
space (space and horizontal tab) to be freelyPand implicitlyPin-
terspersed around major constructs, such as delimiting special
characters or atomic strings.

NOTE: This specification for ABNF does not provide for implicit
       specification of linear white space.

Any grammar which wishes to permit linear white space around de-
limiters or string segments must specify it explicitly. It is

often useful to provide for such white space in "core" rules
that are then used variously among higher-level rules. The
"core" rules might be formed into a lexical analyzer or simply
be part of the main ruleset.

3.2 Alternatives Rule1 / Rule2

Elements separated by forward slash ("/") are alternatives.
Therefore,

```
    foo / bar
```

will accept <foo> or <bar>.

NOTE: A quoted string containing alphabetic characters is spe-
       cial form for specifying alternative characters and is
       interpreted as a non-terminal representing the set of
       combinatorial strings with the contained characters, in
       the specified order but with any mixture of upper and
       lower case..

3.3 Incremental Alternatives   Rule1 =/ Rule2

It is sometimes convenient to specify a list of alternatives in
fragments. That is, an initial rule may match one or more alternatives, with later rule definitions adding to the set of alternatives. This is particularly useful for otherwise-independent
specifications which derive from the same parent rule set, such
as often occurs with parameter lists. ABNF permits this incremental definition through the construct:

```
    oldrule             =/ additional-alternatives
```

So that the rule set

```
    ruleset             = alt1 / alt2

    ruleset             =/ alt3

    ruleset             =/ alt4 / alt5
```

is the same as specifying

```
    ruleset             = alt1 / alt2 / alt3 / alt4 / alt5
```

3.4 Value Range Alternatives   %c##-##

A range of alternative numeric values can be specified compactly, using dash ("-") to indicate the range of alternative
values. Hence:

```
    DIGIT               = %x30-39
```

is equivalent to:

```
DIGIT =                 "0" / "1" / "2" / "3" / "4" / "5" / "6" /
                        "7" / "8" / "9"
```

Concatenated numeric values and numeric value ranges can not be
specified in the same string. A numeric value may use the dotted
notation for concatenation or it may use the dash notation to
specify one value range. Hence, to specify one printable character, between end of line sequences, the specification could be:

```
char-line = %x0D.0A %x20-7E %x0D.0A
```

3.5 Sequence Group   (Rule1 Rule2)

Elements enclosed in parentheses are treated as a single element, whose contents are STRICTLY ORDERED. Thus,

```
elem (foo / bar) blat
```

which matches (elem foo blat) or (elem bar blat).

```
elem foo / bar blat
```

matches (elem foo) or (bar blat).

NOTE: It is strongly advised to use grouping notation, rather
       than to rely on proper reading of "bare" alternations,
       when alternatives consist of multiple rule names or lit-
       erals.

Hence it is recommended that instead of the above form, the
form:

```
(elem foo) / (bar blat)
```

be used. It will avoid misinterpretation by casual readers.
The sequence group notation is also used within free text to set
off an element sequence from the prose.

3.6 Variable Repetition   *Rule

The operator "*" preceding an element indicates repetition. The
full form is:

```
<a>*<b>element
```

where <a> and <b> are optional decimal values, indicating at
least <a> and at most <b> occurrences of element.

Default values are 0 and infinity so that *<element> allows any
number, including zero; 1*<element> requires at least one;
3*3<element> allows exactly 3 and 1*2<element> allows one or
two.

3.7 Specific Repetition   nRule

A rule of the form:

    <n>element

is equivalent to

    <n>*<n>element

That is, exactly <N> occurrences of <element>. Thus 2DIGIT is a
2-digit number, and 3ALPHA is a string of three alphabetic characters.

3.8 Optional Sequence   [RULE]

Square brackets enclose an optional element sequence:

    [foo bar]

is equivalent to

    *1(foo bar).

3.9 ; Comment

A semi-colon starts a comment that continues to the end of line.
This is a simple way of including useful notes in parallel with
the specifications.

3.10 Operator Precedence

The various mechanisms described above have the following precedence, from highest (binding tightest) at the top, to lowest and
loosest at the bottom:

    Strings, Names formation
    Comment
    Value range
    Repetition
    Grouping, Optional
    Concatenation
    Alternative

Use of the alternative operator, freely mixed with concatena-
tions can be confusing.

Again, it is recommended that the grouping operator be used to
make explicit concatenation groups.

4. ABNF DEFINITION OF ABNF

This syntax uses the rules provided in Appendix A (Core).


```
rulelist           = 1*( rule / (*c-wsp c-nl) )
rule               = rulename defined-as elements c-nl
                          ; continues if next line starts
                          ; with white space
rulename           = ALPHA *(ALPHA / DIGIT / "-")
defined-as         = *c-wsp ("=" / "=/") *c-wsp
                          ; basic rules definition and
                          ; incremental alternatives
elements           = alternation *c-wsp
c-wsp              = WSP / (c-nl WSP)
c-nl               = comment / CRLF
                          ; comment or newline
comment            = ";" *(WSP / VCHAR) CRLF
alternation        = concatenation
                      *(*c-wsp "/" *c-wsp concatenation)
concatenation      = repetition *(1*c-wsp repetition)
repetition         = [repeat] element
repeat             = 1*DIGIT / (*DIGIT "*" *DIGIT)
element            = rulename / group / option / char-val /
                     num-val / prose-val
group              = "(" *c-wsp alternation *c-wsp ")"
option             = "[" *c-wsp alternation *c-wsp "]"
char-val           = DQUOTE *(%x20-21 / %x23-7E) DQUOTE
                          ; quoted string of SP and VCHAR
                              without DQUOTE
num-val            = "%" (bin-val / dec-val / hex-val)
bin-val            = "b" 1*BIT [ 1*("." 1*BIT) / ("-" 1*BIT)
]
                          ; series of concatenated bit values
                          ; or single ONEOF range
dec-val            = "d" 1*DIGIT [ 1*("." 1*DIGIT) / ("-"
                     1*DIGIT) ]
hex-val            = "x" 1*HEXDIG [ 1*("." 1*HEXDIG) / ("-"
                     1*HEXDIG) ]
prose-val          = "<" *(%x20-3D / %x3F-7E) ">"
                          ; bracketed string of SP and VCHAR
                              without angles
                          ; prose description, to be used as
                              last resort
```

5. SECURITY CONSIDERATIONS

Security is truly believed to be irrelevant to this document.

6. APPENDIX A - CORE

This Appendix is provided as a convenient core for specific
grammars. The definitions may be used as a core set of rules.

6.1 Core Rules

Certain basic rules are in uppercase, such as SP, HTAB, CRLF,
DIGIT, ALPHA, etc.

```
ALPHA          = %x41-5A / %x61-7A ; A-Z / a-z
BIT            = "0" / "1"
CHAR           = %x01-7F
                     ; any 7-bit US-ASCII character,
                       excluding NUL
CR             = %x0D
                     ; carriage return
CRLF           = CR LF
                     ; Internet standard newline
CTL            = %x00-1F / %x7F
                     ; controls
DIGIT          = %x30-39
                     ; 0-9
DQUOTE         = %x22
                     ; " (Double Quote)
HEXDIG         = DIGIT / "A" / "B" / "C" / "D" / "E" / "F"
HTAB           = %x09
                     ; horizontal tab
LF             = %x0A
                     ; linefeed
LWSP           = *(WSP / CRLF WSP)
                     ; linear white space (past newline)
OCTET          = %x00-FF
                     ; 8 bits of data
SP             = %x20
                     ; space
VCHAR          = %x21-7E
                     ; visible (printing) characters
WSP            = SP / HTAB
                     ; white space
```

6.2 Common Encoding

Externally, data are represented as "network virtual ASCII",
namely 7-bit US-ASCII in an 8-bit field, with the high (8th) bit

set to zero. A string of values is in "network byte order" with the higher-valued bytes represented on the left-hand side and being sent over the network first.

7. ACKNOWLEDGMENTS

The syntax for ABNF was originally specified in RFC 733. Ken L. Harrenstien, of SRI International, was responsible for re-coding the BNF into an augmented BNF that makes the representation smaller and easier to understand.

This recent project began as a simple effort to cull out the portion of RFC 822 which has been repeatedly cited by non-email specification writers, namely the description of augmented BNF. Rather than simply and blindly converting the existing text into a separate document, the working group chose to give careful consideration to the deficiencies, as well as benefits, of the existing specification and related specifications available over the last 15 years and therefore to pursue enhancement. This turned the project into something rather more ambitious than first intended. Interestingly the result is not massively different from that original, although decisions such as removing the list notation came as a surprise.

The current round of specification was part of the DRUMS working group, with significant contributions from Jerome Abela, Harald Alvestrand, Robert Elz, Roger Fajman, Aviva Garrett, Tom Harsch, Dan Kohn, Bill McQuillan, Keith Moore, Chris Newman, Pete Resnick and Henning Schulzrinne.

8. REFERENCES

[US-ASCII] Coded Character Set—7-Bit American Standard Code for Information Interchange, ANSI X3.4-1986.
[RFC733] Crocker, D., Vittal, J., Pogran, K., and D. Henderson, "Standard for the Format of ARPA Network Text Message," RFC 733, November 1977.
[RFC822] Crocker, D., "Standard for the Format of ARPA Internet Text Messages", STD 11, RFC 822, August 1982.

9. CONTACT

David H. Crocker   Paul Overell
Internet Mail Consortium   Demon Internet Ltd
675 Spruce Dr.   Dorking Business Park
Sunnyvale, CA 94086 USA   Dorking
                                    Surrey, RH4 1HN
                                    UK

Phone: +1 408 246 8253
Fax: +1 408 249 6205
EMail: dcrocker@imc.org paulo@turnpike.com

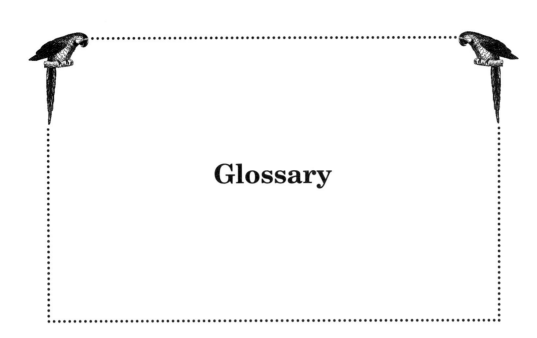

Glossary

AH   Authentication Header
AIN   Advanced Intelligent Network
ANM   ISUP answer message
ANM   SS7 answer message
ANS   answer tone
API   Applications Programming Interface
ARP   Address Resolution Protocol
ASN.1   Abstract Syntax Negotiation One
AVT   Audio & Video Transport
BCF   Bandwidth Change Confirm
BER   Basic Encoding Rules
B-ISDN   broadband-ISDN
BNR   Bakus Naur Form
BRJ   Bandwidth Change Reject
BRQ   Bandwidth Change Request
CAMA-ANI   Centralized Automatic
    Message Accounting-Automatic
    Number Identification
CAS   CPE altering signal
CC   contributor count
CCAF   call control agent function
CCF   call control function
CCIS   Common Channel Interoffice
    Signaling
CCS   common channel signaling
CED   terminal identification
CGN   calling tone

CIC   circuit identification code
CO   central office
COT   continuity test
CPE   customer permises equipment
CRd   Capabilities Request
CRe   Capabilities Request
DLC   data link control
DNS   Domain Name System
DSU   data service units
DTMF   dual-tone multifrequency
E   extension
EO   end office
ESi   escape signal
ESP   Encapsulating Security
    Payload
ESr   Escape Signal
ET   Exchange termination
FDI   feeder-distribution interface
FGB   Feature Group B
FSK   frequency shift key
FTP   file transfer protocol
GCF   Gatekeeper Confirmation
GRJ   Gatekeeper Reject
GRQ   Gatekeeper Request
GS/LS   ground start/loop start
GSM   global systems for mobile
    communications

GSTN   General Switched Telephone
    Network
HDLC   High Level Data Link Control
HF   high frequency
HTML   Hypertext Markup Language
http   Hypertext Transfer Protocol
I/G   individual/group
IAM   Initial Address Message
IC   interexchange carrier
ICMP   Internet Control Management
    Protocol
IETF   Internet Engineering Task Forces
IGMP   Internet Group Management
    Protocol
IGMP   Internet Group Multicasting
    Protocol
IN   Intelligent Network
IntServ   Integrated Services
IP   Internet Protocol
IPDC   Internet Protocol Device
    Control
ISDN   Integrated Services Digital
    Network
ISUP   ISDN User Part
IXC   interchange carriers
KP   key pulse
LANs   local area networks
LEC   local exchange carrier
M   marker
Ma Bell   AT&T
MAC   media access control
MC   Multipoint Controller
MCU   Mulitpoint Control Unit
MCU   Multipoint Central Unit
MDF   main distribution form
MF   multifrequency
MG   Media Gateway
MGC   Media Gateway Controller
MGCP   Media Gateway Control Protocol
MGCU   Media Gateway Control Unit
MGU   Media Gateway Unit
MIB   Management Information Base
MIME   Multipurpose Internet Mail
    Extension
MRd   Mode Request
MRe   Mode Request
MTU   maximum transmission unit
MUX   multiplexing

NANP   North American Numbering Plan
NAP   Network Access Point
NI   network interface
N-ISDN   narrowband-ISDN
NSI   Network Solutions Incorporated
NTP   network time protocol
OSPF   open shortest path first
OUI   organization unique identifier
P   padding
PCM   pulse code modulation
PDU   IP datagram
POT   point-of-termination
PPP   Point-to-Point Protocol
PSTN   Public Switched Telephone
    Network
PT   payload type
PVC   permanent virtual circuit
QOS   quality-of-service
RARP   Reverse Address Resolution
    Protocol
RAS   Registration, admission, and status
RDT   remote digital terminal
REL   ISUP RELEASE
REL   ISUP Release Message
RPC   Remote Procedure Call
RR   Resource Record
RRJ   Registration Reject
RSVP   resource reservation protocol
RT   Routing Tables
RTCP   real time control protocol
RTP   Real Time Protocol
RTP/AVP   RTP Audio/Video Profile
RTP/ID   RTP Termination
RTT   round-trip-time
SCE   service creation environment
SCEF   service creation environment
    function
SCF   service control function
SCN   Switched Circuit Network
SCP   Service Contol Point
SDF   service data function
SDLC   synchronous data link control
SDP   Session Description Protocol
SEP   Signaling Endpoint
SG   Signaling Gateway
SGM   Small Group Multicast
SGMP   Simple Gateway Control Protocol
SGU   Signaling Gateway Unit

SIG Signaling Transport
SIP Session Initiation Protocol
SIP Session Invitation Protocol
SLA Service Level Agreements
SMAF Service Management Access
    Function
SMF service management function
SMS service management system
SMTP Simple Mail Transfer Protocol
SN sequence number
SNMP Simple Network Management
    Protocol
SRF specialized resouce function
SS7 Signaling System Number 7
SSP Service Switching Points
ST start
STP Signaling Transfer Points
TCP Transmission Control Protocol
TFTP Trivial File Transfer Protocol

TOS type of service
TSAP Transport Service Access Point
TTL time-to-live
U/L universal bit
UA user agent
UAC user agent client
UAS user agent server
UDP User Datagram Protocol
UNI user network interface
URI Uniform Resource Identifier
URJ Unregister Reject
URL Universal Resource Locator
URQ Unregister Request
V version
V1 IGMP Version 1
V2 IGMP Version 2
VOIP voice over IP
WAN Wide Area Network
XML Extensible Markup Language

References

[AKRA99]. Akramovich, Ilya, et al. "Megaco MIB", draft-ietf-megaco-mib-00.txt, October 1999.

[ARAN98]. Arango, Mauricio, Huitema, Christian. Simple Gateway Control Protocol (SGCP), Internet Engineering Task Force draft-huitema-sgcp-va-o2.txt.

[ARAN98a]. Arango, Mauricio, Dugan, Andrew, Elliott, Isacc, Huitema, Christian, Pickett, Scott. Media Gateway Control Protocol (MGCP). Internet Engineering Task Force draft-huitema-MGCP-v0r1-01.txt.

[BELL00]. Bell, Robert, et al. Megaco IP Phone Media Gateway Application Profile, draft-ietf-megaco-ipphone-02.txt, February, 2000.

[BERN98]. Berners-Lee, Tim, et al. Uniform Resource Identifiers (URI): Generic Syntax, RFC 2386, August, 1998.

[BERN99]. Bernet, Y, et al. "A Framework for Differentiated Services", draft-ietf-difserv-framework-02-.txt., February, 1999.

[BLAC95]. Black, Uyless. The V Series Recommendations, McGraw Hill, 1995.

[BLAC99]. Black , Uyless. Voice over IP. Prentice Hall, 1999.

[BOIV00]. Boivie, Rich and Feldman, Nancy. Small Group Multicast. draft-boivie-sgm-00.txt, March 2000.

[CUER00]. Cuervo, Fernando, et al. Megaco Protocol, draft-ietf-megaco-protocol-07.txt, February 21, 2000.

[CUER99]. Cuervo, Fernando, et al, Megaco Protocol, draft-ietf-megaco-protocol-01.txt.

[FUJI98]. Fujikawa, Kenji, SDP URL Scheme, draft-fujikawa-sdp-url-01.txt, August, 1998.

[HAND99]. The SIP authors are Mark Handley, Henning Schulzrinne, Eve Schooler, and Jonathan Rosenberg. Their addresses and company associations are available in the final standard (RFC 2543).

[JAND99]. Jander, Mary, "SAL Monitoring Tools", Data Communications, February, 1999.

[JOHN00]. Johnston, Alan, et al. "SIP Telephony Call Flow Examples", draft-ietf-sip-call-flows-00.txt March 2000.

[KNAP00]. Knapf, Eric. "Can They Really Rebuild the PTSN?", *Business Communications Review,* May 2000.

[MA99]. Ma, Gene, "H.323 Signaling and SS7 ISUP Gateway: Procedure Interworking", draft-ma-h323-isup-Gateway-00.txt, October, 1998.

[MIER00]. Mier, Edwin E. and Yocom, Betsy. "Too Many VOIP Standards", *Business Communications Review,* June, 2000. Authors can be reached at ed@mier.com and byocom@mier.com respectively.

[ROSE98]. J. Rosenberg, H. Schulzrinne. Timer Reconsideration for Enhanced RTP Scalability, draft-ietf-avt-reconsider-00.txt, July, 1997.

[SCHU] Schulzrinne, Henning and Rosenberg, Jonathan, "A Comparison of SIP and H.323 for Internet Telepphony", a white paper, hgs@cs.comumbia.edu and jdrosen@bell-labs.com, date not given.

[SCHU99]. Schulzrinne, Henning and Petrack, Scott. "RTP Payload for DTMF Digits, Telephony Tones, and Telephony Signals", Internet Draft, ietf-avt-tones-01.ps.

[SCHU99]. Schulzrinne, Henning and Petrack, Scott. RTP Payload DTMF Digits, Telephony Tones, and Telephony Signals. Ietf-avt-tones-o1.ps, August, 1999.

[SIGN00]. Singh, Kundan and Schulzrinne, Henning. Interworking Between SIP/SDP and H.323", draft-singh-sip-h323.txt, January 10, 2000.

[TAYL98]. Taylor, P., Calhoun, Pat R., Rubens, Allan C. IPDC Base Protocol. Internet Engineering Task Force. Draft-taylor-Ipdc-99.txt.

[TAYL98]. Taylor, Steven, Wexler, Joanie, "Maturing Frame Relay Make New Demands", *Business Communications Review,* July, 1998.

[VAND98]. Vandenameele, Jozef. Requirements for the Reference Point ('N') between Media Gateway Controller and Media Gateway. Draft-vandenameele-tiphon-arch-gway-decomp-00.txt, November 1988.

From the AVT (Audio Visual Transport) Working Group, J. Rosenberg and H. Schulzrinne. See draft-ietf-avt-aggregation-00.txt © The Internet Society.

International Teleconferencing Corsortium, Inc. (IMTC) HTTP://www.imtc.org/main.html.

The information from this section is sourced from the Internet Software Consortium (http://www.isc.org/). Their paper was focused on the potential Y2K problem, and I have not included this part of the paper in my summary. I thank the Internet Software Consortium for this information. As you can see from Table 3-1, they run DNS site F.

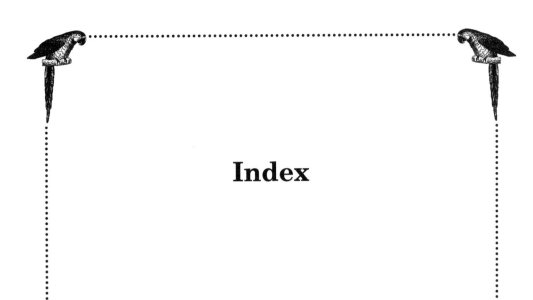

Index

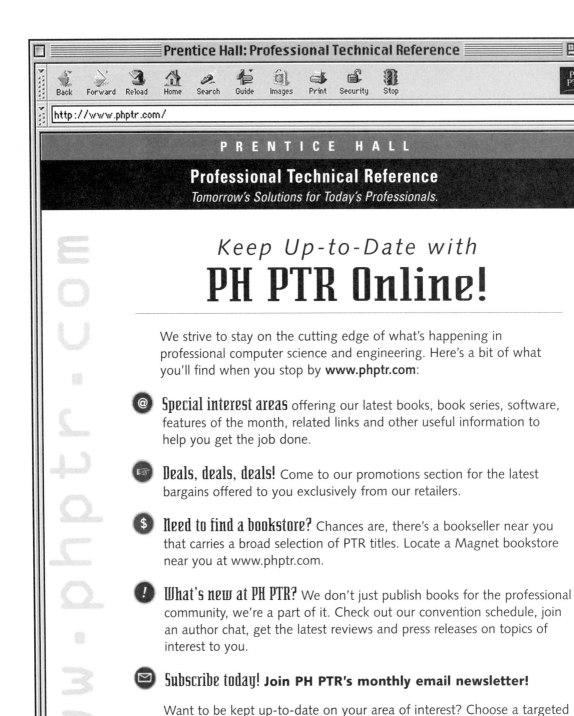